The Teaching of Criminal Law

We can lament the lingering influence of 'old school' doctrine-focused criminal law teaching or we can articulate better ways to teach and study criminal law. The contributors to this fine collection are to be congratulated for taking the latter more constructive path. Developing curricula that extend beyond the traditional 'general principles + homicide + theft' formula, refusing to artificially extract criminal law rules from the practical and procedures by which they are operationalised, taking historical, cultural, political, economic and other contextual factors seriously, valuing Indigenous and feminist perspectives and insights, employing problem-based learning – it is heartening to read that these and other exciting approaches are well on the way to becoming the 'new normal' in criminal law teaching.

Luke McNamara, Professor, Faculty of Law, UNSW
and co-author of D Brown et al, *Criminal Laws: Materials and Commentary on Criminal Law and Process of New South Wales* (Federation Press, 6th ed, 2015)

The Teaching of Criminal Law provides the first considered discussion of the pedagogy that should inform the teaching of criminal law. It originates from a survey of criminal law courses in different parts of the English-speaking world which showed significant similarity across countries and over time. It also showed that many aspects of substantive law are neglected. This prompted the question of whether any real consideration had been given to criminal law course design. This book seeks to provide a critical mass of thought on how to secure an understanding of substantive criminal law by examining the course content that best illustrates the thought process of a criminal lawyer, by presenting innovative approaches for securing active learning by students, and by demonstrating how criminal law can secure other worthwhile graduate attributes by introducing wider contexts.

This edited collection brings together contributions from academic teachers of criminal law from Australia, New Zealand, the United Kingdom, and Ireland who have considered issues of course design and often implemented them. Together, they examine several innovative approaches to the teaching of criminal law that have been adopted in a number of law schools around the world, both in teaching methodology and substantive content. The authors offer numerous suggestions for the design of a criminal law course that will ensure students gain useful insights into criminal law and its role in society.

This book helps fill the gap in research into criminal law pedagogy and demonstrates that there are alternative ways of delivering this core part of the law degree. As such, this book will be of key interest to researchers, academics, and lecturers in the fields of criminal law, pedagogy, and teaching methods.

Kris Gledhill is Associate Professor at AUT Law School, Auckland, New Zealand.

Ben Livings is Senior Lecturer at the Law School of the University of New England in New South Wales, Australia.

Legal Pedagogy
Series Editor
Kris Gledhill, *Auckland University of Technology, New Zealand*

This series consists of high-quality monographs, each of which explores best practice in an aspect of the law school curriculum. Books will cover teaching methods and curriculum design in the main areas of law, how to integrate themes and areas of jurisprudential thought, and wider questions about legal education more generally. With contributions from around the world, this series explores innovative thinking and practice within the context of a generally conservative branch of academia, with the aim of promoting discussion as to how best to teach the various aspects of the law degree and ensure the ongoing validity of the law degree as a whole. Typical topics addressed include the value of variety in teaching methods and curriculum design, how best to incorporate educational research, the role for more practical courses, and the need to ensure that law schools provide degrees of relevance to the needs of students and of society.

The books in this series will be of great interest to academics, researchers and postgraduates in the fields of law and education, as well as teachers of law who may be interested in revising curricula and need guidance in doing so. In addition, the legal profession, and in particular those who regulate entry into the profession, will find much to interest them within the series.

Books in this series:

The Teaching of Criminal Law
The pedagogical imperatives
Edited by Kris Gledhill and Ben Livings

The Teaching of Criminal Law

The pedagogical imperatives

Edited by Kris Gledhill
and Ben Livings

LONDON AND NEW YORK

First published 2017
by Routledge
2 Park Square, Milton Park, Abingdon, Oxon OX14 4RN

and by Routledge
711 Third Avenue, New York, NY 10017

First issued in paperback 2018

Routledge is an imprint of the Taylor & Francis Group, an informa business

© 2017 selection and editorial matter, K. Gledhill and B. Livings; individual chapters, the contributors

The right of the editors to be identified as the authors of the editorial material, and of the authors for their individual chapters, has been asserted in accordance with sections 77 and 78 of the Copyright, Designs and Patents Act 1988.

All rights reserved. No part of this book may be reprinted or reproduced or utilised in any form or by any electronic, mechanical, or other means, now known or hereafter invented, including photocopying and recording, or in any information storage or retrieval system, without permission in writing from the publishers.

Trademark notice: Product or corporate names may be trademarks or registered trademarks, and are used only for identification and explanation without intent to infringe.

British Library Cataloguing in Publication Data
A catalogue record for this book is available from the British Library

Library of Congress Cataloging-in-Publication Data
Names: Gledhill, Kris, editor. | Livings, Ben, editor.
Title: The teaching of criminal law : the pedagogical imperatives / Edited by Kris Gledhill and Ben Livings.
Description: New York, NY : Routledge, 2016.
Identifiers: LCCN 2016016880 | ISBN 9781138841994 (hardcover) | ISBN 9781315731902 (electronic)
Subjects: LCSH: Criminal law—Study and teaching—Great Britain. | Criminal law—Study and teaching—New Zealand. | Criminal law—Study and teaching.
Classification: LCC KD7869.6 .T43 2016 | DDC 345.00711/1—dc23
LC record available at https://lccn.loc.gov/2016016880

ISBN 13: 978-1-138-54317-1 (pbk)
ISBN 13: 978-1-138-84199-4 (hbk)

Typeset in Bembo
by Apex CoVantage, LLC

Contents

List of contributors		vii
Foreword by Anthony Bradney		ix
1	Introduction	1
	KRIS GLEDHILL AND BEN LIVINGS	
2	Building block or stumbling block? Teaching *actus reus* and *mens rea* in criminal law	21
	FIONA DONSON AND CATHERINE O'SULLIVAN	
3	Teaching the elements of crimes	34
	JOHN CHILD	
4	Enhancing interactivity in the teaching of criminal law: Using response technology in the lecture theatre	46
	KEVIN J. BROWN AND COLIN R. G. MURRAY	
5	Using problem-based learning to enhance the study of criminal law	60
	BEN FITZPATRICK	
6	Turning criminal law upside down	72
	JO BOYLAN-KEMP AND REBECCA HUXLEY-BINNS	
7	Criminal law pedagogy and the Australian state codes	83
	THOMAS CROFTS AND STELLA TARRANT	
8	Teaching criminal law as statutory interpretation	93
	JEREMY GANS	

9 Shaking the foundations: Criminal law as a means of critiquing the assumptions of the centrality of doctrine in law   104
ALEX STEEL

10 The challenges and benefits of integrating criminal law, litigation and evidence   116
ADAM JACKSON AND KEVIN KERRIGAN

11 'Crime and the criminal process': Challenging traditions, breaking boundaries   127
PHIL SCRATON AND JOHN STANNARD

12 Context and connection   139
BEN LIVINGS

13 Teaching and learning criminal law 'in context': Taking 'context' seriously   151
ARLIE LOUGHNAN

14 Teaching indigenous and minority students and perspectives in criminal law   162
KHYLEE QUINCE

15 Introducing feminist legal jurisprudence through the teaching of criminal law   173
JULIA TOLMIE

16 Choice   185
KRIS GLEDHILL

17 The absence of regulatory crime from the criminal law curriculum   194
SHANE KILCOMMINS, SUSAN LEAHY, AND EIMEAR SPAIN

18 Conclusion: Looking to the future   206
KRIS GLEDHILL AND BEN LIVINGS

Index   211

Contributors

Jo Boylan-Kemp, Principal Lecturer, Nottingham Law School, Nottingham Trent University, England

Kevin J. Brown, Lecturer, School of Law, Queen's University Belfast, Northern Ireland

John Child, Senior Lecturer in Law, Sussex Law School, England

Thomas Crofts, Professor, Sydney Law School, University of Sydney, Australia

Fiona Donson, Lecturer, Faculty of Law, University College Cork, Ireland

Ben Fitzpatrick, Senior Lecturer, York Law School, England

Jeremy Gans, Professor, Melbourne Law School, University of Melbourne, Australia

Kris Gledhill, Associate Professor, AUT Law School, Auckland, New Zealand

Rebecca Huxley-Binns, Professor, University of Law, Guildford, England

Adam Jackson, Senior Lecturer, Northumbria Law School, Northumbria University, Newcastle, England

Kevin Kerrigan, Professor, Northumbria Law School, Northumbria University, Newcastle, England

Shane Kilcommins, Professor, School of Law, University of Limerick, Ireland

Susan Leahy, Lecturer, School of Law, University of Limerick, Ireland

Ben Livings, Senior Lecturer, School of Law, University of New England, Australia

Arlie Loughnan, Associate Professor, Sydney Law School, University of Sydney, Australia

Colin R. G. Murray, Senior Lecturer, Newcastle Law School, Newcastle University, England

Catherine O'Sullivan, Lecturer, Faculty of Law, University College Cork, Ireland

Khylee Quince, Senior Lecturer, AUT Law School, Auckland, New Zealand

Phil Scraton, Professor of Criminology, School of Law, Queen's University Belfast, Northern Ireland

Eimear Spain, Senior Lecturer, School of Law, University of Limerick, Ireland

John Stannard, Senior Lecturer, School of Law, Queen's University Belfast, Northern Ireland

Alex Steel, Professor, Faculty of Law, UNSW, Sydney, Australia

Stella Tarrant, Associate Professor, Law School, University of Western Australia, Perth, Australia

Julia Tolmie, Associate Professor, Auckland Law School, New Zealand

Foreword

In common law countries, the quantity, quality, and status of research and scholarship about university legal education has grown markedly over the last 50 years. Many countries now have specialist journals devoted to the subject such as the *Journal of Legal Education* in the United States, the *Law Teacher* in the United Kingdom, the *Legal Education Review* in Australia, and the *Canadian Legal Education Annual Review*. In addition to this, there are also numerous articles in general journals, monographs, and collections of essays devoted to the subject in common law countries. In civil law countries, the subject is perhaps less well developed, but even here books such as Carel Stolker's *Rethinking the Law School: Education, Research, Outreach and Governance*, Christophe Jamin's *La Cuisine du Droit: L'Ecole de Droit de Sciences Po: une expèrimentation française*, and Jan Smits's *The Mind and Method of the Legal Academic* show a developing interest in the area.

The interest in university legal education is not surprising. As academics, most of us accept, in various ways and to varying degrees, the truth of Socrates's dictum that an "unexamined life is not worth living". Legal academics, unlike academics in some other disciplines, spend most of their lives both teaching and researching, so it is almost inevitable that they will spend some of their time thinking about what it is they do, why they do it, and how they do it; as importantly, they will spend some time considering how they can combine teaching and research.

If Weber was correct in thinking that only by specialisation can true progress be made, then it is desirable that some legal academics focus on university legal education as at least one of their research fields. Research on university legal education is no different than research in other legal fields. The usual rules of scholarship obtain. There is no more room here for mere assertion or polemic than there is, for example, in the study of restitution or legal positivism. Existing work must be studied, existing ideas must be considered, and wheels must not be reinvented. However, neither does the past determine what we do. Innovation, though not innovation for innovation's sake, can be progress. At the same time, tradition is not wrong simply because it is tradition. What matters, as always, is the quality of arguments that are being made.

Research into university legal education, like any other research, has merit in itself. The search for knowledge is a good that needs no further justification. However, such research can also inform both what researchers do in their own wider work in the law school and also the work of other legal academics. This is what the essays in this collection do. The essays range far and wide, looking at, amongst other things, what can be taught in a criminal law course, the theoretical foundations of such a course, and the technology that might help or hinder learning. Drawing both on research that they have done in the teaching of criminal law, research done by others on university legal education, and research into university education in general, the authors of the essays reimagine the teaching of criminal law.

Collections such as this book should not be read as a prescription for what we must do. Instead, they should be seen as aids to reflection. Whether or not the reader agrees with any or all of the essays in this book is not to the point. It is the fact that the essays take the process of education and learning seriously that matters. As legal academics, we should be thinking about these things. As legal academics we should be taking these matters as seriously as do the authors.

This collection also serves to emphasise one further thing about academic life. We have choices to make about what and how we teach. In different ways, in different jurisdictions, we are all under pressure from a variety of bodies to shape our teaching in ways that are thought to be appropriate. Thinking about the demands that are made of us is what we should do. University law schools do not exist in isolation. They are part of the societies in which they are located. The society's needs as well as the needs of legal professionals and others, including the needs of students, are things that we should consider. Yet, at the same time, academic freedom is not a right but an obligation. If research into learning is taken as seriously as any other kind of research, then we are obligated to teach things that we think are important in the way that we think is most likely to be successful. Collections like this help us as individuals to make these decisions.

Anthony Bradney

Chapter 1

Introduction

Kris Gledhill and Ben Livings

Background research

The origin of this collection of essays is a survey carried out by Kris Gledhill (with the research assistance of Blair McKeown) to identify whether criminal law courses in different parts of the common law world exhibited any significant variety. The survey was prompted by a move from legal practice in England and Wales into the teaching of criminal law in New Zealand some 25 years after studying it as an undergraduate in England and finding that the module was both very familiar – involving general principles and coverage of homicide, assaults, sexual offences, and property offences – and also that it missed many areas of the substantive criminal law that were important in practice. If it was not a coincidence that two far apart law schools taught very similar courses separated by over quarter of a century, but more systemic, obvious questions would arise: why should this be so? Was it a good thing? Another thought naturally prompted would be whether there had been any real thought given to course design in relation to the important area of criminal law.

The methodology of the survey, carried out in 2010, was simple. Law school websites were searched for descriptions of their criminal law offerings. Where one was available, it was reviewed for whether a reference was made to the teaching of general principles and what specific offences were mentioned as being included on the syllabus, with particular note being made of the coverage of homicide, assaults, sexual assaults, and property offences. If the description did not express a particular matter, an assessment was made of whether language was consistent with a particular matter being covered, or unclear or inconsistent. For example, an indication that a course was taught with illustration through homicide and sexual assaults was viewed as inconsistent with the use of property offences; an indication that unspecified offences were taught was classified as unclear, but a reference to teaching "the principal offences" or similar phraseology was classified as being consistent with the teaching of the traditional range of homicide, assaults, sexual assaults, and property offences. Specific note was also made of references to the teaching of other offences as part of the course.

The outcome of the survey can be summarised as follows:

(i) Australia: 30 law school course descriptions were found, and all of them referred to the teaching of general principles (though the University of New South Wales made this a reference to the so-called general principles). Twenty-five course descriptions referred to, or were consistent with, the teaching of homicide, 24 with other assaults, and 23 each with sexual offences and property offences. Where the descriptions were unclear, none was inconsistent with these offences being taught as part of the course.

There was more significant reference than in other jurisdictions to other offences being taught: 10 course descriptions made reference to drugs offences, 4 to driving offences, 2 to public order offences, and 1 reference was made to regulatory offences.

(ii) Canada: 15 course descriptions were located, all of which made express reference to general principles being taught, or used language that was consistent with this; however, there was much less specificity in terms of the references made to specific offences than in other common law jurisdictions. Indeed, there were only 2 express mentions of homicide and 2 of sexual offences. (A review of USA law schools was also done; this similarly found a focus on general principles, and homicide was often the only offence referred to expressly.)

(iii) England and Wales (plus an English law degree at the University of Dundee): 39 course descriptions were found, of which 38 mentioned general principles or used equivalent language, 1 being unclear but not inconsistent. The express references to homicide, assaults, sexual assaults, and property offences were as follows: 30, 28, 29, 31. Others were unclear but not inconsistent, save that the course description for the Aston Business School LLB had a clear focus on corporate offending that seemed inconsistent with assaults and sexual offences (though it covered homicide in the form of corporate manslaughter).

There were limited references to other courses, in the form of 4 references to public order or similar matters, 2 to drugs, and 1 each to prostitution, computer hacking, and trade descriptions.

(iv) New Zealand: there were 5 law schools; all the course descriptions referred to general principles, though only that at Victoria University of Wellington referred specifically to offences against the person and property, while the others mentioned "indictable and selected other offences". As will be seen in the account of the regulatory regime, this language comes from the prescription of the New Zealand Council for Legal Education (NZCLE). Knowledge acquired from the process in New Zealand, whereby the law schools take turns to assess each other's examinations, and discussion with a representative from the NZCLE indicated that the teaching was consistent with the standard model.

(v) Scotland: 7 course descriptions were located and each one mentioned or was consistent with the teaching of general principles, homicide, assaults, sexual assaults and property offences. There were also 4 express references to public order offences and 1 each to offences against morality, involving the course of justice, and drugs.

The survey also considered other common law jurisdictions, with similar results: Hong Kong, Papua New Guinea, Vanuatu, and the West Indies. In Ireland, 3 course descriptions were located, which were consistent with this but did not mention specific offences; the National University of Singapore mentioned that it would "mainly" use homicide offences. Where they were available, course descriptions for South African law schools and 1 in Namibia followed a similar pattern of the traditionally-taught offences.

In short, there was a significant level of similarity across jurisdictions (at least where it could be assessed – Canada, for example, being problematic in this regard, as was Northern Ireland); Australia had the only significant – though minority – use of a range of other offences, though there was a noticeable reference to public order matters in Scotland.

The survey was repeated in part in 2015 in the Australasian jurisdictions, where there had been several new law schools opened, and several schools in Australia adopted a JD model, with consequent opportunities for course design. The results from this shorter 2015 review were as follows:

(i) Australia: 46 criminal law course descriptions were surveyed, with the increase coming both from new law schools and new JD courses at existing law schools. Of these, all used language that was consistent with general principles or, where it was too brief to tell, was not inconsistent with that; this time it was the University of Tasmania that regarded them as so-called general principles. It is also worth noting, given that there are several chapters in this collection that relate to a "law in context" approach to the teaching of criminal law – namely, using it to explain to students that the socio-political factors behind legal structures have to be understood – that 16 course descriptions referred expressly to such an approach being used. Fourteen seemed inconsistent in that they give the impression of the course presenting a more neutral "black-letter" law approach; the other 16 left the law in context approach as a possibility.

In terms of offences covered, 24 course descriptions made reference to homicide and 5 made reference to matters such as "more significant indictable offences". The other 17 were unclear. In relation to other offences against the person, 17 course descriptions were unclear, but the express references were as follows: assaults, 26; sexual assaults, 18; property offences, 27. The other course descriptions, respectively, 3, 11, and 2, used language that was consistent with the teaching of assaults, sexual assaults, and property.

Other offences were mentioned: 13 course descriptions made reference to drug offences, 5 to driving offences, 5 to public order offences, 3 to the growing range of Commonwealth offences, 1 to anti-terrorism, and 1 to regulatory offences. Two course descriptions emphasised coverage of a broad range of offences.

(ii) New Zealand: the 5 law schools that had been surveyed in 2010 remained as they had before, save that VUW had decided to use the same description as the others ("certain indictable offences"); this was perhaps strange, given that the Criminal Procedure Act 2011 (NZ) has abolished the classification of indictable and summary offences. The new AUT Law School did not make this mistake and also made reference to the offences taught: offences against the person and various commercial crimes, including those involving intellectual property.

Again, this revealed limited variety. This is reflected by the contents of the main textbooks, which follow the same pattern, though with occasional exceptions. Texts from earlier years can also be reviewed to assess whether there has been significant change over time. For example, the first edition of the Smith and Hogan cases and materials book, a staple in English teaching, published in 1980, covered the standard range of offences. The same authors' textbook, which may be aimed at a wider audience, has covered public order and a limited range of road traffic offences since its first edition in 1965; initially, it also covered offences against public morals, the administration of justice, and the security of the state, but this coverage changed in the 1990s to coverage of obscenity. In contrast, the new *Smith and Hogan's Essentials of Criminal Law*, published first in 2015, covers just the standard range as the casebook. Ancient books, such as J. H. Beale's *A Selection of Cases and Other Authorities on Criminal Law*, published in 1894 by the Harvard Law Review Publishing Association before drug offending existed, have the same structure.

There is an obvious chicken and egg situation here: do texts reflect what is taught and so meet that need? Or do they limit the ability to teach other areas because the infrastructure is not present? Australian examples seem to suggest the latter: as both Gans and Steel record in their chapters in this collection, academics who wish to teach criminal law courses that differ from the standard approach can write textbooks to support that approach; as such, it is the decision to teach to a different format that comes first.

Posing the question to be explored

The similarity between the various course descriptions might be thought to allow only limited conclusions without any form of more detailed analysis of how courses are taught. At the same time, it seems proper to assume that an academic putting out a course description would seek to capture the essence of how he or she teaches the subject: on that basis, the course descriptions provide a reliable basis for suggesting that there is a stark similarity over jurisdictions. When combined with the structure of most textbooks, which offer little variety in coverage, it confirms that there is a question, noted at the outset, as to why there should be such similarity.

It also suggests a possible concern, should this similarity arise from a failure to consider whether variety in content produces benefits (or the focus on a small range of offences has significant opportunity costs). As to this, there is no good evidence of a process of discussion leading to a consensus as to the best way of teaching criminal law. Rather, there is little material to suggest that law school curricula in general or criminal law courses in particular are designed on a foundation of research that supports how best to secure an understanding of how criminal law operates.

There have been critiques: Alldridge's suggestion that the "traditional" criminal law course was inadequate because it focussed too much on black-letter law questions of responsibility – a critique mentioned more than once in this collection – is 25 years old (Alldridge, 1990). More generally, and in the context of US law schools, Feinman and Feldman suggested, "Most legal educators are anti-intellectual about the area of their primary professional concern"; they suggested that there was an unwillingness even to reflect on the goals of legal education and the content of the curriculum. Part of the evidence they cited for this was that only 1 of 200 legal journals in the United States dealt regularly with pedagogy and that most of the literature was "anecdotal or platitudinous" (Feinman and Feldman, 1984). Simon and others writing in 1999 suggested that the call by Feinman and Feldman had essentially fallen on deaf ears (Simon et al., 1999). Cownie, focussing on England, suggested that the very structure of academia has led to a focus on doctrinal research, such that research on teaching and teaching methodology is a neglected poor cousin (Cownie, 1999).

A consequence of this may be a tendency for university academics to be influenced more by their own experiences as students than by a research-based analysis of how best to teach when it comes to matters such as the content of a core course: familiarity substitutes for academic rigour. There is no doubt there has been some progress, though some would argue that it has been inadequate and others would suggest that a focus on what James terms 'pedagogicalism', whilst welcome in many respects, has led to an uncritical acceptance of what constitutes 'good teaching' (2004). In terms of the places for scholarship to be published, in the USA, Blasi recorded that an explosion of law reviews in the United States up to 1995 had not produced an additional one dedicated to law school pedagogy (Blasi, 1995, p. 397). Outside the United States, the United Kingdoms' the *Law Teacher*, from the Association of Law Teachers, is approaching its fiftieth volume and has been joined by the *Legal Education Review*, which commenced publication in Australia in 1989; both journals produce a significant amount of work relating to pedagogy. But the point remains that there is a limited range of scholarship compared to that on doctrine. Critics can properly argue that this is problematic in light of the significant range of educational scholarship, including as to such matters as the importance of active rather than passive learning. (Blasi, 1995; Schwartz, 2001).

A clear exception to this is the area of clinical legal education, with journals which are replete with material relating to pedagogy and the value of experiential education as a form of active learning. This suggests an explanation for the deficit in other parts of the legal curriculum: clinical legal educators have been able to start with a relatively blank canvas and follow a research-informed process of course design, identifying the graduate attributes they wish to secure, and constructing a course to achieve that. In contrast, in established courses, lecturers will invariably walk into a pre-existing syllabus, familiar to them from their law school days, which may reduce the need that exists in a freshly minted course to think through and plan a course from the bottom-up. But when a course is a central part of any degree, as criminal law invariably is, the need for such informed planning is all the much greater.

Of course, it may be that this is not teaching that is stuck in a time warp. A consistency of approach over jurisdictions and through time in relation to the content of the criminal law curriculum may reflect the fact that the course content is (and since it became settled has been) satisfactory for the purposes of legal education at the academic stage. Nevertheless, it should always be a matter for consideration and discussion as to whether the content of a course remains fit for purpose: this means that, first, the purpose must be identified and, second, there should be analysis of the success of a course in securing this purpose. If this validates the typical structure, that is all well and good, but if it does not, or suggests that the traditional course is neither unique in achieving this or does not do so as well as alternatives, there may be reason to support change.

Regulatory constraints

Another factor that might impact a syllabus is the regulation of content by the legal profession – a quid pro quo for allowing the degree to play its role in the process of admission to the profession. To the extent that this conditions the content of a criminal law offering to the traditional structure, it might also be suggested that this confirms its value, as it has the collective experience of the profession behind it. However, unless there has been a considered process of arriving at the content set by regulation, exactly the same points as have been made earlier apply in relation to this constraint.

The interests of the profession and the academy should align. Both want to have graduates who understand substantive criminal law. For the profession, this understanding is necessary so that lawyers can apply the law, develop it through appellate argument, and contribute to law reform, as the profession regularly does. Legal academics wish for that outcome in light of the importance of having both graduates who go into practice and those who go into policy positions, as well as for the more purely academic outcome of securing an understanding of the law as a whole even if the graduate heads into a different direction.

Given this commonality of interest, pedagogically valid reasons for suggesting that a different structure to the academic criminal law course can secure this understanding of substantive criminal law should be persuasive to the profession's regulators as well. This in turn means that academia cannot simply adopt a stance of passive acceptance of what should be taught on the basis that the regulators prescribe it; rather, there should be discussion between the legal academy and profession as to the content of any prescription.

In any event, the approach to regulation is rarely prescriptive. In the countries from which chapter authors come, the framework is as follows. In New Zealand, Part 8 of the Lawyers and Conveyancers Act 2006 requires the New Zealand Council for Legal Education to set the standards for admission to the legal profession. Sections 274, 278, and 281 of the statute are key and are structured on the basis that those seeking admission have undertaken an academic law degree followed by a professional training course: there is no method for New Zealand students to take a non-law degree followed by a condensed introductory professional exam, as in England and Wales, though law students often take conjoint degrees and thereby undertake tertiary-level education outside law school.

Section 278 of the statute allows the Council to make regulations, under which it has made the Professional Examinations in Law Regulations 2008, which set out the requirements for admission to the fused profession of barrister and solicitor in New Zealand. As consolidated on 1 December 2014, the 2008 Regulations provide that the academic law degree required has to have been approved as a whole by the NZCLE (reg 3(1)(a)), and it must include courses on the legal system, contract, torts, criminal law, public law, and property law (reg 3(1)(b)). The content of the courses is also regulated (reg 3(2) and Schedule 1), but this is done in a way that provides no real restriction. The prescription for criminal law is in the following terms (in Schedule 1): "The general principles of criminal liability. The law relating to indictable and other selected offences chargeable under New Zealand law. Procedure on indictment and summary procedure (excluding Evidence)". As has already been noted, there has been no such thing as an indictable offence in New Zealand since the Criminal Procedure Act 2011 removed that previous classification. The important point for present purposes is that this prescription allows the law schools of New Zealand the academic freedom to choose which offences to teach, given that covering every offence triable before a jury and selected other ones cannot be the meaning of the language.

The situation in Australia is an interesting picture: a more detailed level of prescription from the profession nevertheless offers a level of flexibility and has not prevented a wider variety within the academy than in other jurisdictions. The regulatory framework is multi-pronged, but has developed a level of uniformity in relation to the requirements of the academic stage. In Victoria and New South Wales, the Legal Profession Uniform Law has been adopted: it is set out as Schedule 1 to the Legal Profession Uniform Law Application Act 2014 (Victoria). Part 2.2 includes provisions relating to admission to the profession, including completion of a degree that conforms to the Admission Rules that are developed pursuant to sections 420 and following of the Uniform Law. These are the Legal Profession Uniform Admission Rules 2015, and they in turn adopt standards developed by the Law Admissions Consultative Committee, which is a coordinating body amongst all the jurisdictions in the Commonwealth; these standards can be found as schedules to its Model Admission Rules 2015 and have been adopted also in the other jurisdictions.

What is included under the heading "Prescribed Areas of Knowledge" in relation to criminal law and procedure is the following, which is set out as alternatives:

1. The definition of crime
2. Elements of crime
3. Aims of the criminal law
4. Homicide and defences
5. Non-fatal offences against the person and defences
6. Offences against property
7. General doctrines
8. Selected topics chosen from

    - attempts
    - participation in crime
    - drunkenness
    - mistake
    - strict responsibility

9. Elements of criminal procedure. Selected topics chosen from

    - classification of offences
    - process to compel appearance
    - bail
    - preliminary examination
    - trial of indictable offences

Or topics of such breadth and depth as to satisfy the following guidelines:

> The topics should provide knowledge of the general doctrines of the criminal law and, in particular, examination of both offences against the person and against property. Selective treatment should also be given to various defences and to elements of criminal procedure.

In short, law schools can adopt what looks like the traditional content for a criminal law course, but they can go wider if that is the choice of the lecturer, provided that offences against the person and property are included. One suspects that items one through three and seven through eight on the list would feature in any course.

In the British Isles, the professional bodies in Ireland, Scotland, Northern Ireland, and England and Wales also have standards for the academic stage. In Ireland, both the Law Society of Ireland (for solicitors) and King's Inn (which controls advocates there) have detailed descriptions of the requirements allowed to proceed to the professional stage before admission. For King's Inn, this requires completion of an approved degree or a diploma course offered by the Inn: the degree must include certain topics, but criminal law is not one of these; the diploma course includes criminal law. However, the Inn requires students to pass an entrance exam that covers criminal law, for which the syllabus sets out the traditionally-taught range of general principles and the specific offences of interpersonal violence and property offences, as well as public order offences.

The Law Society of Ireland does not require entrants to have a degree, but it has an entrance examination that includes criminal law and procedure. The substantive offences included in the syllabus match those for advocates. Aside from the inclusion of public order offences, the list is essentially interchangeable with the first part of the Australian prescription set out earlier. The approach of the profession in Ireland is similar to that arising in the USA, where admission to the profession involves passing a bar examination. This involves a multistate bar examination that covers criminal law and has a syllabus for 2016 that includes the standard range of offences against the person and property and also refers to "possession offences". There is no reason to suppose that the regulators in Ireland would be less amenable to the development of a more flexible prescription if academic lawyers suggested that would be a good idea.

In Northern Ireland, the Solicitors Admission and Training Regulations 1988, made by the Law Society of Northern Ireland under powers given to it by primary legislation, require that solicitors have adequate knowledge of criminal law as part of the admission process, but there is no further specificity as to the details of this. It can be secured through a law degree, but it is also possible to undertake a degree in another subject followed by condensed postgraduate study in law (as in England and Wales, described in the following text). Professional training is then required. As for the Bar of Northern Ireland, the standard route to admission is via a Qualifying Law Degree and further professional training. The process of professional training for both branches of the profession is centred at the Institute of Professional Legal Studies in Belfast: its information booklet sets out the list of Qualifying Law Degrees, which can be in English law or Irish law or from one of Northern Ireland's law schools; students must have taken listed core subjects, including criminal law, but there is no specificity as to the content of the course.

In Scotland, membership to the Law Society of Scotland involves either an LLB in Scots law – which requires the degree to include certain topics, including criminal law – or working in a law firm and in both cases passing a Diploma in Legal Practice. There is no prescribed content for the degree-level course in crime; however, the Law Society sets out which components of the degree at each accredited law school have to be studied to secure progress towards membership in the Society. For the other branch of the legal profession in Scotland, the Faculty of Advocates similarly refers only to Scottish criminal law without giving further details in its Regulations as to Intrants of July 1996, as amended in March 2004 and December 2006 (appendix A(1) at p19).

Turning to England and Wales, there is also a split profession, but the Solicitors Regulation Authority and the Bar Standards Board had a joint Academic Stage Handbook (latest edition July 2014), which set out a joint approach. Either profession required students to obtain either a Qualifying Law Degree or any other degree followed by a conversion course that leads to a Graduate Diploma in Law, following which vocational training occurs, which differs according to the profession. (There are also Exempting Law Degrees, which combine a Qualifying Law Degree and the Graduate Diploma.) The Handbook includes an indication that students must be familiar with "the key elements and general principles of the following areas of legal study: . . . iii. Criminal Law" (pp18–19), but there is no further designation of this. This joint approach has recently broken down. However, the Bar Standards Board's Academic Stage Book for 2015–2016 indicates that criminal law is one of the required subjects to be taken at the academic stage but does not specify what it should contain (paragraph 1.7). Information on the website of the Solicitor's Regulation Authority at the time of this writing still refers back to the previous joint statement. In terms of the content of the criminal law course (or indeed any of the other six foundation subjects), the absence of detail grants what Sanders describes as "a huge amount of freedom"; he continues:

> one [qualifying law degree] might concentrate on why and how we criminalise some things and not others, while another might dwell on the meaning of "intention" and the point at which "property" in goods passes from A to B for the purposes of the law of theft. Any one programme might focus on the intellectual or the practical, the doctrinal or the contextual, the UK or the international and comparative.
>
> (Sanders, 2014, pp. 142–43)

In short, the regulatory regime is one that varies from offering no restrictions on what law schools can teach as part of criminal law (UK jurisdictions, New Zealand) to one that involves specificity with flexibility (Australia). Ireland has a practical requirement to teach the standard range of offences because they feature on the admission examination to the profession. However, two points arise: the profession could no doubt be asked to discuss what is prescribed, and the equivalent requirement for the multistate part of the bar exams in the USA does not seem to lead to a concentration on all the offences at the degree level, no doubt because students can be trusted to combine the commercial cramming courses for the bar exams and the general principles learned in the academic degree.

Pedagogical innovation

The level of similarity between criminal law courses outlined earlier does not mean that there is uniformity or that there has been no thought about pedagogy. A series of seminars and workshops at which initial versions of the material outlined earlier was presented and the questions raised discussed revealed instances where people had sought to innovate. Several attendees agreed to write chapters in this collection. No doubt there are others who have thought through how best to assist students to understand substantive criminal law in a way that meets the graduate attributes to which a particular law school aspires.

That leads to the aim of this collection. It is to collate a critical mass of thought as to how best to secure that understanding of substantive criminal law. Chapters deal both with the methodology of teaching and with course content. The reason for this is fairly self-evident: it is to encourage thought and action in that task. This does not mean that we denigrate the traditional course structure or call for its abandonment. Indeed, some chapters are premised on the traditional syllabus. Nevertheless, we are supportive of the message that a 'black-letter' course is a missed opportunity and of the approach of people such as Brown *et al.* (see Steel, chapter 9) and Gans (see chapter 8) who have designed textbooks to support a different approach to teaching. Our central purpose is to demonstrate that there are options for those who wish to teach criminal law in a way that does not merely replicate with updated cases a course that was taught in generations past.

Given this purpose, it is fitting that the first substantive chapter in this collection is 'Building Block or Stumbling Block? Teaching Actus Reus and Mens Rea in Criminal Law' by Fiona Donson and Catherine O'Sullivan, who draw on pedagogical research into "core concepts" and "threshold concepts". The authors begin with a description of the prevailing structure of criminal law textbooks and point to the prominence afforded to the foundational concepts of *mens rea* and *actus reus* in establishing the "general principles" of the criminal law. Donson and O'Sullivan suggest that this "traditional approach" "may impede the development of true understanding by obscuring the impact of public policy on apparently neutral principles". The chapter draws on research the authors carried out on student cohorts exposed to different teaching approaches. This indicated that, under the more traditional model, students were unlikely to gain a true comprehension of the relationship between *mens rea* and *actus reus* until the latter half of the criminal law course, with the "vast majority" taking until the revision period after the end of teaching to get to this point. This is highly problematic if the *actus reus/mens rea* divide is used for its expositive value in revealing the structuring principles of the criminal law. The chapter describes changes that were made to the criminal course in order to combat perceived deficiencies, chief amongst which was to embed coverage of the various *mens rea* standards throughout the course, using different offences to illustrate them, rather than covering them upfront. The expected and desired outcome was a "delayed", but ultimately "more complete and integrated understanding", and Donson and O'Sullivan's findings suggest that integrating study of the various *mens rea* standards with particular offences allowed for policy concerns to be addressed in a less abstract way. For instance, Donson and O'Sullivan point to the "malleability" of the law as an important threshold concept with which students particularly struggle and note the importance of building a "toleration of uncertainty". They also suggest that an ancillary benefit under the reorganisation was the increased breadth of the course.

In 'Teaching the Elements of Crimes', John Child also examines the way in which criminal law is taught through the use of organising principles. Child identifies two paramount aspects to the role of the criminal law teacher: "to teach [a] small subset of offences so as to provide students with a wide and contextual understanding of criminal law in general, and a mechanism through which to understand and analyse other specific offences in the future". The first of these aims comprises a theme that occupies later chapters in this volume, but Child's concern is with the second: devising a mechanism by which to enable an understanding of criminal offences and the ways in which they are constructed and interpreted. He proposes adopting "element analysis", as opposed to the "offence analysis" more familiar in English law schools and which derives from classifying the constituents of offences according to whether they comprise *mens rea* or *actus reus*. Like Donson and O'Sullivan in the preceding chapter, Child suggests that this classification is apt to cause confusion, particularly since the syllabus necessarily moves away from this strict demarcation when it comes to the appraisal of certain offences. Child cites manslaughter and theft as problematic in this respect, though the criticism can be extrapolated to a range of other offences. To counter this, Child proposes a form of element analysis that is capable of universal application to criminal offences and presents this as a matrix. Any analytical mechanism will have downsides when it comes to understanding the criminal law, and Child does not promote element analysis as a panacea, but he makes a convincing case for the adoption of his brand of element analysis in the teaching of the structure of criminal law offences.

In 'Enhancing Interactivity in the Teaching of Criminal Law: Response Technology in the Lecture Theatre', Kevin Brown and Colin Murray suggest adopting the use of interactive technologies in order to add value to the didactic, large-group lecture – a teaching technique that remains common in law degrees despite acknowledgement of its limitations. Brown and Murray give an account of what they describe as an "action-research project" that trialled the use of "real-time classroom response technology", and appraise its "strengths and weaknesses . . . as a means of generating interaction between the lecturer and large cohorts of students within the lecture hall". The aims of the research are highly student-centred, and the outcomes are tested by way of student surveys and are thus presented from the students' perspective. These results demonstrate a high degree of satisfaction in the students' perceptions of the usefulness of the technology. There is a particular focus on improving engagement on the part of the students, and generating interest in the material, and the findings are set in the context of other pedagogical research cited by Brown and Murray which has similar findings. It facilitates discussion, but also might encourage competition amongst the students, which appeared to garner a mixed response. The lecture that remains central to much criminal law teaching, and that is likely to remain so, can nevertheless be made a place for active learning techniques.

Also illustrated in the collection are instances of more wholesale revisions of the style of teaching the criminal law module. In 'Using Problem-Based Learning to Enhance the Study of Criminal Law', Ben Fitzpatrick points to the intuitive appeal of criminal law as a subject that is likely to engage student interest. He writes of feeling "very fortunate to work as an academic in the field of criminal law", but suggests that these inherent advantages should not distract criminal law teachers from an ongoing process of evaluation of the way in which it is taught. Fitzpatrick points to a number of "shortcomings" in the traditional approach to teaching criminal law: it tends to over-emphasise a narrow range of more serious offences, which does not reflect reality, and is not conducive to considerations of procedure in relation to minor offences; it is overly doctrinal and concentrates on substantive legal rules and is thus partial in its account of the criminal law; it is decoupled from "philosophical underpinnings" and "policy contexts", which underplays the political nature of the criminal law. Fitzpatrick advocates the adoption of problem-based learning (PBL) as a means by which to ameliorate these shortcomings. He first provides an account of the principal features of PBL, noting that the "authentic" way in which the issues are framed make for a ready explication of the procedural framework in which the substantive law operates. Importantly, the scenarios employed under this approach are used across sub-disciplinary settings, which helps to inculcate an understanding of the connections that exist between different areas of law. Beyond these, Fitzpatrick also points to other ways in which PBL might add significant value to the teaching and learning experience, such as fostering a collaborative approach to study and problem solving.

In 'Turning Criminal Law Upside Down', Jo Boylan-Kemp and Rebecca Huxley-Binns give an account of a pedagogical approach to the teaching of criminal law that bears a resemblance to some aspects of the PBL approach advocated by Fitzpatrick, this time drawing on practices developed by US-based physics professor Bob Beichner. Boylan-Kemp and Huxley-Binns begin the chapter by describing the classroom in which this method of teaching takes place, which is "unlike any seminar room [the student has] previously seen at . . . university" and designed in such a way as to promote and facilitate group work, supported by technology, and without a central presence for the teacher. The SCALE-UP approach developed by Beichner and Saul (2013) relies upon a high degree of autonomy on the part of the student, who takes responsibility for learning in a student-centred approach that eschews didactic delivery and "passive" learning. In place of this is a "focus on enquiry-based learning", which involves the students working together using a variety of media in order to source material relevant to the problem they have been assigned. Features of the method described by Boylan-Kemp and Huxley-Binns are the non-interventionist approach of the teacher and encouragement for the students to use books and the Internet, amongst other source material, in order to find the information they require.

In their chapter, 'Criminal Law Pedagogy and the Australian State Codes', Thomas Crofts and Stella Tarrant examine teaching criminal law in the context of the Australian Code states, which have implemented a codified criminal law that is in some ways fundamentally different to that of the other jurisdictions covered here. In explaining why this brings with it a need to consider course design, Crofts and Tarrant concentrate on the jurisdictions of Queensland and, principally, Western Australia, which both have statutory regimes derived from the Griffith Code devised in the late nineteenth century. The chapter begins by setting out what differentiates the code jurisdictions from the Australian common law jurisdictions, and then moves to discuss the impact this has on pedagogy. The authors point to the systematic nature of the criminal codes and the centripetal force they exert on all aspects of the criminal law, which also entails a clear view of the hierarchy of courts and the precedential value of their judgments. From here, Crofts and Tarrant ask whether educators teaching in common law jurisdictions might be able to learn from the pedagogical approach adopted in the Code states. They point out that much criminal law teaching underplays the now largely statutory basis of the criminal law across even nominally common law (and particularly Australian) jurisdictions, and even in those that do not have "consolidating acts" of the type that characterise the Australian common law states. As the authors assert, "the imposition of a clear distinction between what courts are doing in Code and common law jurisdictions is unsustainable, except as a matter of emphasis". Crofts and Tarrant suggest that more attention should be paid to the increasingly statutory basis of the criminal law.

Jeremy Gans's contribution ('Teaching Criminal Law as Statutory Interpretation') addresses a similar theme to that explored by Crofts and Tarrant in acknowledging the importance of statutes to the criminal law in every Australian jurisdiction. His chapter also resembles in some respects the integrative approach described by Donson and O'Sullivan, as well as Child's advocation of element analysis. In common with Child, Gans considers the "key skill" for criminal lawyers to be the ability to "determine the meaning of thousands of criminal offences"; since a criminal law course cannot hope to cover anywhere near all of these, the material covered should equip the student with the ability to do this. Teaching the criminal law through statutory interpretation comprises a distinctive approach, and Gans has written a textbook in order to support it (Gans, 2012). The course and text described by Gans are arranged thematically, with 'running examples' providing the subject matter through which to engage with the various concepts, and Gans suggests that the methodology could be adopted in any jurisdiction in which there is a significant statutory basis for the criminal law. Gans describes his approach to the criminal law as a "marriage between the substantive law . . . and core concepts", but there are some perspectives on the criminal law that are not easily accommodated. For instance, Gans concedes that the statutory interpretation approach is "not a natural fit" with some of the more critical approaches that might be taken to the criminal law, such as that offered by Tolmie.

Alex Steel is another Australia-based academic who (along with several co-authors) produces a textbook that deviates from the typical approach (Brown et al., 2015). In 'Shaking the Foundations: Criminal Law as a Means of Critiquing the Assumptions of the Centrality of Doctrine in Law', Steel criticises the traditional model of criminal law teaching, pointing to the standard arrangement of materials as being "presented as an ahistorical, timeless and logical division". The contingency of such divisions is demonstrated by reference to the very different conceptual demarcations found in Blackstone's *Commentaries on the Laws of England*. Steel marks Blackstone's efforts to "idealise the law into a rational system" as the beginning of a project of structuring that has been manipulated by numerous influential commentators over the ensuing centuries. Steel's chapter opens by pointing to the connectedness of the criminal law to other sub-disciplines across the legal curriculum and highlights how this renders an introverted criminal law course an artificial construct. He then describes the way in which the abstraction of the substantive criminal law can be given life by reference to the normative justification for offences and to the socio-political and institutional context in which the criminal law operates. Although Steel points to the usefulness of his approach for a practical, vocational understanding of the operation of the criminal law, the focus is not explicitly on engendering a vocational approach, but rather on presenting a realistic picture of the administration of criminal justice into which the more technical aspects of doctrine can be fitted.

Another aspect of fragmentation to be countered is the placing of substantive criminal law in the wider body of criminal justice. In 'The Challenges and Benefits of Integrating Criminal Law, Litigation, and Evidence', Adam Jackson and Kevin Kerrigan describe Northumbria Law School's experience of teaching criminal law, litigation, and evidence as part of an integrated course offered to first-year undergraduate students. Jackson and Kerrigan point to a "deeper approach to learning" that this helps to facilitate and suggest that it encourages a "decompartmentalisation whereby students are encouraged to think both about the interlinking nature of doctrinal law and procedural rules and the relevance of pervasive skills". The chapter begins by describing the curriculum development that took place at Northumbria Law School in the 1990s, set against the backdrop of contemporary changes to legal education in England. From here, the chapter moves to a discussion of the way in which the integrated course functions, with the authors describing a pedagogical approach that is "designed to introduce students to a mode of experiential learning". To this end, "the delivery of the module is by way of realistic scenarios out of which issues relating to the three elements . . . emerge", with the aim that "doctrinal and procedural understanding" develop concurrently. Throughout, Jackson and Kerrigan emphasise the 'realism' of the material with which students are provided and the importance of practitioner input in the teaching. The authors end by reflecting on the successes of the approach, the challenges that had to be overcome, and the ways in which the model could be improved.

Phil Scraton and John Stannard have a similar aim to avoid any problems of placing criminal law in a silo. They begin their chapter ' "Crime and the Criminal Process": Challenging Traditions, Breaking Boundaries' by setting out the criticisms levelled at the narrow focus of criminal law teaching in 1990 by Alldridge, and note that "it is disappointing that Alldridge's call for a significant reappraisal of Criminal Law teaching has not led to significant change". As they note, students may arrive with enthusiasm about criminal law to be informed that the core learning opportunities will start with the lesson that *actus non facit reum nisi mens sit rea* and that they will have to deal with such earth-shattering questions such as whether a man who takes what in fact is his own umbrella believing that it belongs to someone else is a thief. They go on to describe an approach adopted at Queen's University, Belfast, in which the undergraduate criminal law course was delivered by "fusing" "critical criminology and doctrinal criminal law". The course described was titled Crime and the Criminal Process and was delivered from 2006–13, and it aimed to avoid some of the pitfalls identified by Alldridge. The description of the course is broken down into two sections, with the first intended to introduce students to "foundational debates and dilemmas within academic and popular discourses concerning the context, circumstances, and consequences of 'crime' and criminal justice". Here, Scraton and Stannard attempt to move beyond unhelpful and circular definitions of crime as a "procedural violation", encouraging a wide-ranging social and political understanding of the 'nature and aetiology' of crime, looking to historical influences and media representations of crime and then moving to examine the "theoretical traditions" of criminology. In order to facilitate a greater degree of comprehension, students were asked their personal views about ostensibly minor infringements of the law and thus the role and function of the criminal law itself. The second part of the course was itself split into four sections: the criminal justice system as a State response to "the problem of crime", the institutional and procedural backdrop against and within which criminal law operates, selected substantive criminal offences and the issue of evidence and the proof burden, and, finally, the trial process, sentencing, and appeal.

The approach adopted by Scraton and Stannard involves an emphasis on teaching substantive criminal law as part of a wider context. Other contributions also explain the value of criminal law being taught with an eye on broader social and jurisprudential contexts. In the chapter titled 'Context and Connection', Ben Livings writes about how the introduction of context can improve student understanding. Livings suggests drawing from other sub-disciplinary areas that exist within the legal education curriculum in order to find material that can both provide context for a fuller understanding of the operation of criminal law and achieve the collateral aim of developing an appreciation of conceptual and practical connections that transcends ostensible subject boundaries. Livings posits that the typically atomistic approach of the law degree can engender a fragmented understanding on the part of students and that this inhibits a more holistic and integrated conception of law and the legal system. The chapter starts by setting out some of the forces that shape the curriculum of the law degree and which might impinge upon what can and should be achieved through the criminal law course. Livings points to the traditional doctrinal treatment of appellate judgments as symptomatic of an approach that marginalises the context in which criminal law operates, such as discretionary judgements by police and prosecutors, and the possibility of regulatory alternatives to criminal action. A more imaginative approach to the source material can foster connections with other parts of the curriculum, promote a deeper understanding of criminal law, and facilitate discussion of the "legitimate scope of criminalisation against a pluralistic regulatory and legal backdrop".

Turning to other contextual matters, in 'Teaching and Learning Criminal Law "in Context": Taking "Context" Seriously', Arlie Loughnan questions what it is that we mean when we talk about 'law in context'. Loughnan describes the growth and development of "law in context" in Australia against the backdrop of "black-letter" doctrinal teaching and learning methods, and notes its close ties to the "law and society" and "critical legal studies" intellectual movements. She then outlines four key features of a "law in context" approach: use of a conceptual lens, a historical sensibility, taking account of criminal law's institutional backdrop, and multidisciplinarity. After explaining what is meant by these, Loughnan applies each of them to a 'case study' of the criminal law's treatment of mental incapacity. Loughnan clearly sees great value in a contextualised approach in criminal law teaching, but she also perceives threats to its viability and practice in the "rise of the neo-liberal university", with the prevailing political and financial pressures felt in Australian universities (and indeed more broadly) threatening "institutional commitments to a 'law in context' approach to teaching". Whilst Loughnan concedes that it is "hard to pin down this evocative and talismanic term", she cautions that "law in context . . . seems vulnerable to an evacuation of all substantive meaning", and her chapter serves as a reminder both to value the possibilities it opens and to be mindful of what it means.

Khylee Quince also urges that contextual material must be brought to bear on the teaching of criminal law. In 'Teaching Indigenous and Minority Students and Perspectives in Criminal Law', Quince's concern is twofold: engaging students from indigenous and minority backgrounds and teaching criminal law in a way that inculcates an understanding of indigenous and minority experiences of the criminal law. The approach that Quince advocates provides "the opportunity to critically analyse black-letter criminal law, which is often presented as neutral and non-contestable", and its substantive points can be seen to apply to the experience of ethnic minorities in many jurisdictions. Quince describes the position of Māori in relation to criminal justice, pointing to an "over-representation as offenders and victims" and "under-representation as lawyers, judges, law makers and agents of enforcement". These phenomena need to be understood in terms of the potential dissonance between Māori culture and the practice of law as a colonial imposition, and Quince illustrates this through case analysis, which allows her to demonstrate the possibility for alternative accounts that may not be reflected in orthodox understanding of the practice of criminal law. Quince writes from the perspective of a Māori teacher of criminal law, as somebody with an "insider privilege" that brings both a depth of knowledge of the issues with which the chapter is concerned and a natural platform from which to discuss them. Although subjective experience facilitates the approach she advocates, Quince suggests non-minority teachers should also engage with "contentious matters concerning race or minorities in criminal law; omitting such concerns from the teaching of criminal law amounts to a 'sin by omission'".

In 'Introducing Feminist Legal Jurisprudence through the Teaching of Criminal Law', Julia Tolmie also gives an example of the way in which context can provide valuable insight into the operation of the criminal law. Tolmie focuses on violence against women as an important subject of feminist legal study, pointing to a criminal law that is gendered in terms of offenders and victims, a situation that is compounded by the intersection of this with problems relating to "racism and social marginalisation". Tolmie uses "intimate partner violence" to illustrate patterns of male violence and how this impacts upon women, and particularly those from socially disadvantaged backgrounds. She goes on to explore further examples of ostensibly objective standards that underpin the doctrinal arrangement of important criminal law doctrines, such as "consent", "compulsion" (or "duress") and "necessity". Tolmie argues that understanding such phenomena from a feminist perspective is an important counter to the misleading characterisation of the criminal law as "a neutral body of principles that applies impartially and equally to all individuals", since "formal equality" can result in "substantive inequality". Tolmie emphasises the importance of conveying these ideas to students, arguing that "it is an abdication of [the criminal law teacher's] professional responsibility . . . not to address the subject of violence against women and expose the students to what experts have to say about it". Like Loughnan, Tolmie acknowledges the "countervailing demands" of teaching criminal law, and her chapter raises the important and discussed quandary of what should come first when it comes to assessing priorities in the criminal law curriculum: "technical competence", or a contextualised critical understanding, or whether these are properly conceived of as inextricable and how such concerns can be addressed in the context of a crowded curriculum.

The latter issue is also raised by Kris Gledhill, in the chapter titled simply 'Choice', the central message of which is to assert that, in terms of substantive content, the criminal law's traditional and prevailing concentration on violent and property offending is unnecessarily constrictive. Gledhill suggests that "the teachers of criminal law should cast their net wider and consider making use of a range of other offences" and that a more open-minded approach to the content of the criminal law course brings with it a number of advantages. Gledhill starts by suggesting that the choice as to what to cover in a criminal law course should be underpinned, and shaped, by a consideration of its aims and that this should be underpinned by a sound understanding of research pointing to how this can be achieved. In keeping with this, Gledhill suggests for inclusion two potentially fruitful areas of the criminal law that rarely form a significant part of the curriculum: drugs law and driving law. The first reason advanced for their inclusion as substantive topics of study is the frequency of their respective commission, particularly when counterposed against the relative infrequency of homicide. The second is that drugs law, for example, may provide a "superior palette" for understanding and critiquing criminal law's central doctrines against policy demands. Driving offences can serve a similar function, and provide "a context that is familiar for most, which might assist comprehension". Gledhill's point is not necessarily that these topics should be adopted (though he makes a cogent case for this), but rather that against the backdrop of the permissive regulatory regime outlined earlier, there is little stopping criminal law teachers from conceiving of their subject a little more imaginatively.

Rounding off the collection with a further call to take a perspective that is wider than traditionally so, Shane Kilcommins, Susan Leahy, and Eimear Spain write in 'The Absence of Regulatory Crime from the Criminal Law Curriculum' about a comparatively neglected but important area of the criminal law. They advocate a shift in the content covered in the criminal law course in order to accommodate "regulatory crime". The chapter focuses on Ireland but picks up themes that will be recognised in all jurisdictions. It takes a look at the historical place and importance of regulatory bodies, charting their profusion as the police became increasingly more concerned with "ordinary crime" in the nineteenth century. Kilcommins, Leahy, and Spain portray regulatory concerns that are removed from the prevailing approach to criminal law teaching, which is "rooted in 'crime in the street' harms to individuals" and which only questions this according to a "traditional bifurcated representation of wrongs as either civil or criminal harms". In so doing, the authors argue that the criminal law syllabus is in danger of excluding important material relating to the wide-ranging and serious effects of misconduct that more often elicits a regulatory response, such as banking, corporate, and environmental wrongdoing. Kilcommins, Leahy, and Spain seek to promote understanding of these and point to the different priorities and approaches that often pertain in these contexts, such as a consideration of the merits of relative compliance (as opposed to sanctioning) regimes.

In sum, this collection of material about the pedagogy of criminal law provides a series of ideas for how to ensure that a core part of the law degree is delivered in a way that does not elevate the traditional way of doing things above all else. It illustrates possibilities for those who wish to go back to fundamentals and calibrate a criminal law module that reflects research-based lessons on how best to teach the subject and encourages the conclusion that there may be many ways to do that.

References

Alldridge, P. "What's Wrong with the Traditional Criminal Law Course?" (1990) *Legal Studies* 10 (1) 38–62.

Beichner, R. J. and Saul, J. M. *Introduction to the SCALE-UP (Student-Centered Activities for Large Enrolment Undergraduate Programs) Project* (2013) Proceedings of the International School of Physics, (Online) Available Via: North Carolina State University at https://www.ncsu.edu/per/Articles/Varenna_SCALEUP_Paper.pdf last accessed 02/12/2015.

Blackstone, W. *Commentaries on the Laws of England* (University of Chicago Press, 1979).

Blasi, G. L. "What Lawyers Know: Lawyering Expertise, Cognitive Science, and the Functions of Theory" (1995) 45 *J Legal Educ* 313.

Cownie, F., "Searching for Theory in Teaching Law" in Cownie, Fiona (ed.), *The Law School – Global Issues, Local Questions* (Aldershot: Ashgate, 1999), pp. 41–61.

Feinman, J. and Feldman, M., "Pedagogy and Politics" (1984) 73 *Geo L J* 875.

James, N. "The Good Law Teacher: The Propagation of Pedagogicalism in Australian Legal Education" (2004) 27 (1) *University of New South Wales Law Journal* 147.

Sanders, A. "Poor Thinking, Poor Outcome? The Future of the Law Degree After the Legal Education and Training Review and the Case for Socio-Legalism" in Sommerlad, H and others (eds.), *The Futures of Legal Education and the Legal Profession* (Oxford: Hart, 2015), pp. 139–168.

Schwartz, M. H., "Teaching Law By Design: How Learning Theory and Instructional Design Can Inform and Reform Law Teaching" (2001) 38 *San Diego L Rev* 347.

Simon, M., Ochialino, M. M., and Fried, R. L. "Herding Cats: Improving Law School Teaching" (1999) 49 *J Legal Educ* 256.

Chapter 2

Building block or stumbling block? Teaching *actus reus* and *mens rea* in criminal law

Fiona Donson and Catherine O'Sullivan

Introduction

The typical criminal law textbook has three main sections: first will be general principles, including chapters devoted to the *actus reus* and *mens rea*, and then chapters on particular offences and defences. The ordering of the second and third sections varies by publication; the primacy given to the general principles does not (a notable exception is the thematic arrangement of materials in Wells and Quick 2010). This division of material is replicated in criminal law courses around the common law world and reflects how most academics were taught and now teach the subject, fulfilling the "apprenticeship of observation" in pedagogical practice (Schulman 2005, p. 57).

The instructional reason behind this textbook and course structuring makes sense based on the theory that foundational concepts such as *actus reus* and *mens rea* must be mastered by students at the outset before they can move on to the substantive content of the offences and defences. This is because the offences traditionally-taught in criminal law courses are made up of *actus reus* and *mens rea* elements and defences either focus on a failure to prove the presence of an *actus reus* element (for example, the lack of volitional control in sane automatism) or *mens rea* (for example, insanity) or they add additional layers to the *mens rea* element in order to justify or (partially) excuse the (apparent) wrongdoing on the part of the accused (as with provocation). Unfortunately, in addition to ignoring the existence and operation of strict liability offences, this building block approach is not based on empirical evidence of students' acquisition of criminal law understanding.

In this chapter, we question whether the traditional approach is the best way of teaching students either the concepts of *actus reus* and *mens rea* or the criminal law generally and suggest it may impede the development of true understanding by obscuring the impact of public policy on apparently neutral principles. We will introduce and distinguish between core concepts and threshold concepts and argue that lecturer awareness of the different functions they fulfil will enhance student understanding of the law. We will then explain how an appreciation of these concepts has informed our module design, outline the methodology we used to empirically examine whether our module modification could improve student understanding, and present the results of that research.

Questioning the traditional method

The teaching of *actus reus* and *mens rea* at the beginning of a criminal law module and largely in isolation from the offences and defences in which context the case law exploring them arises means, for example, that students are immersed in murder cases when the *mens rea* of intention is taught before being introduced to the constituent elements of murder or the difference between murder and manslaughter. This is problematic because the symbolic and practical importance of the distinction between murder and manslaughter underpins the often tortuous judicial discussion about the lines between intention, oblique intention, and recklessness.

Our shared impression of teaching criminal law has been that true comprehension of the relationship between *actus reus* and *mens rea* is not gained until the second semester, and often as late as the revision period, long after these foundational concepts are supposedly assimilated. Worryingly, we found, particularly when marking exam papers by weaker students, that the artificial separation of *actus reus* and *mens rea* from the offences and defences means that some students fail to see the criminal law holistically, instead focusing mechanically on the separate elements without understanding how they connect with one another and with other offences/defences. Mid-range students may be able to mask their incomplete understanding by mimicking (Cousin 2006a, p. 5) what they think is required: as such, they can answer exam questions through the ritualised performance of understanding but have not acquired true understanding as they are unable to "adapt their learning to a new context or setting . . ." (Wilson et al. 2010, p. 98).

Wishing to determine whether our impressions were correct, and if so how best to modify our teaching approach, we reflected on how research on threshold and core concepts might inform our understanding of the difficulties our students faced.

Actus reus and *mens rea*: Threshold concepts or core concepts?

Threshold concepts

Meyer and Land, in their seminal work, define a threshold concept as "akin to a portal, opening up a new and previously inaccessible way of thinking about something. It represents a transformed way of understanding, or interpreting, or viewing something without which the learner cannot progress" (Meyer and Land 2003, p. 1). Threshold concepts have five characteristics, four of which are of interest to us in this article. They are transformative, irreversible, integrative, and troublesome. A threshold concept is transformative because the student experiences a shift in perception towards the whole or part of a subject that "may lead to a transformation of personal identity, [or even] a reconstruction of subjectivity" (Meyer and Land 2003, p. 4). A powerful instance is exposure to feminist theory through discussion of the law of rape. In response to the transformation occasioned, students may adopt a new vocabulary that relates to a specific discipline or community of practice (Land *et al.* 2005, p. 58). The discursive effect of threshold concepts includes using terms such as *actus reus* and *mens rea* in the context of criminal law.

The irreversibility of such concepts means that once they are understood, it is difficult to look at the same or similar material without awareness of this knowledge. For example, once fundamental concepts such as the rule of law are grasped, it is hard to imagine reversing that sense of "thinking like a lawyer". The integrative nature of threshold concepts allows the learner to make connections between concepts that were previously "hidden" to them (Cousin 2006a, p. 4). Finally, threshold concepts are troublesome in that their transformative and irreversible effect challenges or contradicts "deeply held or even cherished belief systems" (Ricketts 2004, p. 4).

Their troublesome aspect means that students may get stuck at the threshold and be unable or unwilling to move forward. Land *et al.* describe this as a state of liminality, where students "oscillate between earlier, less sophisticated understandings, and the fuller appreciation of a concept that their tutors require from them" (2005, p. 55). Some students will never acquire the mastery of the threshold concept to allow them to leave this liminal space, but may acquire a superficial understanding which allows them to engage in the mimicry noted earlier and/or students' default position, "[q]uasi plagiarism . . . copying it out of books and shoving it in . . ." (Cousin 2006b, p. 139). Others simply leave the course. The best students progress from a pre-liminal to a post-liminal state, although the time spent on the spectrum of liminality is variable (Kabo and Baillie 2010, p. 308), and the process is not straightforward, with students often moving backwards and forwards between the different states as their understanding develops (Weresh 2014, p. 698).

Threshold concepts in law

Thinking like a lawyer or legal reasoning has been identified as a key threshold concept in law (Åkerlind *et al.* 2010, p. 3). It is transformative and irreversible because "being able to engage in legal reasoning provides students with a sense of self-identity as a lawyer" which cannot be unlearned. It is integrative because it "inculcates students into the integrated nature of the culture of legal argument and the importance of authority and evidence to the efficacy of legal argument." It is troublesome because "it forces students to re-consider, and possibly to change, their preconceptions about what law is and what law can achieve."

However, as thinking like a lawyer is the "aspirational goal of legal education, or a graduate attribute" (Weresh 2014, p. 708), it is a threshold concept for the discipline of law rather than one specific to a subject within it (McDiarmaid and Webster 2010, online). As such, it develops via the acquisition of other threshold concepts. Focusing at the subject rather than the discipline level, Davies and Mangan helpfully suggest that "it may be appropriate to think in terms of a web of threshold concepts" and that threshold concepts may inform and transform the acquisition of subsequent threshold concepts (2007, p. 722).

It is therefore necessary to consider what other precursor threshold concepts are entailed in the study of law generally, and of criminal law in particular. Weresh has identified malleability/contingency as one such concept, which she defines as "an understanding of the latitude or flexibility a lawyer has in articulating legal principles" (2014, p. 719). Integral to her conception of malleability is a belief in the certainty of the law; she assumes a clearly defined set of rules that can be divined through the practice of legal reasoning, which can then be applied in a number of different but legally bounded ways by the student, *i.e.* the law is certain, but students are uncertain about how to use it. Similarly, McDiarmaid and Webster posit the existence of certain uncertainty: "[c]rossing the threshold [of contingency] allows student[s] to recognise simultaneously law's certainty – a quality which its continued credibility requires it to possess – *alongside its essential malleability*" (2010, online), notwithstanding their recognition that the law is a contested narrative.

We, however, reject the proposition that law is certain. There is, for example, significant scholarship on the uncertainty of the criminal law. Writing about how fear is constructed as reasonable or not in gendered and racialised ways in cases of rape and self-defence, Nelson notes "in the absence of critique, explication, commentary and investigation, the law may actually make little sense. The one thing that is consistent with much of the criminal law is its inconsistency" (2004, p. 1282). Indeed, the malleability Weresh identifies is partly due to the law's lack of certainty – an inconsistency derived primarily from the extent to which judges "cloak policy-based reasoning in doctrinal-sounding language" leading them to "treat like cases differently and different cases alike" (Midson 2010, p. 123). Meyer highlights the varying impacts of this on those working with the law:

> [w]hat legal theorists now acknowledge with uneasiness, first-year law students with terror and confusion, and lawyers with prosaic calm is that there may not be a right answer to every legal question. Two reasonable minds, both analyzing the same set of legal materials, may differ as to their proper application.
>
> (1996, p. 1468)

The terror that uncertainty creates in students occurs because it is contrary to their expectation that the law is the application of a set of clearly defined rules. Allen notes that business students "often tell me that they see law as a set of rules that have to be 'obeyed' and followed" (2007, online). This erroneous perception can be compounded by legal education which frequently valorises this rule-bound construction of the law. Sugarman writes that the "common law frame of mind" is that "although the law may appear to be irrational, chaotic and particularistic, if one digs deep enough and knows what one is looking for, then it will soon become evident that the law is an internally coherent and unified body of rules" (1986, p. 26). This is not, however, the reality of the law in practice because "principles are inseparable from interpretation and theory, which are shaped by values" (Midson 2010, p. 128). This disconnect between theory and practice gives rise to student puzzlement: "when is it that s/he is supposed to talk about 'law'; and when is it that s/he can talk about 'policy'?" (Sugarman 1986, p. 27). We have seen this same anxiety in our students who will ask, "But what is the law/the rule/the principle/the test?" The frequent answers – "it depends", or even worse from the students' perspective, "that's a policy decision" – are not the black-and-white responses that students expect.

The toleration of uncertainty, therefore, is a threshold concept that students must internalise as part of the higher skill of thinking like a lawyer, and is, we would argue, clearly operable in criminal law. In light of the fact that the criminal law continually changes in response to judicial decisions, legislative changes, and is constantly under review by policy makers and others, toleration of uncertainty is vital to position students to analyse and critique the law. Moreover, and importantly, uncertainty becomes an important strand in the web of threshold concepts that constitute the disciplinary threshold concept of thinking like a lawyer. This is important because, as Ricketts notes,

> The assumption is made that the thresholds and the knowledge are essentially neutral in nature. . . .
> Even a shallow analysis will reveal that law is about power and politics, and that the assumptions upon which legal truths are built are culturally and politically contingent. Students may have very good reason to resist inculcation into such belief systems.
>
> (2004, pp. 7–8)

Of particular concern for Ricketts is that the transformative nature of legal knowledge may cause students to "lose or fail to develop their capacity to critique" the foundational perspectives of the law (2010, p. 45). James agrees that current understandings of thinking like a lawyer are problematic and suggests reformulating it to "include an appreciation of ethical practice and social justice" (2007, p. 33). He notes that the implicit nature of the threshold concept in most legal curricula can lead to an "absence of critical reflection upon the precise nature of the threshold concept being taught . . ." (2007, p. 35).

The focus on the often hidden policy rationales underpinning the law that is explicit in our understanding of uncertainty thus ensures that as students develop their ability to think like lawyers, that way of perceiving the world is not reified. It also helps students to understand the sources of uncertainty in the law, and it exposes some of the tacit assumptions made in the criminal law in relation to personhood, autonomy, subjectivity, and rationality. Indeed, the entire idea of *mens rea* as we understand it today is infused with enlightenment understandings of rationality. It is therefore not a neutral aphilosophical legal concept but a culturally loaded one.

Core concepts

Core concepts are necessary to bring students to a threshold concept: "[a]core concept is a conceptual 'building block' that progresses understanding of the subject; it has to be understood but it does not necessarily lead to a qualitatively different view of subject matter" (Meyer and Land 2003, p. 4). They are not transformative in nature but are nonetheless essential for student understanding into and beyond the threshold concepts of a subject and wider discipline.

Actus reus and mens rea are key principles within criminal law and reflect conceptual understandings of how it should function. In particular, these include the requirements of a guilty act to ground liability and a responsibility element. Although understanding the role played by *actus reus* and *mens rea* in criminal law is essential to ground students' overall comprehension of the subject, our view is that they do not have enough of the necessary features to be threshold concepts. While the requirement of all characteristics is not essential (Meyer and Land 2006, pp. 6–7), at the very least, their troublesome, transformative, and integrative characteristics are "necessarily interwoven" (Davies and Mangan 2007, p. 712). *Actus reus* and *mens rea* can be troublesome concepts as indicated by the length of time students need to finally grasp the concepts, particularly with the boundaries between various *mens rea* states. However, they are neither integrative nor transformative. It is not the separate concepts of *actus reus* and *mens rea* that are integrative, but the way that they fit together and reflect the wider understanding of establishing criminal fault. These broader concepts need to be understood by students and then worked through in a more structural way as the basic building blocks of the subject. However, if students persist in viewing them in separate blocks, they will fail to see the bigger picture, including the role public policy often plays in their operation. It is when students realise how and why a particular outcome was obtained through the application of various principles and policies that their knowledge and appreciation of the operation of the criminal law is truly transformative.

The application of threshold concepts to our course design

Our exposure to threshold concept research resulted in our decision to modify our module structure. We believed that some small but significant changes to the traditional model of delivery could reduce students' tendency to view *actus reus* and *mens rea* as discrete topics and move them towards a more holistic understanding. First *actus reus* was introduced through a "definitional" introductory lecture. A public order offence (disorderly conduct in a public place: s5, *Criminal Justice (Public Order) 1994*) was selected to illustrate to students how *actus reus* works in a statutory context and allowed us to focus squarely on the *actus reus* components as it is a strict liability offence.

Second, instead of covering *mens rea* in detail, each *mens rea* state is briefly described in the introductory lecture with the promise that the specifics of each will be dealt with organically in the discussion of individual offences. Accordingly, *intention* is covered in murder, *recklessness* in involuntary manslaughter/criminal damage, *negligence* in gross negligence manslaughter, and *strict liability* in public order offences. In this way, *mens rea* states and/or their absence are concretised in, and integrated into, offences as opposed to being separated into abstract *mens rea* blocks.

Third, the order in which some elements were taught was moved. For example, discussion of the coincidence of *actus reus* and *mens rea* was moved to the beginning of the general discussion of *actus reus* to impress upon the students that although the two concepts are separate elements in many offences, when both are present, they need to be understood as operating together.

Fourth, by including public order offences in the first semester, we provided a more comprehensive and nuanced overview of criminal law to our students. Juxtaposing murder/manslaughter against the law of public order not only allows for a deeper understanding of *mens rea* but also creates space to challenge the notion that subjective *mens rea* is the key to understanding criminal law as a whole.

We hoped this subtle shift in emphasis would facilitate improved learning of the core concepts of *actus reus* and *mens rea*. By moving their teaching into the substantive offences, it was expected that whilst there may be a delayed understanding of their overall operation, when that understanding did come, it would be in the form of a more complete and integrated understanding of criminal law. After we applied these changes, we set out to test if they have in fact improved students' experience of learning these core concepts and in doing so began to redress the lack of empirical research into students' experience of learning *actus reus* and *mens rea*.

Researching module changes and student learning

We engaged with students who were studying the modified criminal law module (first years) and with students who had been taught under the old module structure (second years). A short anonymous questionnaire was distributed to first-year students towards the end of their module. Some questions asked for yes/no answers and others required explanations and illustrations. The response rate was around 25%–30% (from a student cohort of 140). We obtained eight volunteers for a more in-depth focus group, which was complemented by another comprising seven second years who volunteered to share their experience of the previous year. We followed up with a fresh first-year focus group of five students two years later once the new structure had become established. Focus group discussions were based on open-ended questions shadowing the anonymous questionnaire already shared with the student body. Despite the small number of volunteers, we were able to achieve gender balance and a mix of younger and mature students. No external limitations were placed on the research; consent was obtained from all involved and anonymity assured. The focus groups allowed us to explore in more detail our students' views on their levels of understanding and the challenges they faced in achieving this. We did this recognising that students may be uncomfortable acknowledging the difficulties they have in their learning/understanding process, particularly in front of classmates. Focus group discussion was therefore sensitive to this issue.

Complexity/uncertainty

As noted earlier, students rarely admit to a lack of understanding, particularly while they are in the process of learning. This was borne out by our findings. Despite the fact that we endeavoured to explicitly raise the concept of uncertainty, students were resistant to talking about their experience in this way. Instead they preferred the notion of complexity. More than 60% of those who filled in the questionnaire stated that the course was more complex than they had expected (25/40). Comments emphasised the fact that complexity was a part of the challenge in developing a clear understanding. Thus students noted that they "believed that it would be more straightforward" and they had "not envisage[d] the complexity of some of the concepts that would be covered in class." Typically, one student stated, "I didn't realise it would be so complicated, thought it would be more clear cut." Another noted that the wider legal/policy framework was an unexpected challenge: "I knew it would be an interesting topic, as the cases would be more than other modules, but I didn't realise the legal framework I would learn surrounding the topics."

Students' reconceptualisation of uncertainty as complexity in the anonymous questionnaires was echoed in the focus groups. When asked directly about uncertainty, one student went so far as to say, "I don't live in that place. I don't do uncertainty. I'm very structured. . . ." The term complexity appeared to be a more comfortable way of framing the idea of uncertainty, as it did not imply lack of ability on their part:

> There's always two solutions I suppose. There's two sides to everything. So I don't think you can be a 100% sure of anything going in. But you have to trust your own instincts too to a certain degree and go with what you think. . . . but if there's something conceptually that I didn't understand I would come back and say that I really don't get this and I need to understand this in order to come up with my own instincts. But where there's a big stone sitting there and I can't get over you know help.

This quote is from a second-year student who had finished the module and yet was still voicing concerns about uncertainty. The student also presents the idea of the threshold concept in an interesting way: the stone is blocking her way, preventing her movement to a better understanding of the subject.

One of the first-year students who had not yet completed the module noted the need to move from the idea that law is clear to understanding that there is space for different answers. Talking in the context of the law of murder and a high-profile case involving a 21-year old controversially convicted of the manslaughter of an 11-year-old neighbour, he said:

> [E]veryone had an opinion, it might not necessarily be a correct opinion, but everyone had one and everyone was talking about it and it just like makes everyone kind of like aware that there is a bit of an issue about it. In black and white you think he killed him, he's guilty, but you know there are other issues that you need to play out and so – I think like in terms of the whole societal perception of criminal law it should be black and white. You think someone's killed, someone's guilty. That's it. But you don't understand the in-between.

Finally, it is worth noting that sometimes students' perceptions of their own level of comprehension can be erroneous. Students self-reported in questionnaires a high level of understanding of *actus reus* and *mens rea* with 90% stating they understood the first core concept and 80% reporting they understood the second. Yet when describing *mens rea* in particular, students slipped into rather simplistic descriptions which emphasised the idea of "thinking about the act", "doing the act consciously". Student "understanding" of *mens rea* was therefore focused on intention with a lack of engagement with recklessness and negligence: "*mens rea* is crucial for criminal guilt as must plan and mean to do it." By way of contrast, focus group students from the same cohort were more aware of the gaps in their understanding, as will be elaborated under the next heading. This confirmed our expectation that the transition from pre- to post-liminal states frequently occurs in the revision period, which was when the focus groups occurred.

Spectrum of liminality

In discussing the process of developing understanding, students recognise that it is a process rather than a moment. Looking back, they are more comfortable saying, "I don't think you have the understanding at the start" and "Everything is side by side. It's listed." Yet they also note that understanding starts to "filter down" as the module develops; this was particularly emphasised by students who had experienced the reformed teaching approach.

Students acknowledged that they engaged in a degree of mimicry, even if they did not recognise it as such. They reported that at the start of the module, there was an element of learning and repeating what they believed was needed: "At the start I definitely learned off but towards the end of the course I started putting it all together." This is a process of transformation from a state of seeking to appear to understand into one in which the student has developed his or her understanding. When asked directly if they thought the course could be passed without being fully understood, many students said yes. Yet they also indicated that this would be insufficient for them in terms of their learning; there was a sense in which mimicry was an unsatisfactory outcome from their studies.

However, when pressed about how the law might be uncertain, for example, with different approaches to causation being developed by the courts, one student noted that this can be particularly challenging when sitting in lectures and hearing that there is no clear rule but that "when you start to do your revision . . . you just kind of learn to accept it's uncertain. I'll put this in my exam and just see where that gets me!"

With hindsight, students could recognise that there was often a delay in developing a clear understanding: "One of the big problems about Criminal is that everyone thinks they know it better than they know it. As you go along you think, oh yeah, I really know it. And then you get to study month and you realise, wow! I don't know this at all." Students reported how understanding came and went: "I know I drowned in *mens rea* when I came back to study and I was just saying what in the name of God – and the penny would have dropped after Christmas when we were doing the stuff but at the same time when I went back over it they were so big, they were chunks – and I just found that it was really, really tough."

Transformative nature of learning

As noted earlier, students had reported that mimicry was an option, albeit an unsatisfactory one. We pressed them to describe what it was like when they came to fully understand the subject. It was at this point that they highlighted the irreversible transformative nature of their learning: "You start thinking differently. Completely differently. Everyday stuff, you know. There's a crime going on everywhere you're looking like. I was obsessed." This is not necessarily a transformation brought about by the threshold concept of uncertainty, but it does indicate the process of change that students experience. Perhaps it is the first step towards the threshold concept of "thinking like a lawyer": stepping into the new arena of knowledge and perception and seeing crimes where once there was just everyday behaviour.

Students also noted that the exposure to policy and theory altered their perceptions around the law and enhanced understanding – "By understanding what is wrong you can see what is right. . . . By hearing different opinions, they don't necessarily go along with each other, they can clash . . . that's good." This explicit engagement with uncertainty allows students to recognise that it is part and parcel of the criminal law and that in order to develop their understanding, they need to accept and engage with wider debates.

Changing the teaching of core concepts

There is clear evidence from the focus groups that the changed module structure has the potential to facilitate improved learning of *actus reus* and *mens rea*. Students who had gone through the traditional approach identified their delayed understanding in this area:

> I thought it was very hard to do the categories of *mens rea* in isolation from maybe actual [offences] – I know there's cases used to explain them but when *mens rea* became much clearer in the second term . . . when you actually put intention to the *actus reus* in a really real way. Because when you're just doing you know recklessness and all the different forms of *mens rea* in isolation from each other it becomes kind of hard to distinguish them in your own mind, especially if you only have *actus reus* to go on and no solid founding.

A first-year student noted that the new structure would prevent the tendency to block off *mens rea* and *actus reus* into discrete subjects: "If you do *mens rea* as a huge topic. People tend to think that one topic is *mens rea*, another topic is murder, another topic is sexual offences, and so on. But kind of doing it as a smaller thing that feeds into everything else is an improvement."

In our view, supported by our findings, integrating *mens rea* into the substantive offences allowed students to understand the interconnected nature of the different parts of the module and gave them a more practical understanding of criminal law rather than an artificially constructed approach.

Conclusion

This research, particularly the focus group discussions – for which we would like to thank our participants for their openness – made us realise that the integration of *actus reus* and *mens rea* needs time to bed down even under our modified, threshold-concept-informed teaching structure. However, awareness of the existence of liminal states means that we can make the transition from pre- to post-liminal easier by letting students know that it will take time for them to acquire the necessary understandings around core and threshold concepts. This is particularly the case in relation to the uncertainty/complexity dynamic inherent in the subject matter. By forewarning students that the material is uncertain and by drawing attention to the multiple strands adopted by the courts and policy makers in developing the law, the threshold concept of uncertainty can be made more manageable for students. Thus, hopefully, the fear of acknowledging uncertainty is reduced. This does not mean that confusion and difficulties are eradicated. Far from it. Rather we are acknowledging that their experience of confusion is to be expected, it is normal, and that it is a process through which they will travel. As Osmond and Turner note, "By legitimising the 'stuck in the bubble' moment, it is possible that students may feel more comfortable in this moment at an earlier stage" (2010, p. 359). This in turn means that students do not give up on the module or the discipline, rather they can identify the cause(s) of that uncertainty and propose solutions that either resolve or accommodate it. In addition, this can create confidence that they will eventually cross the threshold, even if that journey may only take place during the study period just before the exams, as was reported by the vast majority of our focus group participants.

We have offered an explanation of the challenge students face in the development of their understanding of law, particularly criminal law, as being in large part because of their expectation of certainty:

> I suppose, in law in general you're surprised at how complex it is. I expected it to be like this is the law. If you do this, this happens. . . . One of the things I was really surprised about was how unclear it is in some cases.

Recognising the dissonance between this expectation of certainty and the reality of law's inherent uncertainty is important in ensuring that students are not left searching in vain for the rule(s) that will make sense of the conflicting case law, legislation, and wider policy debates. In addition, accepting the liminal nature of students' engagement with this threshold concept and the core concepts of each subject ensures that curriculum design can be tailored to foster student understanding both during the learning process and at the point(s) of assessment. As James notes, law schools generally do not explicitly recognise threshold concepts within their curriculum design (2007, p. 35), and this implicit engagement is replicated at module levels. By identifying threshold concepts, we can allow for the development of teaching that better facilitates student learning for understanding and also eases some of the angst students can experience in coming to terms with uncertainty and the role of policy and pragmatic decision making in the core concepts and key principles they deal with every day in the lecture theatre.

References

Åkerlind, G., Carr-Gregg, S., Field, R., Houston, L., Lupton, M., McKenzie, J., & Treloar, C., "A Threshold Concepts Focus to First Year Law Curriculum Design: Supporting Student Learning Using Variation Theory" in *13th Pacific Rim First Year in Higher Education Conference* (Adelaide, Australia: June 2010).

Allen, V., "A Critical Reflection on the Methodology of Teaching Law to Non-Law Students" (2007) 4 *Web JCLI*.

Cousin, G., "An Introduction to Threshold Concepts" (2006a) 17 *Plant* 4–5.

Cousin, G., "Threshold Concepts, Troublesome Knowledge and Emotional Capital: An Exploration Into Learning About Others" in J.H.F. Meyer & R. Land, eds., *Overcoming Barriers to Student Understanding: Threshold Concepts and Troublesome Knowledge* (London: Routledge, 2006b) 134–147.

Davies, P. & Mangan, J., "Threshold Concepts and the Integration of Understanding in Economics" (2007) 32(6) *Studies in Higher Education* 711–726.

James, N., "Teaching First-Year Law Students to Think Like (Good) Lawyers" in L. Wolff & M. Nicolae, eds., *The First-Year Law Experience: A New Beginning* (Canberra: Halstead Press, 2007) 32–45.

Kabo, J. & Baillie, C., "Engineering and Social Justice: Negotiating the Spectrum of Liminality" in J.H.F. Meyer, R. Land & C. Baillie, eds., *Threshold Concepts and Transformational Learning* (Rotterdam: Sense Publishers, 2010) 303–315.

Land, R., Cousin, G., Meyer, J.H.F., & Davies, P., "Threshold Concepts and Troublesome Knowledge (3): Implications for Course Design and Evaluation" in C. Rust, ed., *Improving Student Learning Diverstiy and Inclusivity* (Oxford: Oxford Centre for Staff and Learning Development, 2005) 53–64.

McDiarmaid, D. & Webster, E., "Contingency and Contested Narrative: A Threshold Concept in Legal Education" (2010) 20 *Directions in Legal Education, UCKLE Newsletter* (online).

Meyer, J. & Land, R., *Threshold Concepts and Troublesome Knowledge (1): Linkages to ways of thinking and practising within the disciplines* (ETL Project, Occasional Report 4, May 2003).

Meyer, J. & Land, R., "Threshold Concepts and Troublesome Knowledge: An Introduction" in J. Meyer & R. Land, eds., *Overcoming Barriers to Student Understanding: Threshold Concepts and Troublesome Knowledge* (London: Routledge, 2006) 3–18.

Meyer, L.R., "When Reasonable Minds Differ" (1996) 71 *NYUL Rev* 1467.

Midson, B., "Teaching Causation in Criminal Law: Learning to Think Like Policy Analysts" (2010) 20 *Legal Education Review* 109–136.

Nelson, C.A., "Consistently Revealing the Inconsistencies: The Construction of Fear in the Criminal Law" (2004) 48 *St. Louis U LJ* 1261–1283.

Osmond, J. & Turner, A., "The Threshold Concept Journey in Design" in J.H.F. Meyer, R. Land & C. Baillie, eds., *Threshold Concepts and Transformational Learning* (Rotterdam: Sense Publishers, 2010) 347–363.

Ricketts, A., "Threshold Concepts in Legal Education" (2004) 26(2) *Journal of Educational Studies* 2–12.

Ricketts, A., "Threshold Concepts: 'Loaded' Knowledge or Critical Education?" in J.H.F. Meyer, R. Land & C. Baillie, eds., *Threshold Concepts and Transformational Learning* (Rotterdam: Sense Publishers, 2010) 45–60.

Schulman, L.S., "Signature Pedagogies in the Professions" (2005) 134(3) *Daedalus* 52–59.

Sugarman, D., "Legal Theory, the Common Law Mind and the Making of the Textbook Tradition" in W. Twining, ed., *Legal Theory and Common Law* (Oxford: Blackwell, 1986) 26–62.

Wells, C. & Quick, O., *Lacey, Wells & Quick Reconstructing Criminal Law*, 4th ed. (Cambridge: CUP, 2010).

Weresh, M.H., "Stargate: Malleability as a Threshold Concept in Legal Education" (2014) 63(4) *Journal of Legal Education* 689–728.

Wilson, A., Åkerlind, G., Francis, P., Kirkup, L., McKenzie, J., Pearce, D., & Sharma, M.D., "Measurement Uncertainty as a Threshold Concept in Physics" in *Creating Active Minds in our Science and Mathematics Students: Proceedings of the 16th UniServe Annual Conference 2010* (Sydney: UniServe Science, University of Sydney, 2010) 98–103.

Chapter 3

Teaching the elements of crimes

John Child*

The criminal law of England and Wales, as with other jurisdictions, is made up of many thousands of offences. Therefore, no more than a small sample could ever be taught within a criminal law module. The task for the academic is to teach this small subset of offences so as to provide students with a wide and contextual understanding of criminal law in general and a mechanism through which to understand and analyse other specific offences in the future. Both aspects are vital to any criminal law module, but it is the mechanism aspect that will be the focus of this chapter.

Our mechanisms for understanding and analysing criminal law are often referred to as the elements of crimes. Essentially, we aim to deconstruct *whole* criminal offences into their constituent *elements*. We do this in order to identify patterns between offences (often referred to as general principles), encourage consistent analysis between offences, provide a vocabulary for commenting on specific parts of offences, provide a structure for independent analysis of future offences, and so on. However, as discussed by Fiona Donson and Catherine O'Sullivan (Ch 2), the identification and use of elements within the criminal law can also be problematic, potentially complicating rather than facilitating analysis and debate.

This chapter explores the teaching of criminal elements over five sections. The first discusses current practice in teaching, textbooks, and in court judgements, highlighting problems of incoherence and inconsistency. The second examines the potential for a universal structure of element analysis and how this can be used in teaching. The third highlights the potential advantages of this, with the fourth highlighting some potential problems. Finally, the fifth provides an overview of element analysis in other common law jurisdictions. The discussion makes use of law and psychology literature to explain and support a number of the points made. However, it should be acknowledged that much of the substance of the chapter has emerged more organically from experience and discussion with colleagues.

---

* I would like to thank Mark Walters, Tanya Palmer, and Colin King for helpful comments on a draft of this paper. The usual disclaimer applies.

Current practice in England and Wales, current concerns

Analysing the criminal law through elements (of one kind or another) is entirely standard practice. In England and Wales, this predominantly focuses on the separation of actus reus (external elements of an offence) and mens rea (mental elements of an offence), which can be usefully referred to as 'offence analysis' (Robinson and Grall, 1983). Discussion of offence analysis generally takes place in the early lectures of a criminal law module and almost universally within the early chapters of textbooks. Students are thereby set up with a toolbox for analysis and a structure through which to make sense of each of the specific offences tackled during their studies. Rather than viewing each 'new' offence as a unique collection of rules, students are encouraged to find order: to separate the offence in terms of actus reus and mens rea, to clarify both sets of requirements, and, through this, to see commonalities and differences between offences. Specifically, these early lectures/chapters use offence analysis to identify and explore the general principles of criminal law: the act requirement, the rules on omissions, the rules of causation, the definition of mens rea terms, and so on.

So far, so good. There is occasionally some dispute about whether a particular requirement should be classified as actus reus or mens rea (Sullivan, 1990), and this may lead to some uncertainties, but offence analysis generally works well in theory. Problems fully emerge, not in theory, but in practice. This is because, having explored the general principles through the mechanism of offence analysis, and having applied this to initial offences (most commonly murder), the mechanism is not consistently applied to other offences. Rather, with teaching and textbooks (understandably) mirroring the much less consistent language and analysis from court judgments, offence analysis is often ignored and/or supplanted with an entirely new mechanism.

Examples of where the actus reus/mens rea distinction is ignored (at least partially) include core offences such as manslaughter and theft. When analysing gross negligence manslaughter for example, we do not identify external or mental elements, rather we focus on duties of care, a breach of these duties, death, and the grossness of D's negligence. When analysing unlawful act manslaughter, we identify an unlawful act, dangerousness, and death, even though these requirements involve a mix of actus reus and mens rea. Even when we analyse offences such as theft, where the terms actus reus and mens rea are often used, the five-part separation of appropriation, property, ownership, an intention to permanently deprive, and dishonesty tends to dominate as our primary analytical tool. This approach to theft is presented as anti-offence analysis because even quite brief reflection on the element of 'dishonesty', often presented unquestionably as a mens rea requirement, reveals a combination of actus reus and mens rea: D's conduct must be dishonest by the standards of honest and reasonable people (external evaluation), and D must appreciate that this is the case (mental evaluation). Even if D believed that her conduct was dishonest, if the jury does not, then the requirement of dishonesty will not be satisfied.

Sidelining the use of actus reus and mens rea in relation to these offences does not impact the substance of the law, and it is important to remember that offence analysis is nothing more than an analytical tool. However, there are negative impacts for students. First, in the absence of a common structure to learn these offences with, the requirements are memorised in isolation, making them more easily confused or forgotten (Bower, 1970). And second, because the general principles are learned through offence analysis, students often fail to apply them to these offences, or require specific additional prompting to do so.

Just as problematic are the occasions where offence analysis is supplanted by an alternative or additional mechanism. The clearest example of this comes through the general inchoate offences and complicity and the mechanism of analysis that distinguishes conduct, circumstances, and results. The approach usually taken here has been referred to as "element analysis" (Robinson and Grall, 1983). This approach is commonly used within the examination of complicity and conspiracy, and it is *essential* for the application of attempts (Criminal Attempts Act 1981, s1) and inchoate assisting or encouraging (Serious Crime Act 2007, Part 2). It is essential for these latter offences because the mens rea requirements of attempt and assisting or encouraging explicitly relate to the elements of the offence attempted, assisted, or encouraged. For example, where D assists P to commit criminal damage, section 45 of the Serious Crime Act 2007 requires D to *believe* that P will complete the *conduct element* of the criminal damage, whereas D need only be *reckless* as to P completing the *other elements* (Child, 2012). In this way, it is essential for students to understand element analysis in order to apply the assisting or encouraging offence, as in our example, to distinguish the conduct element of criminal damage from the other elements. Additionally, because these inchoate offences apply generally across the criminal law (e.g., attempted murder, attempted rape, attempted theft, etc.), students must be able to re-analyse *all* the offences they have studied using element analysis where such offences are attempted or assisted or encouraged. Unsurprisingly, students generally struggle to meet this challenge, and equally unsurprisingly, academics may be tempted to exclude such offences from the syllabus to avoid it.

It should be stressed that the concerns raised in this section do not generally relate to the substance of the law. Despite inconsistent methods of analysis, the substantive rules remain the same. And in this vein, we could simply tell students to embrace the inconsistencies as examples of the evolving and dynamic nature of common law analysis. However, to do so, we must also accept the highlighted difficulties that this causes students and perhaps question whether we should be teaching offence analysis as our introductory method at all. It is my belief that we can at once present the complex inconsistencies of the criminal law to students, whilst also providing them with a universal tool for discussion: element analysis.

Teaching element analysis

The central proposal of this chapter is that we should use a single mechanism for analysis throughout our teaching. Element analysis is preferred because it is essential for the application of certain offences, and because it provides a more precise structure than offence analysis. This approach is adopted throughout my teaching, as well as within the textbook I co-author (Child and Ormerod, 2015). For ease of reference, the seven elements identified through the preferred method of element analysis are presented in chart form in Table 3.1.

As the chart demonstrates, this method of element analysis still makes use of the actus reus/mens rea distinction, but supplements it with the further distinction of conduct, circumstance, and result. Take the example of criminal damage (Criminal Damage Act 1971, s1). The conduct element of the actus reus is the bodily movement required for the offence (e.g., throwing a stone), the result element is the required consequence of that movement (e.g., damaging property, such as smashing a window), and the circumstance element relates to any surrounding required facts (e.g., that the property (window) damaged did not belong to D). Each element is required for liability, in addition to their corresponding mens rea. The final ulterior mens rea element (element 7) is my own addition to the mechanism (Child, 2014) and refers to mens rea requirements that do not correspond to elements within the actus reus (e.g., being reckless as to the endangerment of life, for aggravated criminal damage).

Every criminal offence can be broken down and discussed using this method of element analysis. Certain offences, such as aggravated criminal damage, include requirements within all seven elements. However, this will not always be the case: most offences do not include an ulterior mens rea requirement (element 7), and conduct crimes do not include result requirements (elements 3 and 6). Thus the chart can be used to explore all offences, but this does not mean that all offences must include requirements relating to all elements. Where an offence is analysed, which is not generally discussed using element analysis or even offence analysis (e.g., manslaughter, theft, etc.), such offences can still be introduced using element analysis as a point of consistency before moving on to explain how the offence is alternatively discussed in the courts so that students

Table 3.1

	Actus Reus	Mens rea
Conduct element	1	4
Circumstance element	2	5
Result element	3	6
Ulterior mens rea element		7

are not confused when reading cases. In this way, students are provided with a universal tool for analysis, but they are also taught to engage with the inconsistencies of law in practice.

Advantages of teaching element analysis

There are four principal advantages to teaching element analysis as a universal tool: greater precision when teaching the general principles, greater consistency when teaching as a tool for analysis, more effective teaching as a structure to aid memory, and more manageable for teaching inchoate offences and complicity. Each advantage is presented in turn.

Teaching the general principles

When first introducing the general principles of criminal law, the precision of element analysis can be very useful. For example, when discussing the act requirement, this can be done in relation to the conduct element specifically (elements 1 and 4), avoiding the common student conflation of the act requirement and actus reus more generally. The requirement of coincidence can also be more accurately presented in relation to mens rea coinciding with the conduct element of an offence (element 1), as opposed to the actus reus. When discussing causation, this can be presented as the required nexus between the conduct and result elements within the actus reus (elements 1 and 3), clearly demonstrating how it works within the structure of a result crime. And of particular importance, element analysis also makes it much easier to explain to students that the mens rea of an offence is not necessarily defined by a single term, but may vary between different elements (e.g., intention as to the result element, recklessness as to the circumstance element, and so on). Indeed, the mechanism even facilitates the teaching of mens rea terms, allowing the lecturer to clearly present occasions where a particular term is only relevant to a certain element of the actus reus (e.g., voluntariness and the conduct element) as well as where a term varies in its definition between elements (e.g., knowledge as to circumstances or results).

Teaching a tool for analysis

Element analysis provides students with a toolbox to help them with their studies. Where the task is simple comprehension, element analysis allows students to break down a complex whole into more easily understood sections, which is essential in relation to a lot of complex modern statutes. The mechanism also facilitates focused analysis upon individual elements, highlighting uncertainties, allowing precise comparison between offences, and providing the language necessary for communicating this analysis to a reader. As Robinson has commented on codification more generally, for which he sees element analysis as a central component, structured analysis of legal rules will often expose problems that would otherwise be missed:

> The rambling paragraphs of case opinions and scholarly literature . . . provide a permanent haven for the murky rule. Leaving the law's rules to the shadows of case law and scholarly literature, where there is never a clear target, means less likelihood of seeing and correcting law's flaws.
> (Robinson, 1998)

Element analysis also provides a universal method of analysis that can be used by students when discussing other offences in the future. In this way, element analysis can help avoid the criminal law module becoming an exercise in memorising a set of offences that may change over time, and instead enables students to develop skills that can be (re)applied throughout their current and future analysis of the criminal law.

Teaching a structure to aid memory

Having stated that criminal law modules should avoid becoming exercises in memory retention, it should nevertheless be acknowledged that memorising the detail of offences can play a significant part in exam performance. In this regard, there is clear support within the psychology literature that memories are more effectively stored and retrieved where they are associated with an analytical framework (Bower, 1970; Reed, 2012). Element analysis provides that framework. For example, rather than simply trying to remember all the various requirements for murder, students can work through the offence logically in their minds: are there any required circumstances? What mens rea is required for these? Are there any required results? What mens rea is required for these? And so on. This process aids students when they are trying to remember what they have learned as well as exposing gaps in their knowledge (hopefully before the exam!) that they should investigate further.

Teaching inchoate offences and complicity

Academic discussion of the general inchoate offences and complicity has, over time, become reliant on element analysis, which is needed to break down the complexity of these offences and describe how they work. We see this, for example, across the range of recent projects in this area carried out by the Law Commission of England and Wales (Law Commission, 2006, 2007a, 2007b, 2009), where the Commission employs element analysis both within the discussion of the law as well as within its proposals for law reform. In order for students to engage with such material, it is important that they understand how to use element analysis.

Beyond this, as discussed earlier, the use of element analysis within offences of attempt and assisting or encouraging is not *simply* analytical. Rather, it is essential to use element analysis in order to apply these offences in practice: we must distinguish the elements of the principal offence attempted, assisted or encouraged in order to know what mens rea is required in relation to them. This necessity has developed through case law for attempt (*Khan* [1990] 2 All ER 783), where the courts have isolated the circumstance element of a principal offence for separate treatment, and through statute for assisting and encouraging (Serious Crime Act 2007, Part 2), where the conduct element must be distinguished.

Given the role of element analysis within these offences, the mechanism becomes essential for any teaching in this area. It is possible, of course, that the teaching of element analysis could be restricted to lectures on inchoate liability and complicity, and I believe that this is common practice in many institutions in England and Wales. The problem with this approach, however, is that the general inchoate offences and complicity apply across the criminal law (e.g., attempted murder, assisting theft, accomplice to a sexual offence, etc.). Therefore, isolating the teaching of element analysis to these topics effectively asks students to relearn all the offences they have encountered within the criminal law course using this new mechanism of analysis as well as learning how the mechanism itself works. Where element analysis is introduced from the beginning, and where it is used consistently within the analysis of each substantive offence, the challenge for students when learning the inchoate offences and complicity becomes considerably more manageable.

Problems with teaching element analysis

Despite the advantages of element analysis, it is important to recognise that there are several problems highlighted in the literature; problems that can be mitigated but not entirely resolved. The two major issues that I would like to discuss here are those relating to consistency between legal sources and the internal coherence of element analysis.

Problems of consistency

Element analysis is not standardly used by courts or commentators when discussing most criminal offences in England and Wales. Although it is routinely used in more codified common law jurisdictions such as the United States and Australia (US Model Penal Code; Australian Criminal Code), scepticism about the usefulness of element analysis in England and Wales has severely limited its application. Therefore, as discussed earlier, it would be inappropriate to teach students the criminal law using element analysis alone. Rather, in order to maintain the benefits of internal consistency (i.e., using element analysis to discuss each offence), whilst also enabling students to engage with the analysis of courts and academic commentary (i.e., analysis that rarely uses element analysis), it becomes necessary to discuss two mechanisms of analysis when teaching each new offence (i.e., element analysis and whatever form of analysis is most commonly employed in relation to the particular offence).

This approach presents a number of challenges. For students, learning two mechanisms for each offence represents a significant increase in what they are expected to learn and an increase based on form rather than substance. Thus it is questionable whether spending additional time on mechanisms for analysis detracts from alternative discussions – discussions which could focus more directly on the substance of those offences and the normative questions that underpin them. Additionally, problems can emerge for students who confuse and conflate the different mechanisms within their analysis of offences, both in their learning as well as in their discussion. For academics teaching criminal law, similar problems emerge in relation to additional material and time constraints, which mean that compromises are always necessary when considering what material to include or exclude. It can also be challenging, particularly across larger teaching teams, to ensure consistency between lecturers.

Although these problems of consistency are important, they should not be overstated and can be minimised. First, if inchoate offences and/or complicity are taught, as surely they must be, then teaching multiple mechanisms, including element analysis, is already essential: the question is simply where within the course this teaching should come. Second, even if these general offences are not taught, teaching multiple mechanisms can have pedagogic value. This value manifests in a number of ways. The main advantage of element analysis as an additional mechanism is that it provides a point of consistency and a detailed tool for analysis (points discussed earlier), but it also helps to demonstrate the role of such mechanisms (including their flexibility) as distinct from substantive legal rules. For example, where students have struggled with the element analysis of a particular offence, confusing or conflating it with other mechanisms, it is useful to remind them that (general offences aside) the use of multiple mechanisms is not essential in every case. Indeed, when applying or discussing an offence, students should be encouraged to *choose* whichever mechanism they deem most appropriate, making decisions about whether the additional detail of element analysis will facilitate or confuse their argument.

Problems of coherence

Element analysis has attracted considerable and sustained criticism for its perceived incoherence as a form of analysis, with commentators stressing the difficulty of objectively distinguishing elements. Such criticism has been discussed across the common law world, but has had particular impact in England and Wales (Buxton, 1984; Duff, 1996). Taking the offence of criminal damage, for example, a lack of precise rules for distinguishing elements makes it difficult to say whether the result element of this offence is simply 'damage', with the issue of 'ownership' classified as a circumstance; whether the result element is 'damage to another's property', with no distinct circumstance; or even whether the result could be 'damage to another's property caused by D'. These confusions are particularly important when applying general inchoate offences that rely on such distinctions to identify mens rea, but they are also problematic for anyone using element analysis to discuss any aspect of an offence. This criticism has been central to the underuse of element analysis in England and Wales generally, and it remains a strong reason against its use within teaching. In short, the mechanism may raise more questions than it answers.

Several responses can, and have, been given to this line of criticism. These range from early denials that the problem exists (Williams, 1983), partial acceptance of the criticism (Law Commission, 2006, 2007a, 2007b), through to a more general acceptance of the criticism, followed by detailed re-constructions of element analysis (Child, 2014; Robinson and Grall, 1983). However, none of the approaches have fully undermined the criticism, and certainly not without introducing additional complexity.

Such criticisms are not, however, fatal to the usefulness of element analysis. This is because, although any proponent of element analysis must acknowledge a degree of uncertainty when separating elements, the removal of such uncertainty is not *essential* for a mechanism of analysis. It is debatable whether such uncertainty alone should be sufficient to undermine the stricter and more substantive use of element analysis within the general inchoate offences and complicity (a debate for another time), but mechanisms of analysis generally are used to aid discussion rather than create rigid distinctions. Indeed, as was identified in the first section of this chapter, the more traditional mechanism of offence analysis also lacks complete objectivity when separating actus reus and mens rea.

It should also be emphasised that even the debates created by current uncertainties in relation to element analysis are not always trivial, but have themselves often proved useful in unlocking areas for important normative investigation. For example, if we need to identify and distinguish the conduct element of an offence, then this leads us to question what we mean by 'conduct', including what the role of conduct is within the construction of an offence and the assigning of criminal responsibility, what the role is (if any) of the act requirement within criminal law, and so on (Moore, 1993). Equally, where we separate the result element of offences as something caused by D's conduct, then this can often lead to questions of responsibility and moral luck (i.e., whether the law should assign additional blame where D's attempted harms have come about and corresponding leniency where they are (for whatever reason) thwarted (Alexander et al., 2009). In these ways, and through many other examples, the focus of element analysis and the distinctions it draws seem to be appropriate, and even where uncertainty arises, that uncertainty will often stem from and represent an important and interesting normative question that might otherwise have been missed.

Element analysis and other common law jurisdictions

This chapter has focused on teaching criminal law in England and Wales, but much of the debate applies equally to other common law jurisdictions. This section provides a brief overview detailing the role of element analysis within other selected jurisdictions. Although element analysis often plays a greater (or certainly more established) role within many such jurisdictions, similar criticisms regularly emerge.

In certain jurisdictions, we see the use of element analysis for analytical purposes, or within law reform proposals, but without its consistent application in law. This is apparent in Canada and Hong Kong, for example, where Law Reform Commissions have recommended the use of element analysis within the definition of inchoate offences and/or mens rea definitions, but without legislative success (Law Reform Commission of Canada, 1987; Law Reform Commission of Hong Kong, 1994).

In other jurisdictions, such as Australia, New Zealand, and America, the use of element analysis is relatively advanced. In Australia, the Model Criminal Code (MCC) uses element analysis to define fault terms (Div 5) and for the presumption of fault (Div 5.6), and the courts have employed it to define inchoate liability (*Evans* [1987] 48 SASR 35). In New Zealand, the 1989 Crimes Bill used element analysis to define inchoate liability, an approach later employed by the Supreme Court in *L* [2006] 3 NZLR 291. Perhaps the most entrenched use of element analysis, however, can be found in America. The US Model Penal Code uses element analysis to define all fault terms (§2.02), as well as within the definition of attempts (§5.01). This structure has been adopted in all but two of the US jurisdictions where reform has occurred and has been described as 'the most significant and enduring achievement of the Code's authors' (Robinson and Grall, 1983).

Each of these jurisdictions, however, have also seen problems with element analysis and explicitly questioned its usefulness. In Australia, for example, commentary to the MCC describes the problems of defining element analysis (Commentary s202), and despite the initial acceptance of the approach for inchoate liability in *Evans*, this case was effectively overruled just five years later in *Knight* (1992) 175 CLR 495. In New Zealand, despite judicial endorsement in *L*, a review of the 1989 Crimes Bill highlighted a number of concerns about the objective and coherent application of element analysis, with the Consultative Committee eventually recommending offence analysis alone (1991). Even in America, despite 'remarkable' acceptance of element analysis (Gainer, 1987), issues are still raised about the 'fuzziness' of the definition of the conduct element in particular (Moore, 1993; Robinson and Grall, 1983). The problems here mirror those identified in the previous section of this chapter.

Conclusion

This chapter advocates the adoption of element analysis in the teaching of criminal law. Particularly when it comes to the approach that prevails in England and Wales, this amounts to a significant change in the way we analyse, and teach the analysis, of such law. Teaching element analysis as a consistent tool of analysis is challenging, both in terms of the mechanism's own internal coherence as well as the lack of similar analysis and debate (for many offences) within surrounding court judgments and within other academic material. However, the potential benefits are clear. Element analysis provides students with a tool for understanding, remembering, and engaging with the many and varied inconsistencies of the current law; with a tool for consistent and precise analysis.

By setting out the advantages and disadvantages of element analysis, the intention was not simply to say that one outweighs the other. The mechanism of element analysis outlined in this chapter clearly needs further work, and can be improved. However, I contend that the problems highlighted earlier (both in England and Wales and beyond) are not terminal to the usefulness of element analysis, and the debates they raise have generally invigorated legal scholarship rather than stifling or confusing it. The idea here is to choose a mechanism that provides the most promise for improving student learning and to work further on that mechanism to improve it, both as a general tool for analysis, and as a teaching aid.

One of the biggest challenges in teaching law students (and, I suspect, teaching more generally) is to prevent the subject from becoming simply about memorising a bland set of legal rules, or even about memorising and repeating the analysis of others. Rather, we want law students to actively engage with the law and the normative questions that underpin it. It is my belief that the lack of consistent analysis within current legal teaching creates a barrier to this endeavour, creating confusion and encouraging compartmentalism. The argument advanced in this chapter is that the consistent teaching of element analysis provides one means of breaking down that barrier.

References

Alexander, Kessler and Morse, *Crime and Culpability: A Theory of Criminal Law* (CUP, 2009).
Bower, 'Organizational factors in memory' (1970) *Cognitive Psychology* 18.
Buxton, 'Circumstances, consequences and attempted rape' (1984) *Criminal Law Review* 25.
Child, 'Exploring the mens rea requirements of the Serious Crime Act 2007 assisting and encouraging offences' (2012) *Journal of Criminal Law* 220.
Child, 'The structure, coherence and limits of inchoate liability: The new ulterior element' (2014) *Legal Studies* 537.
Child and Ormerod, *Smith and Hogan's Essentials of Criminal Law* (OUP, 2015).
Duff, *Criminal Attempts* (OUP, 1996).
Gainer, 'The culpability provisions of the MPC' (1987) *Rutgers Law Journal* 575.
Law Commission, *Conspiracy and Attempts* (Law Com No 318, 2009);

Law Commission, *Participating in Crime* (Law Com No 305, 2007a);
Law Commission, *Conspiracy and Attempts* (Consultation No 183, 2007b);
Law Commission, *Inchoate Liability for Assisting and Encouraging Crime* (Law Com No 300, 2006);
Law Reform Commission of Canada, *Re-Codifying Criminal Law* (Report 30, 1987).
Law Reform Commission of Hong Kong, *Report on Codification* (Topic 26, 1994).
Moore, *Act and Crime: The Philosophy of Action and Its Implications for Criminal Law* (OUP, 1993).
New Zealand Crimes Consultative Committee, *Crimes Bill 1989: Report of the Crimes Consultative Committee* (Wellington, 1991).
Reed, *Cognition: Theories and Applications* (CENGAGE learning, 2012).
Robinson, 'In defence of the Model Penal Code: A reply to Professor Fletcher' (1998) *Buffalo Criminal Law Review* 25.
Robinson and Grall, 'Element analysis in defining liability: The Model Penal Code and beyond' (1983) *Stanford Law Review* 681.
Sullivan, 'Bad thoughts and bad acts' (1990) *Criminal Law Review* 559.
Williams, 'The problem of reckless attempts' (1983) *Criminal Law Review* 365.

Chapter 4

Enhancing interactivity in the teaching of criminal law
Using response technology in the lecture theatre

*Kevin J. Brown and Colin R. G. Murray**

Introduction

Over the last two decades, digital technology has played an influential role in shaping the institution of the United Kingdom (UK) Law School. Access to the Internet, email communication, electronic research databases, and online learning platforms are shaping how students learn and how staff teach and research. Despite these changes, the didactic large-cohort lecture survives in many UK law schools as the primary method of delivering material, particularly in core modules of undergraduate programmes. With a rapid expansion of the number of undergraduate students studying law in the UK in recent years (Spencer, 2013), this reliance upon the lecture is unlikely to change. Whilst these traditional lectures are, at least from the perspective of university resource management, an efficient means of transmitting information, they do little to stimulate independent thought or to develop students' skills at processing such information (Beard, 1970, pp. 104–105). Technology has had some impact on the typical large-cohort law lecture. Presentation software, such as PowerPoint, has become popular and can, according to some studies, increase levels of student engagement and enthusiasm in lectures (for a summary of research studies, see Susskind, 2005). Moreover, lecture capture and playback facilities are becoming more common, with advocates arguing that the technology allows students to reprise complex material that they found difficult to process in class leading to improved exam performance for some (Terry, 2015). Neither development, however, fundamentally alters the didactic mode of delivery inherent within the lecture format (Baer, 1997, p. 128).

This chapter examines the strengths and weaknesses of real-time classroom response technology as a means of generating interaction between the lecturer and large cohorts of students within the lecture hall. Research has found that

---

* The project upon which this research is based was funded by the Newcastle University Innovation Fund. Our thanks to Ben Middleton (University of Sunderland) and Kris Gledhill (AUT Law School, Auckland) for their advice and encouragement regarding earlier drafts of this chapter. Any errors remain our own.

both lecturers and students find establishing genuine interactivity to be problematic in this teaching environment due to a range of social, psychological, and logistical factors (Black, 2005). We begin by exploring the role of interactive lectures in the context of legal education and in particular the Socratic method of lecturing. The chapter then examines the growing body of literature, both general (Simpson & Oliver, 2007) and specific to legal education (Easton, 2012), which identifies the capacity of Classroom Response Systems (CRS), popularly known as "clickers", to generate interactivity in large-group teaching. The remainder of the chapter explores an action-research project (Zuber-Skerritt, 1992, pp. 1–2) conducted at Newcastle Law School (UK) that integrated educational technology into core undergraduate law lectures in both Criminal Law and Public Law in an effort to enhance our student body's in-class engagement. In light of this experience, we evaluate whether the application of CRS technology offers an alternative to traditional methods of encouraging class participation in large-cohort lectures and some of the shortcomings of this approach.

Generating interactive law lectures

However laudable the intention to allow students to hone and voice their own opinions in lectures might be, in UK law schools, open questions to the massed ranks of students in a core undergraduate lecture rarely elicit rapid or direct responses. When a response is proffered, and it often will be if the academic perseveres (the wounded silence of an unanswered question can only be endured for so long), particular students tend to monopolise such interchanges, potentially alienating others from the process. Chastened by such experiences, many academics reluctantly settle into a didactic mode of delivery, despite its attendant problems of student passivity and disengagement (Garside, 1996). Traditional modes of lecture delivery are buttressed by the promise of active student discussion of course material in subsequent small-group sessions. The use of these staff-intensive, small-group sessions (seminars or tutorials) varies according to institution, but in general, they are much less frequent than the large-cohort lectures.

One time-honoured solution to these problems, particularly in US law schools, is to employ the Socratic method of teaching in lectures, through which all students are expected to attend class prepared for discussion on the topic at issue and particular students are called upon by the lecturer to engage with a series of questions and responses drawing out issues for the remainder of the class (Kerr, 1999, p. 118). Under the traditional form of the Socratic method, the risk of being chosen to answer questions before the entire cohort, and the knowledge that some students will be chosen to do so, incentivises the entire student body to attend class prepared to engage in debate, advancing lectures beyond the exposition of basic concepts and key facts. The imperative of transforming students into professionals, primed to conduct a legal discussion with a judge in a courtroom, has sustained the use of the Socratic method in US postgraduate legal education (Sullivan et al., 2007, p. 3). If it is effective, the Socratic method should heighten student preparation for class, whilst the question-and-answer discussions hone students' legal reasoning skills and their capacity to engage in academic debate on legal issues. It can, however, rely upon the potential for humiliation to encourage preparation and debate by engaging students in competition with each other and potentially undermining the development of cooperative learning (Marshall, 2005, pp. 14–15). As a result, the Socratic method risks compelling students to approach their education as a process of learning sufficient legal trivia to fend off questions rather than developing their capacity for active debate and critique (Kerr, 1999, p. 125). The Socratic method has not gained much traction within the lecture theatres of UK law schools. Much of the impetus behind the approach was blunted by the UK's separation of the academic study of law at the undergraduate level and subsequent professional education. A UK law degree, unlike a US law degree, is not necessarily preparation for a back-and-forth dialogue with a judge across a courtroom. In addition, the fact that law is taught largely as an undergraduate subject in the United Kingdom means that such students are younger, less mature, and new to university life in comparison to their US counterparts (Klein, 1991, p. 635). Therefore, many lecturers view the Socratic method as an inappropriate learning tool in the UK law school context.

CRS provides an opportunity for lecturers looking for an alternative or additional method of engaging students in interactive lectures. Turning Technology, producers of a version of this technology, claim that their CRS system is 'designed to achieve superior levels of student engagement with compelling instruction that leaves a lasting impression in and outside of class' (https://www.turningtechnologies.com/higher-education). Small wireless radio handsets and latterly smartphone apps (Law & Devon, 2014) allow students to state their agreement or disagreement with a proposition or to select which multiple-choice option enumerated on the lecture slides they believe to be correct. Each response device is barcoded and can be registered to an individual or group of students for a period of time (from the duration of a lecture to an entire academic year).

As a discipline, law's "traditional focus upon analytical problem solving should . . . [place it] at the forefront of clicker use and experimentation" (Easton, 2009, section 4). And yet, despite the opportunities opened up by interactive educational technology, efforts to enhance the reflective aspect of law lectures by engaging the student body in discussions upon aspects of law reform and development face ongoing difficulties. Catherine Easton has catalogued the factors inhibiting the use of interactive educational technology in law lectures. She identifies, in particular, fears that CRS use detracts from the time dedicated to delivery of course content (Easton, 2009, section 2.3.1), concerns over control of the classroom during interactive sessions (Easton, 2009, section 2.3.2), and worries over the challenge of adapting to new technology (Easton, 2009, section 2.3.3). To these not-inconsiderable impediments might be added a concern that clickers could replicate some of the shortcomings of the Socratic method in prioritising the recall of facts (for example, case names or relevant sections of statute) over the interpretation of material (Auster & MacRone, 1994) and in making the learning environment more competitive. In our action-research study, we wished to explore with our students whether the reported advantages of CRS outweighed the perceived negatives.

Our classroom response system project

During the 2011/2012 academic year, we integrated TurningPoint CRS into lectures for Public Law and Criminal Law, core modules in Newcastle University's undergraduate law degree taught at Stage 1 and 2, respectively. Both modules had a class size of 150. Multiple-choice-question slides were incorporated into these modules' PowerPoint presentations at the conclusion of each module topic. Once students have selected the option which they believe to be correct using their response handset, the lecturer can display the overall cohort results on screen. By enabling academics to monitor cohort responses in this way, CRS technology allows them to immediately address common misconceptions. At the end of a quiz, the system also ranks handsets by proportion of correct answers and allows the lecturer the option of displaying a leader board of high-scoring teams. This facility allows academics to recognise and praise strong performances. Following CRS-enabled lectures, lecturers can save the quiz results and produce detailed reports on question responses, allowing them to track individuals or small groups of students who consistently fail to answer questions correctly and direct them towards further support.

For all the studies attributing pedagogical benefits to CRS-enabled lectures (see Denker, 2013; Evans, 2012; Krumsvik, 2012), less research has considered how best to employ this educational technology. In our project, we adopted different models of application in our respective lectures. Public Law lectures used an individualised model by which every student who agreed to take part in the TurningPoint exercises did so through a handset registered to them personally. TurningPoint exercises in Criminal Law lectures, by contrast, were conducted using a group model, by which 'Law Firms' of four to six students answered questions as a team following discussion. Our aim was to assess the relative merits of a group model which supported co-operative learning over a more competitive individual model. In theory, these approaches would not only develop different learning processes but also generate different learning outcomes. Our research questions were:

1) How do students respond to the use of CRS in large-cohort law lectures?
2) Does the method by which CRS is employed alter student perceptions of lectures?
3) Having been introduced to CRS, how regularly would students like it to be used, if at all, in future classes?

Student opinion was assessed through qualitative and quantitative analysis. Towards the end of the academic year, questionnaires were distributed to students to gauge their impression of the usefulness of TurningPoint handsets as learning aids, at stimulating in-class discussion, and as a feedback mechanism. In addition, the questionnaire asked for their opinion as to the degree to which CRS should remain a feature of teaching on these modules. Across the Criminal Law and Public Law classes, 173 students responded: 68 Criminal Law students (48% response rate) and 105 Public Law students (70% response rate). These responses were anonymised and the qualitative data analysed using Statistical Package for the Social Sciences (SPSS) software. In order to gain further information, a randomised selection of students were invited to participate in focus groups (Krueger, 2009), one for each cohort. Focus group questions followed the model laid out in the cohort questionnaires. Responses were recorded and transcribed, anonymised, and analysed using Nvivo software. Throughout the trial, we also met on a regular basis to share our experiences of using CRS, including any technical or practical difficulties we had encountered, to discuss the effectiveness of different types of multiple-choice questions, and to report our impressions of how students appeared to be engaging with CRS technology.

Project outcome: Ease of use

The first question we asked was the extent to which the students agreed that the 'TurningPoint device was easy to use'. With only minimal instruction on the use of CRS, 95% of the participant students nonetheless agreed or strongly agreed with the statement (Table 4.1). Only one student strongly disagreed, with a further seven disagreeing. All but one of the students who reported difficulty with the technology came from the Public Law cohort in which each individual student had been issued with a handset.

There was a consensus from the focus group participants that the devices were generally straightforward to use, though some raised the issue of the ease of 'knocking' the device to a different radio frequency, meaning that the response from that handset is not picked up by the receiver. Whilst it is straightforward to reset the device, this non-communication does not become apparent until the final results for the session have been processed. Based on these results, we introduced an information slide into any CRS-enabled lecture that advised students to set the radio signal to the correct channel. In subsequent years, this test allowed students to check whether the battery on a particular handset was spent.

None of the students in either cohort were registered as having any sight or hearing impairments, which could potentially have impacted their participation

Table 4.1 The TurningPoint device was easy to use

	Strongly Disagree	Disagree	Agree	Strongly Agree
Public Law (n = 105)	0	7	43	55
Criminal Law (n = 68)	1	0	17	50

in the CRS-enabled session. Nevertheless, as lecturers, we made adjustments to our delivery of the sessions in case of any non-registered students. The CRS-enabled devices had a raised button in the centre to allow for ease of navigation by touch. Each question and the possible answers were read out aloud as well as being presented visually on the slide. The results of each poll were also read out by the lecturer to the class.

As for the preparation of the sessions, with some basic training, Turning-Point was straightforward to use in terms of both designing the slides and employing the handsets in lectures. Occasionally, the technology would cause the lecture theatre computer to freeze briefly (though not to crash). The main logistical concern was the length of time required to distribute and collect the devices at the beginning and end of class, particularly in Public Law, in which all students had individual handsets. We could not let students keep handsets between classes, as they were needed for other CRS-enabled sessions within the Law School. Even if more units were available, the likelihood of them being forgotten because not all lectures featured TurningPoint exercises would have dissuaded us from issuing the devices to students on a long-term basis. Handsets occasionally went missing: six were lost over the course of the academic year from Criminal Law, but none during Public Law sessions in which handsets were allocated to students by name. Occasionally, and in particular when the CRS session was mid-class, students would forget to return handsets at the end of the lecture but would almost invariably bring them to the next lecture.

At the time of the study, we were the only two out of 25 lecturing staff to regularly use CRS within our lectures. However, as the project progressed, students discussed the use of CRS amongst themselves and with other staff members. Consequently, a number of colleagues sought information and training on using CRS. Within a year, the number of staff using the technology had increased to half a dozen across five modules.

Project outcome: Enhancing engagement

The questionnaires subsequently asked the students to indicate the extent to which they agreed that 'the use of TurningPoint made the lectures more interesting'. Fully 51% of participants strongly agreed, whilst a further 45% agreed with the statement (Table 4.2). Only 4% disagreed. This appears to be a strong endorsement of the use of the technology by the students.

The focus groups provided further evidence that students considered that CRS use made lectures more engaging and that the discussion generated by TurningPoint exercises was relevant to the questions at issue (a concern noted with regard to in-class discussions which are not directly monitored by the lecturer; Biggs, 2002, p. 65):

> I tend to sit quite far back in the lecture theatre and there's always a danger that some people do sit behind us and just talk throughout the lecture, but

Table 4.2 The use of TurningPoint made the lectures more interesting

	Strongly Disagree	Disagree	Agree	Strongly Agree
Public Law (n = 105)	0	3	58	44
Criminal Law (n = 67)	0	2	45	20

> as soon as Kevin brought the TurningPoint out everything like that stopped. And everybody was focusing and it was quite nice to actually have a lecture where the people weren't talking and when they were talking they were talking about relevant material for the topic.
>
> *Criminal Law Focus Group*

> I think that something that's a lot more interactive is worth two [traditional] lectures, because you're more likely to remember them and you're more likely to engage in the issues rather than just having them spoken to you, if you will.
>
> *Criminal Law Focus Group*

One student emphasised the importance she and her friends attached to lectures involving CRS:

> I think it makes the lectures more important. A lot of people skip the odd few lectures because they just say oh, I'll get the slides and I'll read the book and I'll do it myself. So it's not so bad. But when you miss a lecture like that, you can't get that back.
>
> *Criminal Law Focus Group*

Other research studies have also found that the use of CRS in lectures noticeably increases interest and engagement across disciplines (Auras & Bix, 2007; Bates, Howie & Murphy, 2006; Cole & Kosc, 2010; Salemi, 2009). In an era when the availability of social media and the Internet on wirelessly enabled devices can distract students in lectures, CRS-enabled sessions serve to focus student attention on the subject matter (Cole & Kosc, 2010, p. 397).

Project outcome: Engaging co-operative approaches to learning

The survey also asked students about the extent to which they agreed that 'the use of TurningPoint made me more willing to discuss this subject with other students'. In response, 80% either agreed or strongly agreed with the statement, whilst 20% disagreed or strongly disagreed (Table 4.3).

Table 4.3 The use of TurningPoint made me more willing to discuss this subject with other students

	Strongly Disagree	Disagree	Agree	Strongly Agree
Public Law (n = 105)	3	24	59	19
Criminal Law (n = 67)	4	2	36	25

The Criminal Law focus group emphasised the value of CRS for generating discussion:

> I really enjoyed discussing with all of my friends, because I know I'll remember that in my exams because I remember having the conversation about it. So I'm far more likely to remember that than reading it.
> *Criminal Law Focus Group*

A typical Criminal Law module will contain subjects of controversy and sensitivity such as sexual offences. Some students tend to be wary of expressing their views on such issues, especially in front of a large cohort of peers. Using CRS allows students to feel more comfortable in expressing opinions in lectures, as emphasised in the following statement from the Criminal Law focus group:

> I personally am not bothered about putting my hand up, but I know people that are and they feel a little bit unsure about something, maybe they're just uncomfortable with sort of expressing their opinion that boldly, but giving it anonymously is a good way because people don't particularly watch you push the button, you can say what you really think. And especially with some things in criminal law, people do have really controversial opinions that perhaps they don't want to air because they're quite personal to them.
> *Criminal Law Focus Group*

In a criminal law lecture that was examining the issue of intoxication and rape, students were asked using CRS whether they agreed that a woman who becomes intoxicated is at least partially responsible if she was raped. This question has been asked in a number of national and international surveys (see, for example, Amnesty International, 2005). When the results from the question were displayed, revealing a clear division of opinion, there were audible gasps. There then followed several minutes of class debate in which a significant number of students participated. This outcome is in line with previous studies into the use of CRS, which have also found that it can be useful in generating in-class discussion amongst students (Auras & Bix, 2007; Campbell & Monk, 2012; Mollborn & Hoekstra, 2010).

Our project, however, indicated a marked divergence between students who had experienced the individual model of CRS in Public Law and those who had experienced the group model in Criminal Law. Most of the substantial minority of students who did not believe that CRS-enabled sessions had made them more willing to discuss the subject with other students were Public Law students. As one concluded,

> [I]n the end you're doing a degree for yourself, you're not doing your degree to be better than everyone else. . . . And if I would say a negative point to the technology, it would be that it introduced feelings of competition between people which surely isn't what a degree is about.
>
> *Public Law Focus Group*

Using CRS-enabled sessions to generate a form of individuated norm-referenced formative assessment in Public Law harnessed students' achievement motivation, but with this came the attendant risks of "killing collaborative learning" (Biggs, 2002, p. 62). Whilst many students valued the process of in-class exercises, some disliked the resultant competitive learning environment. The approach adopted in Criminal Law, by grouping students together into teams, placed a stronger emphasis on co-operative drivers to learning than on competitive drivers. This is not to say that the latter were removed from the process; student engagement was encouraged by using scoreboards to display which groups performed the best at the end of each quiz, but scoring highly on the quizzes required students to work together. This mixture of competitive and cooperative elements seemed to strike a chord at least with some students:

> I think with being a law school or whatever, everybody is slightly competitive. So knowing what the topics were in advance and knowing there's a prize or whatever . . . I did the revision before having the lecture. Whereas before if it was a revision lecture and it was going through, I'd bring the notes in, but I wouldn't be engaging as much. So that was quite good.
>
> *Criminal Law Focus Group*

Only the top-five performances were identified, meaning that these scoreboards did not operate as a tool for naming-and-shaming individuals or those groups which struggled with the questions.

Project outcome: Enhancing student confidence

Students were also invited to express their opinions on the extent to which CRS impacted on their confidence in their knowledge and understanding of the subject. The results of this were mixed (Table 4.4). Whereas 80% of students agreed or strongly agreed that 'the use of TurningPoint improved my confidence in the subject', 20% disagreed or strongly disagreed. Again, the proportion of students

Table 4.4 The use of TurningPoint improved my confidence in the subject

	Strongly Disagree	Disagree	Agree	Strongly Agree
Public Law (n = 102)	0	38	55	9
Criminal Law (n = 66)	1	9	40	16

disagreeing was considerably higher under individual-model CRS (Public Law) than under group-model CRS (Criminal Law).

When the issue of confidence was explored further in focus groups, students explained that the use of TurningPoint sometimes made them identify gaps in their knowledge or understanding:

> It helps you to practice your recall of the material, because you only have a limited time to do it, and obviously you have that sense of . . . success if you do well.
>
> *Public Law Focus Group*

> If I got a bad score then it made me determined that it was time to try and get a good one and try and get in the top five [leader board]. So I thought it was good.
>
> *Public Law Focus Group*

The practice of both lecturers during the TurningPoint quizzes was to provide an explanation as to why a particular answer was correct. This allowed students who had selected the incorrect answer to understand where they had gone wrong. The following was a free-text comment from the survey questionnaire:

> The TurningPoint tests are a useful way to show the key points I haven't understood or have mixed up and I find the discussion of the answers afterwards is really helpful.
>
> *Free-Text Comment in Survey Questionnaire*

In other words, most students agreed that CRS-enabled sessions provide an opportunity to receive formative feedback on knowledge and understanding of core concepts whilst a topic is still being taught, generating a 'teachable moment' at which the lecturer can intervene to correct misconceptions (Easton, 2009, section 2.2.3). A number of students, however, noted that due to the excitement of the quiz, students would often be particularly talkative at the moment answers were revealed, which meant that hearing the explanation might sometimes be difficult:

> It would be more beneficial if people were quiet when lecturer is explaining the answers because it is hard to concentrate!
>
> *Free-Text Comment in Questionnaire*

In subsequent years, this issue was addressed by our allowing more time for the commotion generated by responses to settle before we delivered explanations to the class.

Project outcome: Level of CRS use

Whilst the general response to the use of TurningPoint in lectures was positive, there was less of a consensus among the two student cohorts as to the limits on the use of CRS-enabled sessions. Students were asked if they would like to see TurningPoint used in the regular seminars of no more than 12 students at Newcastle Law School which require advanced preparation of responses to pre-set questions. The two cohorts were more divided in response to this question, with 59% of those completing the questionnaires strongly agreeing or agreeing that they would 'like to see TurningPoint used in seminars', whereas 41% disagreed or strongly disagreed.

Data from the focus groups as well as free-text comments suggested that this division in opinion related to whether students perceived that CRS was necessary to generate discussion, or whether discussion arose naturally within the seminar format:

> TurningPoint would be excellent for sparking discussion in seminars. I think this would be a very good idea.
>
> *Free-Text Comment for Survey Questionnaire*

> In my view the entire point, as far as I'm concerned, of a seminar, is to facilitate discussion amongst a small group. And I definitely think if you were to implement TurningPoint . . . it would detract from what I feel is the crux of seminar teaching.
>
> *Criminal Law Focus Group*

Although almost all students enjoyed the use of CRS to assess class opinion on an issue or to conduct in-class tests at the conclusion of a topic, when asked whether they would like to see the technology used in every lecture, 65% of respondents to the questionnaires said that they would not, evidencing concerns over 'clicker fatigue' (Easton, 2009, section 3.3). A follow-up statement asked students whether or not they agreed that if 'TurningPoint was used in all classes I would get bored of it'. Opinion was divided, with 48% of students agreeing or strongly agreeing that they would get bored and 52% disagreeing or strongly disagreeing. The focus groups and some of the free-text comments from the questionnaire survey confirmed that, at least for some students, the provision of some CRS-enabled sessions enhanced a mixture of lectures and seminars but did not substitute for either:

> Little bit of a novelty isn't it, having it every so often breaks things up a bit, rather than if it was every lecture.
>
> *Public Law Focus Group*

> It would get tedious to use it in every lecture and every module.
> *Free-Text Comment from Survey Questionnaire*

Such comments indicate a risk that the overuse of CRS would diminish its capacity to stimulate learning (Heaslip *et al.*, 2014, 22). From our experience of the trial, if the quiz lasted more than 15 minutes in total (six multiple-choice questions, allowing time for discussion and feeding back on response patterns), students would begin to disengage.

Conclusions

No one teaching method will suffice to engage all students, all of the time. The wide range of approaches to learning in large cohorts require lecturers to utilise a variety of methods to support as many students as possible (Boyle *et al.*, 2009; De Groff & McKee, 2006; Haar & Hall, 2002). That axiom notwithstanding, the potential impacts upon student learning of the systematic application of CRS technology in law lectures are threefold. First, in line with previous studies, we found that by adding 'variety in the lecture presentation' (Easton, 2009, 2.1.4), use of CRS can make lectures more engaging for a broad spectrum of the student body and thereby increase student attentiveness and attendance. Second, as a formative assessment technique, lecturers will be able to assess student answers over the course of several lectures and identify those students who regularly struggle with key concepts, enabling the lecturer to investigate the cause of these misconceptions and, as necessary, direct the students towards additional support. An individual-response model of CRS, in particular, allows lecturers to assess student attendance and potentially identify students who may be struggling with a module. Third, if a team-response model of CRS is employed, the lecturer can harness co-operative drivers for learning by encouraging critical engagement with legal issues through stimulation of collaborative discussion of foundational concepts and problem solving with their peers. Although CRS technology is not a panacea for all the problems of the large-cohort lecture as a learning environment (and we have outlined some the limitations we encountered in this chapter), we would nonetheless encourage all academics who want to break free from a didactic model of delivery in their criminal law lectures to experiment with the use of this technology.

Bibliography

Amnesty International (2005). 'UK: New poll finds a third of people believe women who flirt partially responsible for being raped' Available at: http://www.amnesty.org.uk/press-releases/uk-new-poll-finds-third-people-believe-women-who-flirt-partially-responsible-being

Auras, R., & Bix, L. (2007). 'Wake up! The Effectiveness of a Student Response System in Large Packaging Classes'. *Packaging Technology and Science* 20: 183–195.

Auster, C. J., & MacRone, M. (1994). 'The Classroom as a Negotiated Social Setting: An Empirical Study of the Effects of Faculty Members' Behavior on Students' Participation'. *Teaching Sociology* 22: 289–300.

Baer, W. (1997). 'Teaching Strategies and Accommodations for Students with Learning Disabilities'. In Hodge, B.M. and Preston-Sabin, J., eds., *Accommodations or Just Good Teaching?* (pp. 126–131). Praeger.

Bates, S.P., et al. (2006). 'The Use of Electronic Voting Systems in Large Group Lectures: Challenges and Opportunities'. *New Directions in the Teaching of Physical Sciences* 2: 1–8.

Beard, R. (1970). *Teaching and Learning in Higher Education.* Penguin.

Biggs, J. (2002). *Teaching for Quality Learning at University.* Open UP.

Black, L.W. (2005). 'Dialogue in the Lecture Hall: Teacher–Student Communication and Students' Perceptions of Their Learning'. *Qualitative Research Reports in Communication* 6(1): 31–40.

Boyle, R., et al. (2009). 'Law Students are Different from the General Population: Empirical Findings Regarding Learning Styles'. *Perspectives: Teaching Legal Research and Writing* 17: 153.

Campbell, C., & Monk, S. (2012). 'How do we get Students Talking in First Year Courses? Engaging Students using Learner Response Systems'. *Society for Information Technology & Teacher Education International Conference*, 3541–3546.

Cole, S., & Kosc, G. (2010). 'Quit Surfing and Start "Clicking": One Professor's Effort to Combat the Problems of Teaching the US Survey in a Large Lecture Hall'. *The History Teacher* 43(3): 397–410.

De Geest, G., & Dari-Mattiacci, G. (2013). 'The Rise of Carrots and the Decline of Sticks'. *The University of Chicago Law Review* 80: 341–393.

De Groff, E.A., & McKee, K.A. (2006). 'Learning Like Lawyers: Addressing the Differences in Law Student Learning Styles'. *Brigham Young University Education and Law Journal*, 499.

Denker, K.J. (2013). 'Student Response Systems and Facilitating the Large Lecture Basic Communication Course: Assessing Engagement and Learning'. *Communication Teacher* 27: 50–69.

Easton, C. (2009). 'An Examination of Clicker Technology Use in Legal Education'. *Journal of Information, Law and Technology*, 3.

——— . (2012). 'Employing a Classroom Response System to Teach Law: A Case Study'. *European Journal of Law and Technology*, 3.

Evans, H.K. (2012). 'Making Politics "Click": The Costs and Benefits of Using Clickers in an Introductory Political Science Course'. *Journal of Political Science Education* 8: 85–93.

Garside, C. (1996). 'Look Who's Talking: A Comparison of Lecture and Group Discussion Teaching Strategies in developing Critical Thinking Skills'. *Communication Education* 45: 212–227.

Heaslip, G., et al. (2014). 'Student Response Systems and Learner Engagement in Large Classes'. *Active Learning in Higher Education* 15: 11–24.

Kerr, O. (1999). 'The Decline of the Socratic Method at Harvard'. *Nebraska Law Review* 78: 113.

Klein, S.R. (1991). 'Legal Education in the United States and England: A Comparative Analysis'. *Loyola LA International & Comparative Law Review* 13: 601–641.

Krueger, R.A. (2009). *Focus Groups: A Practical Guide for Applied Research.* Sage.

Krumsvik, R. (2012). 'Feedback Clickers in Plenary Lectures: A New Tool for Formative Assessment?'. In Rowan, L. and Bigum, C. eds., *Transformative Approaches to New Technologies and Student Diversity in Futures Oriented Classrooms* (pp. 191–216). Dordrecht: Springer.

Law, R., & Devon, J. (2014). 'The Use of Smartphone Technologies by Students in the Education Environment'. *EDULEARN14 Proceedings*, 3948–3957.

Marshall, D.G. (2005). 'Socratic Method and the Irreducible Core of Legal Education'. *Minnesota Law Review* 90: 1–17.

Mollborn, S., & Hoekstra, A. (2010). '"A Meeting of Minds": Using Clickers for Critical Thinking and Discussion in Large Sociology Classes'. *Teaching Sociology* 38: 18–27.

Salemi, M.K. (2009). 'Clickenomics: Using a Classroom Response System to Increase Student Engagement in a Large-Enrolment Principles of Economics Course'. *Journal of Economic Education* 40: 385–404.

Simpson, V., & Oliver, M. (2007). 'Electronic Voting Systems for Lectures Then and Now: A Comparison of Research and Practice'. *Australasian Journal of Educational Technology* 23: 187–208.

Spencer, B.J. (19 Dec 2013). 'While the US Law School Bubble Bursts, the UK Law School Bubble Grows'. *Huffington Post*. Available at: http://www.huffingtonpost.co.uk/brian-john-spencer/uk-law-school_b_4473341.html

Susskind, J.E. (2005). 'PowerPoint's Power in the Classroom: Enhancing Students' Self-Efficacy and Attitudes'. *Computers and Education* 45(2): 203–215.

Terry, N., *et al.* (2015). 'The Impact of Lecture Capture on Student Performance in Business Courses'. *Journal of College Teaching & Learning* 12(1): 65–74.

Zuber-Skerritt, O. (1992). *Action Research in Higher Education: Examples and Reflections* Kogan Page.

Chapter 5

Using problem-based learning to enhance the study of criminal law

Ben Fitzpatrick

Introduction

I feel very fortunate to work as an academic in the field of criminal law. The subject is a guaranteed conversation starter; it is something on which everybody has an opinion. In a similar way, it is not hard to persuade students to engage with criminal law – the subject pretty much sells itself. It is rare that there is a complaint that criminal law is 'dry'. In those kinds of conditions, it can be easy to become complacent. The fact that students demonstrably engage with the subject and find it interesting is of course positive, but it should not get in the way of asking questions about whether the subject is optimally constructed and whether students have the most appropriate learning opportunities.

I will be arguing in this chapter that there are some shortcomings in the conventional approach to learning in 'criminal law', and in legal education more broadly, that alternative configurations exist, and that problem-based learning (PBL) is suitable as the general basis for a law curriculum and the teaching of criminal law because it is an approach that makes connections between the substantive law and different domains of inquiry.

The size and shape of 'criminal law'

To demonstrate that, notwithstanding the prominence of conventional approaches, a range of different legitimate accounts of 'criminal law' are possible, including a broadly conceived approach, the starting proposition is that a curriculum/programme/module has no objective existence independent of the choices which are made as to how to populate it. It is 'constructed', and not in a purely 'academic' manner. To use the words of a colleague, a module is 'a vessel for credit': modules and programmes are, in part, institutional, administrative mechanisms for packaging and badging certain learning opportunities and experiences. The 'curriculum' and the 'subject' may well have a more 'academic' than administrative flavour, but they remain constructs.

As such, the contents of curricula, programmes, modules, and subjects are matters of choice, rather than inevitable. Not that you would necessarily know this when considering criminal law. Criminal law as a subject, and the 'criminal law module' which sits in many law programmes, often entails a fairly standard narrative. The journey takes the learner from the so-called general part – those rules and principles which apply to all or to a substantial proportion of offences (for example, the general rules regarding *actus reus* and *mens rea*) – to the 'special part' – those rules and principles which denote and identify the content of specific offences and defences.

The predominance of this narrative suggests that it is not to be dismissed lightly. It underlies the structure of many textbooks designed for learners in criminal law. However, it is not beyond challenge (see Alldridge, 1990 for a particularly wide-ranging critique, and Fitzpatrick, 2014). It is not absolutely clear what the scope of the general part actually is, either in terms of breadth or depth. Thus, Shute and Simester (2002) seem to countenance a different scope from Williams (1961). We might also query the extent to which the principles of the general part really are of general application (see e.g., Farmer, 1995, pp. 765–766). For example, there is a plausible argument that 'causation' (which may or may not sit in the general part) means different things in different contexts, rather than having a truly unitary meaning which sits across all result crimes (Norrie, 2001, ch. 7; Padfield, 1995). Beyond challenges based on coherence, we can identify other sensible criticisms of the standard 'criminal law' narrative and, by implication, a number of factors which might inform alternative conceptions of the subject.

First, it seems to entail disproportionate emphasis on certain – more serious – offences. This is in part an empirical criticism that the study of criminal law does not capture the 'truth' about what crime looks like in the world. At a more ideological level of criticism, the emphasis on serious crimes at the expense of minor offences deflects attention both from the procedural shortcomings in the manner in which justice institutions deal with minor offences (on which, see McBarnet, 1981) and from the potentially serious effects of victimisation in the context of offences formally styled as 'minor'.

Second, the standard journey can be heavily doctrinal and, in jurisprudential terms, disproportionately positivistic. Whilst perfectly consistent both with academic rigour and with robust coherence testing of the criminal law, legal doctrine tells only part of the story. The full richness of criminal law is arguably brought out most effectively by the discussion of its connections with other areas of law and other disciplinary and jurisprudential ways of seeing law and the world.

Third, and linked to the second criticism, the standard approach prioritises substantive rules of criminal law over their connections with other cognate areas of law. So, for example, there may be little sustained engagement in a criminal law module with rules of criminal procedure or evidence, notwithstanding that key procedural concepts – such as the burden and standard of proof – are integral to an understanding of how real-world effect is given to the substantive rules. Similarly, there may be little in the way of dealing with prosecutorial decision-making, which can impact significantly on the way in which the substantive rules of criminal law are tested, and even sustained or undermined, in practice. Sitting beneath these instances of procedural neglect is a deeper, conceptual problem: substance and procedure are arguably not distinct (Fletcher, 1998, ch. 1) in the way that locating them in separate modules might imply.

Fourth, the standard approach might decouple the substantive rules of criminal law both from their philosophical underpinnings and from the policy contexts in which they operate. The questions of what makes a crime a crime and of the justifications for criminalisation may well be addressed through a relatively cursory engagement with a staple such as the Hart–Devlin debate (Devlin, 1959; Hart, 1963) and the question of the extent to which criminal law should encroach into domains of behaviour which may appear to be, at first look, private. However, much more may be missed; for example, an engagement with criminal justice policy can help to shed light on how and why certain philosophical priorities in criminal law might prevail over others. In addition, sitting behind the broad issue of criminal justice policy is the question of *power*: who gets the chance to define what is criminal and what is not? Disproportionate focus on the substantive rules can deflect attention from the acutely political questions of how and why, and through whose choice, the criminal law is as it is.

In a similar vein, the standard journey may also drive an artificial wedge between the substantive rules and the sometimes competing rationales which determine social and institutional responses when they are breached. So a typical criminal law module may have little to do with the sentencing process and, similarly, little to do with the key philosophies which inform sentencing, and which, by extension, must inform the content of the criminal law itself (see e.g., Giles, 1991, p. 216).

The standard journey may also envisage criminal law as a relatively clearly bounded domain. This can obscure some of the enquiries which can be made at the boundaries of criminal law and the question of how we distinguish between 'criminal law' and 'not criminal law'. So there are questions about the relationship between the 'lower end' of criminal law and 'anti-social behaviour', which may justify coercive interventions even in the absence of crime properly so-called and involve criminal penalties for non-compliance. At the 'top end', we might ask where the domain of criminal law ends and that of anti-terror law begins, but the State seeks to maintain a distinct domain of anti-terror law, in which incursions into and deprivations of liberty which would ordinarily be associated with criminal law are undertaken. This distinctiveness is *intended* to facilitate the circumvention of some of the constraints – most notably the due process protections available to suspects – of conventional criminal justice.

When it comes to the definitional boundaries of the criminal law, we might want to devise a distinctive identifier which allows us to say, categorically, this is (or is not) a 'criminal law' matter. Perhaps we might point to the involvement of the State as *the* feature. But what would we then make of the tendency of restorative processes to devolve the resolution or management of criminal matters to parties themselves? Perhaps we might point to the presence or potential for *punishment* as the defining characteristic of criminal law. But what would we then make of the punitive features of other domains of law, such as exemplary damages in tort?

The key message from this section is that 'criminal law' can be constructed in a range of different ways and that the most satisfying are those which are broadly conceived and which explore the connections between different domains. Problem-based learning is a good pedagogic vehicle for operationalising such an account of criminal law, for forging further intellectual connections within the law curriculum, and for facilitating other benefits for learners of criminal law.

Problem-based learning, the law curriculum and 'criminal law'

Just as a broad account of 'criminal law' can lead to a productive reimagining of the 'subject' or the 'module' through its engagement with connections and relationships which might be missed in a more orthodox approach, so a curriculum designed around problem-based learning (PBL) can open up the possibility of exploring connections between 'criminal law' broadly conceived and other 'subjects' (also broadly conceived). There may also be a range of other benefits to criminal law learners from a PBL approach, which relate to motivation, the nature of learning countenanced by PBL, citizenship and employability in general, and effective criminal legal practice. Its challenges are also noted.

There are various different conceptions and a range of different learning activities and approaches that might make credible claims to the 'PBL' label (see, generally, Boud and Feletti, 1997). Rather than detailing demarcation disputes around what 'counts' as PBL (see Barrows and Wee Keng Neo, 2007), some features at its heart can be identified by contrasting it with a conventional approach to learning law (and other disciplines). The latter places the lecture at the start (and arguably the heart) of the learning cycle. The lecture involves students being introduced to and having their first formal learning encounter with specific content – maybe core principles, a series of key cases and statutes, and conceivably some critical commentary on those principles and sources. Ordinarily, students then undertake further research, such as engagement with prescribed or broader reading of other statutes and cases and secondary sources such as journal articles. The learning cycle would usually conclude with a smaller group activity – typically a tutorial or seminar in which the *application* of the relevant legal principles and associated arguments to problem scenarios and to more open-ended, discussion-type questions could be tested.

Despite its significant historic pedigree, the following risks attach to a conventional approach. First, the model sets off on a *transmissive* footing: lecturers give content to students in lectures. Moving from the role of recipients of information to active, independent learners (a position to which many academics would claim to be committed) can be difficult for students, and it can be difficult for academics to develop their own practice in ways which allow this to happen. Second, the model offers no inherent incentive for students to collaborate; an individual could – at least in a formal sense – 'succeed' without having to work effectively with others. The third problem with a conventional approach is that it entails and reinforces artificial distinctions between different modules and hence between different areas of the curriculum, and so it involves a limiting perspective on the nature of law as a discipline. The fourth problem, which flows from the artificial segmentation of the curriculum, is that the scenarios which students work with in their smaller group activities can be lacking in authenticity. Scenarios are stylised and contrived to 'constrain' them to their modular context. The distance from the scenario to the real world can be exasperating for students and staff. Moreover, every inauthentic and frustrating learning activity is a missed opportunity to engage more richly with how legal issues play out in the real world.

The starting point of PBL, on the other hand, rather than the lecture, is a scenario (the 'Problem' (*P*BL) on which the 'Learning' (P*B*L) is 'Based' (PB*L*)). Scenarios may take a variety of forms: a set of facts (in that respect, looking not unlike a conventional seminar problem), a bundle of correspondence, a newspaper report, a piece of audio, an image, or an extract from a policy document. Whatever the 'scenario' is, it is intended to serve as a trigger for students' interest and as the focus for their discussion. Students consider the scenario in a small-group, tutor-facilitated session. The discussion may be very open in terms of its content, but it has clearly defined steps (Moust, Bouhuijs and Schmidt, 2007). The PBL process in use at York Law School (see Fitzpatrick and Hunter, 2011; Grimes, 2014; York Law School, undated) was modelled on that used in Hull York Medical School and draws on the process at Maastricht University (see, for example, Moust, 1998). In a nutshell, the PBL process entails students

1. ensuring that the group shares an understanding of the terms of the scenario
2. defining the scenario in a way which will frame the rest of their discussion
3. pooling as wide as possible a range of ideas of what issues might be raised by the scenario
4. arranging those ideas systematically in order to identify key themes
5. drawing from the themes a set of questions – sometimes referred to in this context as learning outcomes or learning objectives – which will form the agenda for the work conducted by the group over the current learning cycle

The role of the tutor to this point is not to provide the 'right answer' to students, but to facilitate the students through the stages of the process in order that they reach suitable learning outcomes themselves.

Step 6 of the process involves the students spending the learning cycle accessing learning resources or activities in order to support their enquiries. They might attend lectures, access readings and other materials, and collaborate with each other. The learning cycle concludes when the group reassembles with their tutor (for example, a week after the initial meeting in which steps 1 to 5 were undertaken) for a session in which the key task – step 7 of the process – is to report out to each other and to the tutor on their progress against the agenda of learning outcomes which they formulated at the start of the cycle. This discussion can be used to identify ongoing learning needs and appropriate follow-up tasks. The group then moves to a new scenario and the next learning cycle begins. There are also regular opportunities for the group of students to take stock of their progress and to reflect on the effectiveness of their individual and collective learning strategies and approaches.

The process might be represented in an abridged form as follows in Figure 5.1. So, for example, a scenario might comprise a pair of (real or constructed) newspaper reports or extracts, the first on the passage through Parliament of a Bill on assisted dying and the second on the journey of a British citizen to seek assisted dying from a provider in another jurisdiction. Perhaps the extracts also refer to the House of Lords debates in which the Bill is subject to scrutiny and the views of campaigners on various sides of the assisted dying argument. Such a scenario, considered by a group of students using the PBL process, might lead

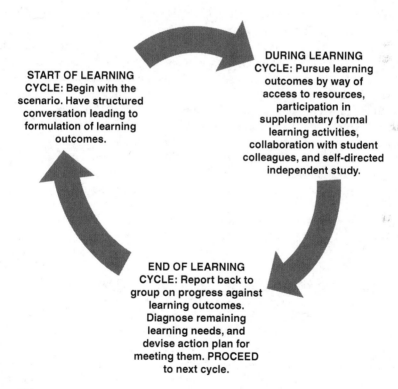

Figure 5.1

to a series of learning outcomes addressing, for example: (i) the current scope of criminal offences involving assisted dying; (ii) prosecution policy and practice in relation to such cases; (iii) policy and moral arguments in relation to different modes of regulated assisted dying; (iv) the process of lawmaking and whether special considerations might apply in morally controversial areas; and (v) the roles of Parliament and, more particularly, the role of the House of Lords – and, by extension, of second chambers in general – in lawmaking.

A well-designed scenario would allow these questions to emerge reasonably naturally through the PBL process, framed in whatever way the group saw fit (subject to the tutor helping the group to 'stay on track' and to arrive at questions which would allow them to address the relevant aspects of the programme). The group would then use the learning outcomes as their work agenda before reporting back to each other at the conclusion of the cycle.

So why is this an improvement on a conventional approach?

Starting with the content of the scenario, some of the learning outcomes relate to a broad conception of 'criminal law'. There are questions of substantive law – the definitions of particular offences – and a 'criminal procedure' outcome – namely, prosecution policy and practice. A further outcome is targeted at policy and moral arguments about the scope of criminal law.

Other outcomes, those to do with lawmaking and the role of second chambers, relate to issues which would ordinarily be 'housed' in other modules – 'public law', for example. The scenario provides an authentic vehicle for bringing Criminal and Public Law modules together in a shared activity, an idea that is not exclusive to PBL (see Giles, 1991, p. 223) but usefully acted on through PBL (Wong, 2003, pp. 165–166, offers an example).

Authenticity refers to the 'messiness' of a well-designed PBL scenario (see, for example, Duch, 2001) and reflects the way that legal issues arise in the world: they do not respect academically constructed modular boundaries. It is good that opportunities arise to see issues from different areas of the curriculum arising in the same context, most obviously for students who go into legal practice: it is important that 'criminal law' practitioners can see the links between, for example, the criminal allegation and the tort claim, or between the stop and search policy and the human rights claim. Scenarios constructed, for example, through simulated files might be helpful in this respect. Moreover, irrespective of their future practice intentions, we should not unreasonably require students, expressly or by implication, to respect modular boundaries. Students bring their prior experiences of the world to their learning and are unburdened in the way that staff might be by supposed distinctions between say, procedure and substance, or tort and contract. How frustrating it must be for the student who raises the interesting and insightful point to be told that they must defer their interest until next term's lecture in a different module, or to be told that their point is interesting and insightful but not 'relevant'. Authenticity can diminish the frustrations that students might otherwise experience in a more conventional seminar scenario; in short, authenticity supports motivation.

By constructing learning activities around a range of scenarios, curriculum designers can step away from standard textbook narratives of subjects – including criminal law – and build a curriculum from different intellectual blocks. Scepticism towards the standard narrative of criminal law does not mean that anything goes. 'Messy' scenarios give designers an opportunity, for example, to identify key *themes* which transcend individual modules and in the context of which the scenarios and their associated learning outcomes can make most sense. Perhaps the scenario about assisted dying laws might sit within a broader theme about *rights* or *competing interests* – a context where claims to individual autonomy might, under certain circumstances, be traded off against supposed broader social interests or where the interests of others (in this instance, the interests of vulnerable people) call for protection.

The idea of a thematic criminal law *module* is clearly plausible. Giles (1991) discusses the implementation of such a module, while a module built around the work of Lacey and Wells (1998) or Norrie (2001) could reasonably claim thematic status. The next step would be the thematic *programme* or *curriculum*. Perhaps other scenarios with which students engage around the same time as the assisted dying scenario could also align with the theme of competing interests: the next scenario involving criminal law might concern the possibility of the testimony of a fearful witness being admitted notwithstanding the absence of the witness from the trial. Maybe the fear could arise in the context of a neighbour dispute about noise pollution which has escalated into something more serious. Such a scenario opens the door to exploring a broadly conceived criminal law further through the vehicle of laws of evidence, which manage the relationship between parties to the criminal process. This could be set against the background of, for example, a thematically linked nuisance claim (through which learners encounter criminal law and tort/property law in the context of a shared learning activity) in which party A seeks to curtail the rights of party B to do as they (B) wish on or with their (B's) own property. The content and level of abstraction of the themes themselves might be up for grabs – rights, responsibility, power, equality – whatever – but they might be selected and deployed such that at any given time, the bulk of students' learning activities are associated with that theme.

So PBL serves as a vehicle – and for sure, other vehicles may work just as well – for operationalising an account of 'criminal law' which is conceived in broad terms, is of equal intellectual validity to, and, dare I say, is more interesting than those available in conventional contexts. It also fosters connections between criminal law and other domains of the curriculum. This might also operate as a useful brake on one of the malign tendencies of curriculum and module design – growth by default. It is far easier to grow a module year to year, to add to the case list, and to the 'list of interesting issues' than it is to systematically confront and control the parameters of that module. The upshot for learners is an accretion of content, more and more 'stuff' to learn in less and less depth. Designing a PBL curriculum in the way implied in this account calls for ruthlessness in relation to content and means that great caution must be exercised before 'tampering' with one area because of the potentially serious impacts on other areas. This may render coherent curriculum development especially resource intensive, but this problem has to be weighed against its value in preventing untrammelled, and unconsidered, growth.

Other potential advantages of PBL speak in some respects more broadly than just to criminal law. It can be genuinely student-centred (see, for example, Barrows and Tamblyn, 1980) by involving an approach to learning which sees staff not (exclusively) as expert providers of content to recipient learners, but as co-workers and co-learners. Students can, with staff *support* (rather than exclusively *direction*) not merely work on the *answers* to interesting questions but also identify those *questions* for themselves. Often, the richest learning is in identifying what is interesting about a scenario and establishing what questions would need to be asked to find out more about it. PBL allows students the opportunity to do this in the context of a *process* which is itself sufficiently defined to help students remain, where necessary, within the requirements of the curriculum.

The student-centredness of PBL does not remove the need for scaffolding, particularly in contexts other than formal learning activities. Learning is at risk if students do not know what they are supposed to do outside classes. On the one hand, too much direction can be stifling and passivising. On the other hand, too little can lead to excessive floundering. PBL, in the model I have described here, might provide a 'way through' which gives students sufficient (but not excessive) support through, for example, the regular rhythm of the PBL cycle through which students can become accustomed to the idea of working up and working through their own research agenda on a regular basis. The very fact that the core of learning is framed by *their* research agenda as well as by staff prescription is a constant reminder to students that they have ownership both of the process and of the content of learning. Furthermore, the themes to which I referred earlier, and which form the conceptual underpinning of the curriculum, might provide anchoring points for students so that any concerns about where a particular scenario 'fits' in the curriculum can be allayed. This can be especially useful if the comfort of the textbook-driven journey through a subject or subjects is not available.

The extent and nature of the support for students in PBL, and the opportunities for regular reflection on how learning is (or is not) happening, can help to foster a positive disposition towards independent study and can engender habits and attitudes which are consistent with fruitful self-directed lifelong learning. In the context of criminal law, broadly conceived, these habits can be conducive to active citizenship (it is good to understand the coercive power of the State and its purported justifications) and, I would suggest, to effective, reflective professional practice. Much criminal lawyering is learnt 'on the job'; the experience of PBL could provide a template for criminal lawyers which supports their candid self-reflection and development as practitioners. Moreover, the practice of criminal law may not involve a great deal of close focus on substantive law. This should allay the concern that 'coverage' in a PBL curriculum may be limited (Szabo, 1993 alludes to this concern). Better, I would argue that emerging practitioners have the skills to find and interpret law and a variety of critical lenses through which to view it that go beyond merely knowing a wide range of legal rules.

A further potential benefit of PBL is its dependence on *collaboration*. The central place of the *group*, meeting regularly in formal sessions – and conceivably interacting informally in a variety of ways at other times – links successful student performance to effective co-working. The student-centredness of PBL also implies a broadly egalitarian arrangement between students and staff. Clearly, the nature of institutions and the necessity of assessment mean that hierarchy persists in various forms and contexts. However, the role of staff – as facilitators rather than content-dispensers – can oil the wheels of student-student collaboration as well as fostering a culture in which students can proactively interact with staff as members of the same community of scholars and practitioners. The value of collaboration itself might lie both in the ethical approach to learning it can support; collaborative learning calls for a continued recognition of the roles of others, and their relationships with one's own role. Collaboration also fosters skills which are in demand in the workplace; a student who can demonstrate success in working with a range of people on complex projects has a good employability story to tell. Moreover, the capacity for recognition of the roles and experiences of others may have an especial ethical resonance in the practice of criminal law, where practitioners may be working with people in situations of acute disadvantage, difficulty, or distress.

It pays not to be naive about PBL. There are competing views on whether it works – and competing views about what it means for it to 'work'. I would argue that to 'measure' PBL solely against conventional outcomes from conventional curricula is possibly to miss the point, since PBL is not merely a different vehicle to get to the same place. Rather, it is a different conception of education which calls for different measures of success. But, like conventional accounts of criminal law, conventional educational indicators cannot be merely ignored, and it is important not to take the supposed benefits of PBL as inevitably given. Aspects of the debates around the effectiveness of PBL are examined by Strobel and van Barneveld (2009), who suggest that PBL can claim some success against conventional indicators such as knowledge retention and performance and skills-based activity. It is of course important to remain sensitive to context and the difficulties attendant in 'reading across' a success from another situation or institution into one's own practice.

PBL can challenge the expectations of students and staff in relation to their roles and responsibilities in the learning process. Students may find the lived experience of student-centredness challenging. Staff might struggle to 'step aside' in the way that PBL calls for. The journey from the focal point of the learning experience as a content-transmitting subject expert to a different place in which the emphasis is on collaborating with others to facilitate learning is unsettling (see, for example, Savin-Baden, 2003).

There are further challenges posed to staff through the reappraisal of the relationship between different subjects which is envisaged by PBL. The connections between different areas of the curriculum which PBL prompts can be energising and can stimulate collaborations among staff. At the same time, 'conventional' academic working cultures may be resistant to this kind of development. This resistance can be compounded by institutional arrangements such as modular structures, which might hinder the type of intellectual boundary-crossing suggested by PBL. The emphasis on obtaining academic credit by way of assessment in *individual* modules can also get in the way, as can an institution's internal funding model in which departmental funding might be linked to student enrolment at the module level. The success of PBL, along the lines of the model described, depends on overcoming the forces of insularity and 'territorialism' which can inhibit the collaboration that should underpin learning design in this context. Developing a boundary-crossing PBL programme or curriculum is easier if, at the modular level, individuals and teams are willing to be imaginative about 'their own' subjects. I suggest that a broad conception of 'criminal law', of the nature outlined in this chapter, can be part of that.

References

Alldridge, P. (1990) 'What's wrong with the traditional criminal law course?', *Legal Studies*, vol. 10, no. 1, pp. 38–62.

Barrows, H.S., and Tamblyn, R.M. (1980) *Problem-Based Learning: An Approach to Medical Education*, New York, Springer.

Barrows, H.S., and Wee Keng Neo, L. (2007) *Principles and Practice of a PBL*, Singapore, Pearson.

Boud, D., and Feletti, G.I. (eds.) (1997) *The Challenge of Problem-Based Learning*, 2nd edn, London, Kogan Page.

Devlin, P. (1959) *The Enforcement of Morals*, London, Oxford University Press.

Duch, B.J. (2001) 'Writing Problems for Deeper Understanding' in Duch, B.J., Groh, S.E., and Allen, D.E. (eds.) *The Power of Problem-Based Learning: A Practical "How To" for Teaching Undergraduate Courses in any discipline*, pp. 47–58.

Farmer, L. (1995) 'Bringing Cinderella to the ball: Teaching criminal law in context', *Modern Law Review*, vol. 58, no. 5, pp. 756–766.

Fitzpatrick, B. (2014) 'The place of criminal law in contemporary legal education Part 1: Thoughts from a CEPLER workshop', *Ed Lines*, 30 September [Blog]. Available at https://benfitzpatrick1.wordpress.com/2014/09/30/the-place-of-criminal-law-in-contemporary-legal-education-part-1-thoughts-from-a-cepler-workshop/ (Accessed 4 November 2015).

Fitzpatrick, B., and Hunter, C. (2011) 'Problem-based learning in a new law school', *Directions* (UK Centre for Legal Education Newsletter), no. 22 (Spring).

Fletcher, G.P. (1998) *Basic Concepts of Criminal Law*, New York, Oxford University Press.

Giles, M. (1991) 'Teaching criminal law', *The Law Teacher*, vol. 25, no. 3, pp. 214–226.

Grimes, R. (2014) 'Delivering legal education through an integrated problem-based learning model–the nuts and bolts', *International Journal of Clinical Legal Education*, vol. 21, no. 2, pp. 1–26.

Hart, H.L.A. (1963) *Law, Liberty and Morality*, London, Oxford University Press.

Lacey, N., and Wells, C. (1998) *Reconstructing Criminal Law: Critical Perspectives on Crime and the Criminal Process*, 2nd edn, London, Butterworths.

McBarnet, D. (1981) 'Magistrates' courts and the ideology of justice', *British Journal of Law and Society*, vol. 8, pp. 181–197.

Moust, J.H.C. (1998) 'The problem-based education approach at the Maastricht Law School', *The Law Teacher*, vol. 32, no. 1, pp. 5–36.

Moust, J.H.C., Bouhuijs, P.A.J., and Schmidt, H.G. (2007) *Introduction to Problem-Based Learning: A Guide for Students*, Groningen, Wolters-Noordhoff.

Norrie, A. (2001) *Crime, Reason and History: A Critical Introduction to Criminal Law*, 2nd edn, London, Butterworths.

Padfield, N. (1995) 'Clean water and muddy causation: Is causation a question of law or fact, or just a way of allocating blame?', *Criminal Law Review*, pp. 683–694.

Savin-Baden, M. (2003) *Facilitating Problem-Based Learning: Illuminating Perspectives*, Maidenhead, SRHE and Open University Press.

Shute, S., and Simester, A.P. (eds.) (2002) *Criminal Law Theory: Doctrines of the General Part*, Oxford, Oxford University Press.

Strobel, J., and van Barneveld, A. (2009) 'When is PBL more effective? A meta-synthesis of meta-analyses comparing PBL to conventional classrooms', *Interdisciplinary Journal of Problem-Based Learning*, vol. 3, no. 1 [online]. Available at http://dx.doi.org/10.7771/1541-5015.1046 (Accessed 2 November 2015).

Szabo, A.B. (1993) 'Teaching substantive law through problem based learning in Hong Kong', *Journal of Professional Legal Education*, vol. 11, no. 2, pp. 195–210.

Williams, G. (1961) *Criminal Law: The General Part*, 2nd edn, London, Stevens and Sons Limited.

Wong, Y.J. (2003) 'Harnessing the potential of problem-based learning in legal education', *The Law Teacher*, vol. 37, no. 2, pp. 157–173.

York Law School (undated) *York Law School Guide to Problem-Based Learning* [Online], UK, University of York. Available at https://www.york.ac.uk/media/law/documents/pbl_guide.pdf (Accessed 4 November 2015).

Chapter 6

Turning criminal law upside down

Jo Boylan-Kemp and Rebecca Huxley-Binns

Imagine, dear reader, that you are a second-year law student and it is a couple of weeks before the start of the academic year. You are required to study Criminal Law as a half-year module and have no prior knowledge of the subject matter. You have received an email from your criminal law teachers (whom you have not yet met), who have asked you to watch a few short videos, which they have recorded and uploaded to YouTube:

1   An explanation of the basic laws of joint unlawful enterprise (2:30 minutes)
2   An introduction to the offence of theft (6 minutes)
3   The law governing appropriation (9 minutes)
4   An exploration of the law defining dishonesty (7:30 minutes)

When you attend your first criminal law workshop, you walk in to a room which is, in layout, unlike any seminar room you have previously seen at your university; it contains four round tables, each seating nine people and with plug sockets and network cables coming through the middle of every table. You take a seat, hoping to know somebody from the previous year but finding yourself at a table with all new faces, and you are given a short story to read by your tutor. It is by far the shortest problem question you've ever seen in a legal education setting. Two hours later, you are thrilled to have cracked the back of the law governing theft and joint unlawful enterprise without having stopped talking, going on Google, Wikipedia, and (eventually) LexisNexis and Westlaw. You have relied on your peers for their input and their criticism; you have made assumptions about the law and about facts, which you have had to correct, and you've started to think critically about the concepts of both appropriation and dishonesty in the criminal law. This is the question that has engaged you for the past two hours:

> *Two Boswell sisters, Chevorne Boswell and Shantelle Boswell were in their Claire's Accessories in Lexport. Chevorne picked up some gold-hoop earrings. Shantelle told Chevorne to put them in her pocket. Chevorne was about to put them in her pocket*

when she noticed the shop assistant had seen her. Chevorne then put the earrings back. Both Chevorne and Shantelle ran out of the store.

What, if anything, can Chevorne and Shantelle be charged with?

Now, become yourself again and allow us to explain what we did and why we did it when teaching the Criminal Law module at Nottingham Law School in 2013.

We were given the opportunity to run a pilot scheme within the undergraduate Law School after some of the university senior managers, in pursuit of innovative teaching methods, had toured a number of universities in North America. In one they had been introduced to a physics professor called Bob Beichner. In the mid-1990s, Beichner had decided to trial a new approach to teaching and learning; it was an approach that directly contradicted the traditional and common-place pedagogic practice of the didactic delivery to a passive audience and which instead transferred the focus away from the lecturer and onto students by putting them directly at the heart of their learning experience. Beichner had combined a number of tried and tested pedagogic practices, such as group-work, peer-review, problem-based learning, and flipped-learning, in such a way that a cooperative and collaborative learning environment was created which encouraged students to assume autonomous responsibility for their learning. Beichner termed this new teaching approach 'SCALE-UP', which now stands for 'Student Centred Active Learning Environment with Upside-down Pedagogies'. (Other permeations of the acronym exist, but this is the current preferred one). It has been adopted successfully by a number of universities worldwide. Our senior managers were so impressed with this student-centred learning approach that they assembled a team of academics, librarians, technicians, and estates' managers and found space at both of the university campuses to be re-purposed into SCALE-UP classrooms.

The learning environment in a purpose-built SCALE-UP classroom is different than the standard teaching room layout found within most universities, as described earlier. As well as the round tables, plugs and network connections, each wall has a mounted screen, which can be linked so all students can see what is projected on to the screens without having to move; there are moveable whiteboards; there are laptop computers available for student use (with a ratio of one to be shared between three students) in case students do not have access to their own suitable devices; and, perhaps most importantly, there is no dedicated tutor podium or desk to act as a focal point within the room. Student collaboration and teamwork are encouraged.

The set-up of the learning environment is important; just as at a dinner party, a round table allows you to talk to everyone else seated at the table, a rectangular table restricts your conversation to only those seated directly next to or opposite you. Which set-up makes for the more interactive, stimulating dinner conversation? Our guess is that you would agree round tables encourage more inclusive conversation and debate. The SCALE-UP classroom layout, therefore, is designed to encourage and facilitate student interaction and engagement with their peers. However, even without access to a dedicated learning room with round tables, you can still utilise the teaching methods to make a traditional classroom layout work for the SCALE-UP learning approach.

By engaging the students in an active process of enquiry and discovery, a deeper form of learning occurs, as the thought processes used and the skills engaged in working through a problem to find the answer mean that the student understands not only the ultimate answer (if there is one, or perhaps alternative ones) to the question but also the reasoning behind the answer(s); they go through the process of trial and error in working and discovering the route to the result and, therefore, they fully understand the process required to get the answer.

When confronted with the Chevorne and Shantelle problem (noted earlier), most students immediately concluded that because neither sister had left the store with the earrings, no theft had occurred. They sought confirmation from the tutors that this was true and were surprised when the tutors refused to affirm or deny the accuracy of the conclusion. In fact, the students were disconcerted when the tutors responded, "If you're sure, feel free to leave". Luckily (because we don't know what we would have done if they had left), none did. Instead, the students went from gut instinct to looking at the law and to digging more deeply into the issues. We appreciate that we had already laid the groundwork for this by asking them to watch the YouTube videos listed above, so they relied on their preparation and used their textbooks to define and start to analyse the offence of theft (some simply Googled it, which, as a starting point, was fine too). They began to appreciate that they really had to dissect the ingredients of the offence, which took them to the primary sources of section 3 of the Theft Act 1968 (UK) and the case authorities of *Gomez* [1993] AC 442 and *Hinks* [2001] 2 AC 241. So, with very little prompting, students were voluntarily searching for primary source material on their journey towards the answer to a legal problem. What was great to see from the tutor's perspective was the generosity of those students in the room who had done A-level law in sharing their knowledge and understanding with those who hadn't. What we cannot capture on paper is how active and noisy the room was as the students discussed the problem. There was, however, a real lull when the students realised that Chevorne had appropriated the earrings, which were property belonging to another, and that she had done so dishonestly and with intent; which is, technically, a theft. They knew it didn't feel like one, so they wondered if they had got the law wrong. It was interesting to observe that they did not want to question the law, but rather wanted to question their own understanding of it. At this point, the tutor led a short whole group discussion about the rightness of the decision in *Hinks*, and as the students had started to think critically about the law, they then all felt they were ready to end the workshop. To their surprise and dismay, the tutor then asked whether Shantelle had any criminal liability. To cut a long story short, by the end of the first two-hour workshop, the students had a basic understanding and knowledge of theft and accomplices, had analysed the problem and evaluated the law, and were intellectually both stimulated and exhausted.

The purpose of the student contact time in the SCALE-UP classroom is to focus on enquiry-based learning, and this means we had to 'flip' the classroom. This is where the traditional lecture is delivered online outside the classroom so the learning activities in the classroom are more active and include those we might otherwise describe as 'homework'. How the tutor imparts information prior to the workshop is entirely down to the tutor's personal preference. Some tutors record short bite-sized videos capturing the basics of a particular principle or case (we ended up with over 30 short videos on YouTube); some will make podcasts; some will make PowerPoint presentations with an embedded voice recording. The beauty of this flipped-learning method is that the students get to choose where and when they access this information, which means that they can control their learning so it takes place in a manner that suits their own personal style. One student may choose to watch a video first thing in the morning whilst still in pyjamas; another student may decide to watch the same video once he or she has finished work or after visiting their friends. By providing students with the choice as to how they learn, they are more likely to engage with the process and remember more than when they are required to sit in a lecture theatre at a time prescribed for all (Bergmann & Sams 2012). The other advantage of providing the materials in this way is that students can watch and re-watch the video (or other medium) as often as they want, so if they are unsure of a particular point or they miss something the first time around, then they have the chance to look at it again, and again.

One of the fundamental features in the SCALE-UP classroom is casting the role of the tutor as a facilitator. Lecturers traditionally have taken centre stage in the lecture theatre, and tutors have equally taken control of and led the seminars, directing the discussions, answering student questions, and providing the correct answers for students to take a record of in their class notes. In a SCALE-UP classroom, however, the tutor is merely a facilitator of discussion between students and does not dominate the contact time. The real work of the tutor in a SCALE-UP environment is in the preparation of the online lectures and the workshops (see the following text), which is considerable. Because the students work collaboratively in the workshop environment, with the tutor nudging them in the right direction and reminding them of the existence of the legal databases and the importance of going beyond Google and Wikipedia, it is the tutor's imagination and creativity in designing the workshop activities which takes the time. The learning in the workshop is so active, and the relationship between the students is so dynamic that the tutor genuinely takes a back seat until the plenary concluding comments at the end. Initially, some students were reluctant to control their own learning, and as soon as they had a question, they would raise their hand and ask the tutor. So we decided as a matter of principle not to answer student questions until we were satisfied they had made sufficient efforts to work the answer out for themselves; this was, of course, unless our intervention was needed to correct a fundamental misunderstanding of the task or the law. A common response to a student question, therefore, was something along the lines of, "Good question; if you still don't know in eight minutes, then call me back and show me what you have done to find out. I promise I will tell you the answer if you haven't worked it out". The lazier students were particularly perturbed by this response, but on the whole, the students understood why it was important for them to know the answer and not just for them to be told the answer; and it was rare that we did eventually have to supply it.

Another difference in a SCALE-UP class is that the students had textbooks, mobile devices, and Internet-enabled laptops in the room with them, and we actively encouraged use of them. We are aware from discussions with colleagues that some tutors at higher education institutions forbid student use of technology in their classrooms, which means that online resources the students could use to research legal answers to particular questions are not accessible. Instead, students are normally required to research independently in advance, both online and from hard-copy textbooks, take notes on vast quantities of information, and come to class with fully prepared answers, but no textbooks and no devices. The contact time is then traditionally spent dissecting the student's application of their researched knowledge to the required preparation. We do not dispute that such application and analysis is, of course, a fundamental part of the learning journey. However, the SCALE-UP approach challenges whether this is the best use of class contact time and the best way to ensure an active, dynamic, and effective learning environment for students – especially as some students simply come to class with a blank sheet of paper and write down what the tutor says with perhaps little comprehension of its meaning.

Research undertaken in 2011 (Sparrow, Liu and Wegner), and cited by Beichner in a keynote conference address at Nottingham Trent University in 2014, indicates that the human brain is evolving to take account of the easily-accessible external database of information (i.e. the World Wide Web), as it appears that people are becoming less adept at remembering information but instead have a more developed ability to find the knowledge they require. When teaching SCALE-UP, the tutor has to embrace the fact that information, including the law, is fleeting, disposable, and fit for a purpose that may be transient, but that the skills the students need to develop are their ability to identity the issue, find the law, apply the law accurately, evaluate it, and then reach an informed conclusion. The SCALE-UP approach embraces this by developing reliance upon technology and encourages the students to use online, and other, sources in the classroom.

This may be a seismic shift for some tutors, as they may have spent years telling students to put their phones away and pay attention, but with the SCALE-UP approach, students are encouraged to stop listening to (relying upon) the tutor and to 'get out there' (figuratively) and find the answers to the question through the use of all available sources; this approach also fits better with current student behaviours and their increased reliance upon technology. Technology need not always be a negative, disruptive influence in the classroom.

Most students used the University-provided laptop computers (kept in a locked cabinet when not in use) or brought their own laptops or digital devices, both to record their own notes and to access the Internet for research (we rarely had to ask them to log off Facebook). Each two-hour workshop ended with a 20-minute, student-led plenary where the outcomes of the activities were fed back to the rest of the group. We had the use of several A1-size portable whiteboards and many of the groups preferred to record their structures and reasoning on the boards and then take photographs of the boards for their later consideration or during revision.

Beichner's recommendation in the SCALE-UP room is to allocate the students into teams of three, where one student assumes the role of the 'scribe' (responsible for recording the group discussion and findings), a second student is the 'organiser' (responsible for developing a strategy for the undertaking the task), and the third acts as the 'critic' (tasked with acting as a devil's advocate and questioning the strategy decided on, the information found, and decisions taken and conclusions reached). However, after careful consideration, we decided instead to allow students to exercise autonomy – in where they sat, with whom, and how they might tackle the activities. We cast the student groups into roles according to the nature of the activity, so in one workshop, they might have to provide advice to the police on a charge; in another they had to prepare a report from a junior lawyer on a point of law; or an analysis of a defence strategy to an accused; or a closing speech to the jury, as either prosecution or defence, or a skeleton argument to a judge.

As well as flipping the learning and recasting the role of the tutor to facilitator, the criminal law SCALE-UP at Nottingham Law School also turned the traditional syllabus upside down. As is shown in other chapters of this collection, and subject to exceptions, criminal law modules generally structure the learning in what appears to be a logical way; most start with an introduction to the general principles or theories of criminal law, and this might include, for example, the harm principle or the principles of fair labelling, which is then followed by an introduction to actus reus, mens rea, and strict liability. Thereafter follows an examination of a range of serious offences, followed by an examination of the general defences, and then an examination of joint unlawful enterprise. The problem with this structure is that it encourages students to think of the criminal law in silos. That is, that the offences exist separately to the defences, that the defences exist separately to offences, and that joint liability exists separately to individual liability. This is unrealistic because, of course, offences and defences and various modes of liability arise simultaneously, and their interaction needs to be handled by a competent law student and lawyer with confidence.

We also assert that this curriculum design makes learning criminal law far more complex and technical than it needs to be and presents unnecessary challenges to students in learning the law. Although there may be strong arguments that students need to be able to identify elements of the actus reus separately from elements of the mens rea and that concepts of subjectivity and objectivity within the discussions of mens rea need to be mastered for a high-level understanding of criminal theory, it is quite clear that a competent undergraduate law student who can accurately identify the elements of any given criminal offence should be able to apply those elements (whether actus reus or mens rea) to sets of complex facts using accurate authority so as to reach a reasoned and informed conclusion as to the criminal liability of an offender that will satisfy the learning outcomes for most criminal law modules. We do not assert that mastery in depth of criminal theory is without value, but we do assert that such in-depth theoretical examination of criminal law often carries the risk that students complete a module without the actual ability to apply existing knowledge and understanding when confronted with a criminal offence with which they are not familiar. This is significant, given that criminal law modules will often examine, at most, 30 criminal offences (if we include all the variations on non-fatal offences against the person, all types of homicide, and property crimes, and there are potentially more if we include inchoate offences) and there are probably over 10,000 criminal offences in England and Wales. Many students' success in a criminal law module might not be best described as competence in criminal law in general. We think the SCALE'd-UP criminal law student is better able to tackle the unknown criminal law in the future with confidence and ease, than a traditionally-taught student.

There is a further, fundamental problem with the traditional structuring of criminal law; this is to do with student expectation. Many students reading law as an undergraduate will not previously have studied law. They will, however, have watched television programmes that feature criminal offences, because these do tend to make the best legal dramas, and have started to develop a limited understanding of criminal law, albeit with a skewed perspective. What happens then is that students approach the study of criminal law with very different expectations than when they start to study land law or trusts, with which they are not familiar and for which they have no, or very low, expectations. What students learn in their first few crime classes totally fails to meet their (admittedly unrealistic) expectations. How different the reality of criminal law study is from the perception held in the mind of a new criminal law student. If this were the only problem with structuring criminal law in the traditional way (failing to meet or manage student expectation), there might not be any reason to call for a new approach to the criminal curriculum. However, given the other arguments made earlier in terms of teaching criminal law in silos and making the study of law unnecessarily technical, it is clear that there was merit in examining whether there is a better way to learn criminal law.

In May 2013, we set aside one full working week to start to plan teaching criminal law in the SCALE-UP method. Thankfully, we were already familiar with the concepts of problem-based learning (PBL). We also decided early on that using contact time with students in the SCALE-UP classroom for traditional lectures would be an awful waste of active learning opportunities and that, therefore, we would move the traditional lectures into digital format available on a private channel on YouTube. Therefore, we knew that this meant we had four hours contact time per week for workshops where students would collaborate in answering problem-based questions of criminal law. Other than these basic framework boundaries, the curriculum was tabula rasa. However, all this knowledge did not prevent us from starting at the traditional beginning and trying to create problems based on actus reus issues, such as contact, result, or circumstance crimes, and mens rea issues involving subjective and objective states of mind. We quickly realised, though, that these exercises were artificial; we were sacrificing the reality of criminal conduct in society at the expense of a theoretical model which simply did not work in the SCALE-UP classroom. So we started from scratch and wrote the questions so as to reflect the realities of what happens in life, which means that the offences would not be artificially distinguished in workshop questions and that students would be introduced to different offences and defences and joint liability all coexisting in the same workshop question from the very first workshop onwards.

What follows (Figure 6.1) was one of the students' most popular workshop activities, not just because of the medium but also because it was so effective in getting students to focus on the legal (not just the factual) issues by identifying the (potential) complainants, defendants, and offences committed.

How a Blackpool stag do changed my life forever...

Cherry (not her real name) was a working girl whose whole life changed following the events of one man's stag do. Cherry tells '*Have a rest* magazine' about the weekend she can never forget.

We met them in a bar near the Blackpool Ballroom. There were eight of them all together; each wearing a bright pink T-shirt saying 'Dylan's stag do – July 2013.' I was with Roxie, one of the girls I usually work with. We always work in pairs just to make sure that nothing happens to each other. We thought they looked like they might be up for some female company so we went over to them and asked if they wanted to buy us a drink or two. They said "yeah, come join us", so we did.

After a bit we went back to their hotel. A few of the lads called it a night and it ended up being just Roxie and me left with just two of them, Wayne and Kyle. They both seemed to want to take things further and they asked if we wanted to go back to their room. We said "sure, but it'd cost them".

When we got to their room Wayne got out a box that had things like handcuffs, whips and a couple of blindfolds in it. Roxie and I said we'd give it a go but that it'd cost them another £100 if they wanted to use stuff like that on us. Wayne told Roxie to strip naked, then he tied her to the bed and started to whip her. Kyle asked me to tie him up and perform a number of sex acts on him, which I did.

We then took it in turns to perform various sadomasochistic acts on each other – they got increasingly weird – Wayne even asked me to use a razor to make small cuts all over his legs and back.

After I while I ended up having sex with Kyle. We didn't use a condom as he said he didn't like the feel of them. I said okay but that it'd cost him another £50.

Figure 6.1

The next morning as Roxie and were leaving we saw a couple of the lads getting their breakfast. The young one, Billy, hadn't got any eyebrows and Roxie asked him what happened. He told us that Dylan and Ethan, who he was sharing a room with, had thought it would be really funny to use some hair removal cream on his eyebrows when he asleep. He was really upset about it as he said he looked like an idiot – which he did a bit.

It was when we were talking to Billy that one of the other lads said to me "I hope you didn't give Kyle a good seeing to last night – he's just had a bit of bad news from his doctor."

I asked him what he meant but he wouldn't say any more. It was only when I had my regular check for STDs that I found out what he was talking about – I'd caught HIV from Kyle!

If I'd have known he was HIV+ I'd have never had unprotected sex with him. He knew and he didn't tell me – I can't believe that someone would do that to another person.

He must have known the risk and just decided not to tell me about it. I'm now stuck with this illness for the rest of my life and it's all his fault! I can't work anymore. I hate him - he's ruined my life!

Have a rest magazine contacted Kyle to hear his side of the story, but he declined to comment.

Figure 6.1 (Continued)

What follows is the written script of a podcast which was played to the students at the start of their fifth week (of 12) of study. The podcast was played to the whole group once and made available on the Virtual Learning Environment for playback as necessary. The story of poor Billy is part of a bigger tale of woe of the Boswell family (Chevorne and Shantelle, mentioned earlier, are his sisters), who feature throughout the criminal law module, getting involved in various criminal behaviours. The instructions for the 'Billy' problem were simply to consider, first, if any offence in English criminal law was made out and, second, if there was an arguable defence (and if there was, on whom the burden of proof lies). Feel free to use or adapt Billy's story, but please acknowledge the source:

PC LEWIS: Interview date is 16 October 2013. Time is 20:14. For the benefit of the tape, there is present in the interview room PC Lewis, no 4607 and PC Phillips, no 3318. Also present is Billy Boswell, aged 18, and the duty solicitor, Mrs Cracknell.

So, Billy, why don't you tell us all about it? We know you did it, so it'd be easier for everyone if you just told us exactly what happened.

BILLY: Well I knew about Mildred and that she'd got some money as my Aunt Jade had talked about her. My Aunt Jade's a nurse like, and she helps people out and looks after them. She's real good at it. Aunt Jade liked Mildred, said she was a nice old lady who just wanted to tell someone her stories.

I knew who Mildred was cos me and Aunt Jade had bumped into her in the market place one Saturday afternoon like. Aunt Jade was taking me to get some trainers for me birthday. I'd seen some really nice blue Puma ones, and she said she'd get me them cos I'd been doing really well in school and that I deserved a treat for me birthday. We saw Mildred, and she was buying some fruit from the veg bloke. Aunt Jade said hello and waved. She smiled at Aunt Jade but I don't think she noticed me cos I was a little bit behind as I'd been looking at some DVDs on another stall.

I feel so bad. She seemed like such a nice old lady. I feel terrible about what I did to her. Can you tell her I'm sorry? Please?

PC LEWIS: What did you do to her Billy? What happened on Sunday night?

BILLY: I, I, followed her didn't I? Saw her walking down the road to the bank, and I followed her cos I knew she'd got money. Aunt Jade said her house was dead nice like and that she'd obviously got some cash when her husband had died. So I followed her to the cash machine and watched her take out some notes and put it in her bag. She looked like she'd taken out lots of money so, I just went for it. I snuck up behind her and grabbed her shoulder, not rough like but just so she knew I'd got hold of her, and I said, "Please can I have you bag, Mildred?"

She was so scared. She asked how I knew her name, and I said it didn't matter but that she just had to give me her bag and nothing bad would happen. So she gave me her bag and I took it and ran away as quick as I could like. I did say I sorry to her like before I ran away though, cos I was, I am sorry. I'm really, really sorry. I've never done anything like that before. Never.

PC LEWIS: So why, Billy? Why did you take Mildred's bag?
BILLY: It was Kyle. I did it cos of Kyle.
PC LEWIS: Who's Kyle?
BILLY: Kyle's. Kyle's me dad. But I don't call him dad. He don't deserve that name.
PC LEWIS: Okay. So tell us what Kyle did that made you take Mildred's bag.
BILLY: He said that he owed Shylock money and that I had to sort it for him and give him £200 to pay Shylock off. I know that Shylock is a loan shark and

that he's a right nasty piece of work. Everyone on the estate knows it. So Kyle said that if I didn't get him £200 before Monday that he'd hurt Bruno. I love Bruno so I had to do it like.

PC LEWIS: Who's Bruno?

BILLY: Bruno's me dog. He's the only one out the lot of them who loves me. I'd do anything for him, and I couldn't let dad hurt him, could I?

PC LEWIS: Did Kyle say thing else to you, Billy?

BILLY: Yeah, he also said that if I didn't get him the money that he'd tell me brothers, Ethan and Dylan, that I like boys, you know, like that, and I'm don't, I'm not gay or anything, I like girls. But they'd believe Kyle; they wouldn't have believed me no matter what I said, and they'd be horrible to me if they thought I was gay, cos they hate gays like. And that's why I did it, cos of what Kyle said.

PC LEWIS: Okay, Billy. Have you told us everything? Is there anything else we should know?

BILLY: No, that's it all. Can you tell Mildred I'm really, really sorry like.

Briefly, this exercise gave students the opportunity to consider the offence of robbery and the defence of duress by actively engaging with some of the key case law in the topic.

In conclusion, the SCALE-UP learning model is very rewarding – for tutors and for students. We have data on student achievement – which compares very favourably with a module studied on the 'traditional' approach at the same time. Setting a variety of seminar tasks through various media kept student interest-levels and attendance high; they never knew what to expect. In fact, engagement was so enthusiastic that we were often asked to keep the noise levels down by tutors in adjacent teaching rooms.

References

Beichner, R. J. & Saul, J. M., 2013, *Introduction to the SCALE-UP (Student-Centered Activities for Large Enrolment Undergraduate Programs) Project*, Proceedings of the International School of Physics, (Online) Available Via: North Carolina State University at https://www.ncsu.edu/per/Articles/Varenna_SCALEUP_Paper.pdf last accessed 02/12/2015

Bergmann, J. & Sams, A., 2012, *Flip Your Classroom: Reach Every Student in Every Class Every Day*. International Society for Technology in Education.

Burke, Debra D., 2015, Scale-Up! Classroom Design and Use Can Facilitate Learning. 49(2) *The Law Teacher* 189–205.

Sparrow, B., Liu, J., & Wegner, D. M., 2011, Google Effects on Memory: Cognitive Consequences of Having Information at Our Fingertips. 333 *Science* 776–778.

Chapter 7

Criminal law pedagogy and the Australian state codes

Thomas Crofts and Stella Tarrant

Introduction

In Australia, there are two criminal law traditions: the state criminal codes and the common law. Sir Samuel Griffith drafted the first of the state criminal codes for Queensland in 1897, and this has proven influential in the development of others. This Code has made a unique contribution to criminal law jurisprudence, and although in many ways the Griffith Code may be regarded as not so different from the consolidation Acts found in the Australian common law jurisdictions (and New Zealand), there are some key differences. First, the Code aims to be an organised, systematic presentation of the main aspects of criminal law, which includes the principles of criminal responsibility, not only specific offences. Second, the Griffith Code makes statute law the *only* source of offence liability in Western Australia and the only source of liability for indictable offences in Queensland. This chapter will begin by discussing the nature of the Griffith Code before examining how these distinct features profoundly influence the criminal law pedagogy in code states. It will conclude by reflecting on the relevance of these teaching practices for common law jurisdictions.

The Griffith code and common law jurisdictions

While the efforts to codify English criminal law in the nineteenth century did not lead to the adoption of an English criminal code, they were successful in some of the British colonies. In the Australian context, this has been explained as partly due to the fact that "[t]he process of reception of English criminal law, abusive executive influences, and a less developed bar and bench, meant fewer obstacles to codification" (Wright 2008, p20). In 1896, Sir Samuel Griffith, chief justice of the Supreme Court of Queensland, prepared a Digest of the Criminal Law of Queensland and followed this a year later with a Draft Criminal Code. His draft was heavily influenced by the English Draft Criminal Code of 1880 prepared by Sir James Fitzjames Stephen, by the New York Penal Code of 1881 and by the Italian Penal Code of 1889; the last of these he describes as "in many respects the most complete and perfect Penal Code in existence" (Griffith 1897, pvii; see also Cadoppi and Cullinane 2000, p116). This Draft Code was enacted as the Criminal Code of Queensland in 1899 and adopted shortly afterwards as the Criminal Code of Western Australia in 1902. It was amended and re-enacted in 1913. This Code was also influential on the Criminal Code of Tasmania (1924) and, to a lesser degree, the Criminal Code of the Northern Territory (1983), as well as a number of African colonial codes (see Cadoppi and Cullinane 2000, p116).

The Code is not designed to be a collection of all the criminal laws in operation; as Griffith notes, such a task would be impossible (1897, piv). But what the Code is designed to do, and to a large extent does, is rationalise, simplify, and systematise the criminal law (Griffith 1897, ppiv–v). The Code gathers the criminal law together to 'make sense of it' in one statute. Before going any further, it should be noted that the Australian common law states do have 'consolidating statutes', such as the *Crimes Act 1900* (NSW), *Crimes Act 1958* (Vic), and the *Criminal Law Consolidation Act 1935* (SA), which begs the question of whether there is a significant difference between the two traditions. As with the codes, the Australian consolidation Acts do not contain all aspects of the criminal law, but they do draw together much of it and in this sense may be regarded as similar to criminal codes. It is no doubt true that even in the 'common law' jurisdictions, "[m]ost cases in most courts are cases in which all or most of the . . . law that is applied. . . . has its source in the text of a statute" (Gagelar 2011, p1). Thus many of the differences between code states and the common law jurisdictions with consolidating statutes are differences of degree. Nevertheless, there are differences between codes and the common law, we have found, that affect how the criminal law is conceived in the different Australian jurisdictions and which influence criminal law pedagogy. We explain the two important differences in more detail: First, the conceptual systematisation of the codes distinguishes them from the common law. This feature is often overlooked by those unfamiliar with the codes. There is a clear logic and progression to the Griffith-based Criminal Codes, which to a degree is lacking in the consolidation statutes in the common law states.

The scheme of the Griffith Code is apparent in its structure. Although there are some differences, the *Criminal Code* (Qld) and the *Criminal Code* (WA) follow a similar basic structure. Part 1 (Qld)/I (WA) concerns general matters that are relevant to the whole of the criminal law. This includes the definition of terms used throughout the Codes (Codes, Ch 1), detail on when and to what degree a person can be held to be a party to an offence (Codes, Ch 2), an explanation of when and where the Codes are applicable (*Criminal Code* (Qld) Ch 4, *Criminal Code* (WA) Ch 3), and general provisions on criminal responsibility (Codes, Ch 5). Parts 2–6 (Qld)/II-VI (WA) of the Codes contain the offence provisions and, as such, detail the elements of the offences, explaining what needs to be proven to convict a person of the relevant offence. Within each Part, there is a clear structure. For example, Part VI, Division II (Injuries to Property) of the *Criminal Code* (WA) begins with Chapter XLV defining terms relevant to offences in this division (including matters which affect liability specific to these offences) before moving to a Chapter XLVI which contains the offence definitions. Part VII contains provisions establishing liability for an offence where, although an offence has not actually been committed, there was preparation towards committing that offence. Part 8 of the *Criminal Code* (Qld) contains sections relating to criminal procedure. In 2004, the provisions of this Part of the Western Australian Code were moved to other enactments such as the *Criminal Procedure Act 2004* (WA) and the *Criminal Investigation Act 2006* (WA). This structure of the Griffith Code relies significantly on the inclusion of the general provisions on criminal responsibility. Griffith aimed to provide a system for the interpretation and application of criminal law and, in doing so, expounded fundamental principles which underlie criminal law and which could be applied to all offences – creating what some might label a general part and a specific part to the criminal law.

The second significant difference between the Griffith Code and the common law jurisdictions is that under the Griffith Code, all criminal liability for offences – or indictable offences in Queensland – (except one, the common law offence of contempt of court) has its source in a statute. This arrangement is created by ss4 and 7 of the *Criminal Code Act 1913* (WA) and ss5 and 8 of the *Criminal Code Act 1899* (Qld), the Acts to which *The Criminal Code* (WA) and the *Criminal Code* (Qld) are attached as Schedules. In Western Australia, s4 provides, "No person shall be liable to be tried or punished in Western Australia as for an offence, except under the express provisions of the Code, or some other statute law of Western Australia. . . ." Section 7 provides, "Nothing in this Act or in the Code shall affect the authority of courts of record to punish a person summarily for the offence commonly known as 'contempt of court'". This does not mean, as already noted, that the Code covers all aspects of the criminal law, but the Codes determine that the only source of liability is legislation and that all legislation is subject to the general principles enunciated in Chapter 5 (s36 *Criminal Code* Qld and WA), (although in Qld some sections of Chapter 5 do not apply to regulatory offences). As such, we can see that the Code provides a clear system for determining liability to be applied to the whole criminal law. In contrast, in the common law states, the common law, as a source of liability, can 'protrude' in the gaps left by legislation. The clearest example of this is *mens rea*, the common law doctrine that determines the mental element of an offence, which is implied, alongside statutory provisions.

If we dig deeper into these ideas, the imposition of a clear distinction between what courts are doing in code and common law jurisdictions is unsustainable, except as a matter of emphasis. As Griffith points out (Griffith 1897, piv), it is impossible for any code to cover all of the criminal law. And when courts interpret statutory provisions, they actually create law in a real sense, in that they determine which interpretation, of different possibilities, *is the law*, (Gagelar 2011) and that is an exercise of common law jurisdiction. Nonetheless, at a working level, the fact that the Griffith Code limits the source of offence liability to statute does affect criminal law jurisprudence, and pedagogy, in code states.

The inclusion of the rules governing criminal responsibility is a key feature of the Griffith Code. It plays a part in both distinctions between the Code and common law that we have explained: it is part of the systematic nature of the Code and it makes the limitation of offence liability to statute law comprehensive. Griffith found the concept of *mens rea* to be unclear and therefore aimed to replace it with general principles. The common law presumption of *mens rea* developed in *He Kaw Teh v R* (1985) 157 CLR 523 is not one which has been adopted by the code jurisdictions. The "Griffith Code enacted what was at the time thought to be the common law position of objective criminal responsibility and has remained faithful to that position as a general proposition" (Goode 2002, p157). That is, whereas the mental element of criminal responsibility at common law is constructed through *mens rea*, supplemented by defences and excuses, in the Griffith Code, it is established through the provisions of Chapter 5, specific 'intent' requirements in the Code where they are attached to particular offences and any defences and excuses specific to offences. As noted by Hayne J (dissenting) in *DPP (NT) v WJI* (2004) 219 CLR 43 at 82, this inclusion of criminal responsibility principles, and therefore the lack of need for proof of *mens rea*, was for Griffith a key feature of the Queensland Code (*Widgee Shire Council v Bonney* (1907) 4 CLR (Pt 2) 977 at 981):

> It is never necessary to have recourse to the doctrine of mens rea, the exact meaning of which has been the subject of much discussion. The test now to be applied is whether this prohibited act was, or was not, done accidentally or independently of the exercise of the will of the accused person.

Pedagogy under the codes

We have stressed that the differences between code and common law jurisdictions should not be overstated but that there are important differences: the centrepiece of code jurisdictions is a schematic statute (a code) which, significantly, in the case of the Griffith Code, incorporates general principles of criminal responsibility, not just the conduct elements of specific offences, and the *whole* of the substantive criminal law in Western Australia (and with respect to indictable offences in Queensland) is statutory law, so there is no confusion about whether a court is interpreting legislation or exercising its common law (as a source of law) jurisdiction.

The distinctive features of the Griffith Codes have shaped the pedagogy in law schools in the code states. Or, it may be truer to say they *are shaping* the pedagogy. It has taken a surprisingly long time to conceptualise criminal law doctrine truly from the perspective of the codes (Tarrant 2013) and the same has been the case for the teaching of criminal law. Our observations are drawn from our teaching of criminal law in Western Australia. We believe we have developed a distinctive pedagogy drawn from the nature of this code jurisdiction but, even in the twenty-first century, this has involved realising and then altering some traditional modes of teaching suitable for a common law framework. For generations, in Western Australia there was a tendency to approach the teaching of code law with methods derived from common law pedagogy. For example, as late as the early 2000s, criminal law students in Western Australia were taught from a textbook that explained, in detail, and as a threshold concept derived from cases, the doctrine of *mens rea* as an introduction to constructing liability – and there was no ensuing analysis of Chapter 5 of *The Criminal Code* which was designed to replace the concept of *mens rea*. Rather, *He Kaw Teh* (1985) 15 A Crim R 203, a foundational common law case on *mens rea*, was extracted at some length (Whitney, Flynn, and Moyle 2000, pp9–13). This reveals that the idea that primary principles are located in High Court pronouncements is very deep seated (for a contrasting approach see Edwards, Harding, and Campbell 1992, Ch 6).

Further, as we have suggested, the Griffith Code has been underestimated as a scheme of criminal liability and so, even insofar as it has been made a primary reference, it has tended to be conveyed to students as a 'collection of offences' that can be approached mechanistically (see Edwards, Harding, and Campbell 1992, pp1–13, Ch 9). We believe the impetus to develop further the distinct pedagogy necessary for teaching criminal law of the state codes, is supported now by the greater number of code-trained academics who are available to teach in these jurisdictions. It has also been supported by the national Model Criminal Code movement which, in the 1990s and early 2000s, enhanced interest in the idea of criminal law as a statutory scheme. And the most recent support for continuing development of an appropriate code pedagogy in Australia comes from the movement to ensure law students are adequately trained in statutory interpretation now that so much of the law in all jurisdictions is created by legislation (see Council of Australian Law Deans 2015).

So what is distinctive about a course that teaches the criminal law of the Griffith Code? We give three illustrations of teaching practices (and opportunities) that arise from having a schematic statute (a code) as the centrepiece of the jurisdiction and the fact that all substantive criminal law has its source in legislation.

First, the comprehensive, schematic nature of a code lends itself to being the organisational framework of a criminal law course. Its scheme is the framework for conceptualising the elements of liability in each offence. Moreover, the notion of the 'elements of an offence' in code jurisprudence is, as discussed, the idea of what constitutes liability in full. It does not, for example, include the idea of a list of (conduct or circumstance) elements found in legislation that must then be supplemented by an implied mental element (where none is expressed) for liability to be constituted. 'Elements' of an offence under the Griffith Code are all those required for liability. All the elements (in this comprehensive sense) of every offence created by the Code are expressly stated in the one Act.

This framework, we find, lends itself to a clear exposition of the law and is the basis for repeated practice for students in reading statutes as part of the process of learning the substantive law. With every offence, the provision creating the offence must be located. Then it must be reconstructed as a list of elements, including the mental component, which usually inheres in an element of "unlawfulness" in the offence-creating provision. For example, s313 of the *Criminal Code* (WA) creates the offence of "unlawful assault": "assault" is defined in s222 and an assault is "unlawful" unless "authorised or justified or excused" (s223). Criminal responsibility principles, which determine whether the assault was authorised, justified, or excused, can be found in the later Parts of the Code (for example, self-defence (s248) and provocation (s246)), and in Chapter 5 (for example, unwilled act (s23A), accident (s23B), mistake (s24)).

Thus with each offence covered in the course, students have practised reading statutory terms and reconfiguring them to achieve a list of elements they must express in a way that imports no change in meaning. Moreover, the principles of criminal responsibility in Chapter 5 are graphically part of the Code and have force with respect to every offence. (s36) Therefore, liability for an offence can only be constructed by reading the statute as a whole.

Furthermore, although Chapter 5 is almost unwaveringly referred to as containing 'defences' and 'excuses', suggesting exculpatory principles to be considered (logically) *after* primary responsibility has been established, we are moving towards teaching the principles in Chapter 5 as elements of an offence, in the sense that relevant requirements in Chapter 5 are necessary to constitute liability. The rules relating to onus of proof – evidentiary and persuasive – which underpin the classification of these principles as 'defences' and 'excuses' is taught as a distinct layer of knowledge rather than something that implicitly alters the nature of the structure of criminal liability. That is (as reflected in Hayne J's comments quoted earlier), the principles in Chapter 5 create the fundamental mental states which must be present if criminal liability is to attach to a person. Nowhere in Chapter 5 are the principles of criminal responsibility described as defences or excuses. They are part of the primary structure of criminal responsibility.

Second, where the whole of a course is anchored in legislation, each inquiry within the course begins by locating the primary relevant provision, is at all times 'attached' to that provision, and concludes with that provision. Cases have a defined and specific place within the inquiry about the relevant statutory language. This does not mean all inquiries are a discussion of a statutory provision explicitly; analyses of cases are often complex and while immersed in those analyses, there is no statutory provision in sight. However, there is always a clear thread of reasoning that keeps case discussions linked to the Code. This relationship is taught persistently, throughout the course, partly through the teaching structure (we begin each topic, offence, problem, etc., with Code provisions) but also incidentally, in the classroom. For example, we frequently stop a detailed discussion of cases in tutorials (or the explanation of a case in a lecture) to ask students, 'Which word(s) in the Code are these judges now interpreting?' We also use a trope of the 'leaping off point' to teach the primacy of the statute. There is always a point at which the Code provisions – offence creating, definitional, surrounding context – are exhausted and the court's role begins: to apply, or to interpret and then apply. This aspect of the course is, of course, a constitutional principle in action: the separation of powers. This observation is made to students periodically throughout the course.

Third, a distinctive component of a Griffith Code criminal law course that arises from the entirely statutory source of the law is the emphasis that is required to be placed on the status of each case authority; that is, the emphasis on court hierarchies and relative authority of persuasive decisions. All criminal law courses must teach this, but we have found there is a particular opportunity in code jurisdictions because the 'landscape' of relative authority among all case law is clear cut. Codes create very firm jurisdictional boundaries in the sense that the territorial scope of legislative power also defines the limit of the courts' jurisdiction. In contrast, in jurisdictions where the common law, as a source of law, applies, there is binding judicial authority beyond the legislative jurisdiction of the Parliament (Zimmermann 1995, pp96–97). Where no common law applies (as a source of law) there are no binding case authorities except those emanating from that local jurisdiction and made by courts within the jurisdiction's court hierarchy (including appellate courts). This is the case with any statute (see Finn 1992, pp7–8), not just Codes. However, where the common law is no longer a source of criminal liability unattached to legislation, the distinction between binding and persuasive authority, and the relative weights of persuasive authorities, are easier to see and less easy to confuse. Whether a High Court decision from a 'common law jurisdiction' is binding on another 'common law jurisdiction' depends on whether the High Court was deciding a question at common law or was interpreting a statute, and this is sometimes a complex distinction (for example, see *Babic v R* (2010) 28 VR 297) not always clearly delineated. Thus, while the distinction between binding and non-binding decisions and between the relative weights of non-binding decisions may create a complex matrix in a code jurisdiction, the matrix itself appears in clear relief.

This means we teach some cases as much for identifying sources of law and the status of authorities as for substantive criminal law. *Bolitho v Western Australia* (2007) 34 WAR 215 is a good example of this. The Court of Appeal in that case interpreted the meaning of the element of 'intent to defraud' in s409 of the *Criminal Code* (WA). It considered the question of whether 'intent to defraud' in the offence created by s409 was limited to an intention on the part of an accused to deprive a person of interests related in some way to their property or economic entitlements, or whether it was wider than that, including an intention to deprive a person of *any* kind of interest. Ms Bolitho had induced a woman to believe that she, Ms Bolitho, was an orthopaedic surgeon (which she was not) and, on the strength of that belief, the woman allowed Ms Bolitho to undertake treatment on her injured shoulder. Bolitho intended to deprive the woman of her personal autonomy but not of her property or economic interests. Most of the majority judgement is taken up with a discussion of the common law cases on 'intent to defraud', and students are directed to consider what can justify this. They then examine the Court's treatment of the cases in the context of the Court's statutory interpretation exercise. The words of s409, which appear in their plain meaning and in the context of s409 as a whole to be extremely broad, are examined in the context of their legislative history. The offence was reformulated in 1990 in a legislative reform that repealed a number of specific-context fraud offences and enacted this general offence. The Court's conclusion was that the Parliamentary intent behind 'intent to defraud' in s409 was to enact a provision with the same meaning as that phrase carries at common law. This conclusion opens the door to considering all the relevant common law cases, including the foundational House of Lords cases such as *Re London and Globe Finance Corp Ltd* [1903] 1 Ch 728 and *R v Scott* [1975] AC 819.

It is stressed to students that the court is not applying (and has no constitutional power to apply) that common law; it is going to those cases for 'information' about what s409 means, justified by the Court's conclusions about the legislative intention in the provision. Then students are asked, 'Why, then, is the Court of Appeal also discussing the case of *Peters v The Queen* (1998) 192 CLR 493 at length?' *Peters* is a High Court case dealing with the Commonwealth *Crimes Act 1914* offence of conspiracy to defraud. What can justify reliance on the law in that Act? Students are then directed to the *Bolitho* Court's analysis of *Peters*: one element of the Commonwealth offence is 'intent to defraud', the same words as in the *Criminal Code* (WA). The High Court has interpreted the phrase in the Commonwealth Act to carry the same meaning as the phrase at common law. Therefore, again, students are shown that the Court of Appeal in *Bolitho* can utilise the law in a wide range of cases but only in circumscribed ways. It has no constitutional mandate to *apply* that law but is justified in seeking 'information' from the common law about what the words in the *Criminal Code* (WA) mean.

Pedagogy under the codes: Relevance for common law jurisdictions

The remainder of the chapter is a reflection on whether the approach to teaching we have developed for the Griffith Code has resonance for common law jurisdictions and indeed whether differences are a question of degree rather than of substance. Distinctive characteristics of the Code have made the approaches to teaching we have described necessary: a criminal law course in Western Australia *must be* a course in statutory interpretation, because specific provisions in the *Criminal Code Act* (those quoted earlier) have terminated the common law as a source of liability. An approach more likely to underpin the pedagogy in common law jurisdictions is one that treats criminal law as a complex balance between the common law and parliamentary law. However, codes and the common law jurisdictions' consolidation Acts are statutes: their constitutional natures are the same; they create the same relationship between the courts and parliament. The parliament creates and the courts interpret, law. Wherever any statute speaks, it supersedes the common law.

This being so, the pedagogy we have identified as arising from teaching in a Griffith Code jurisdiction may well have some relevance, and resonance, in other jurisdictions. We have pointed to the Code as providing an organising framework for our courses, a statutory 'anchor' allowing for persistent practice in reading and understanding how legislation works, and the vehicle for learning not only substantive criminal law but the complex relationships between binding and varyingly persuasive authorities. A consolidation Act does not provide an overarching framework for a criminal law course, in that it is not systematically arranged and does not include general principles of criminal responsibility. But it may provide a basis for the other practices. Where an offence is created by a section of a consolidation Act, the section must be reconfigured into a list of elements. These must be interpreted by ascertaining their meaning by reading the words of the provision in their statutory and extrinsic context. This is the same statutory interpretation project as required for a code.

With respect to being a vehicle for teaching the relative authority of law from different jurisdictions, again the same principles of statutory interpretation apply to consolidating Acts. The jurisdictional authority of any statute is defined, in that it corresponds to the reach of the enacting parliament; all case law from outside that jurisdiction's court system is persuasive only. Analysed in this way, this aspect of statutory interpretation – knowledge of the precise status of each case, for the interpretive exercise at hand – is as essential to the criminal law in common law jurisdictions as it is in Code states. As a vehicle for teaching this skill, in a first-year law subject, however, a consolidation Act may not be as suitable as a Code. The more complex mix of statutory and case-derived law makes the exercise itself more complex.

Thus, although we have found the Griffith Code particularly suited to teaching statutory interpretation skills within the criminal law course, the need for most aspects of those skills also arises with consolidation Acts (or any statute). Finally, we have noted that the common law method and forms of reasoning have informed criminal law pedagogy in code states in an unhelpful way; it has taken time to frame teaching to accurately reflect the centrality of the statute (the Code). It may be, despite more and more criminal law having its source in legislation in all jurisdictions, that the habits of common law legal thinking are informing pedagogy relating to consolidation Acts. In other words, the same 'reversal' as we have endeavoured to achieve in a code jurisdiction, from case-centred method to the primacy of the code may be relevant in common law jurisdictions with a consolidating Act as its centrepiece.

Conclusion

There are many similarities between the Australian criminal law consolidating Acts and the Griffith Code. However, we have found that the systematic nature of the Code provides a clear organising framework for teaching criminal law. It assists in the teaching of the structure of criminal liability and provides persistent practice in, and understanding of, how a statute operates as law. Further, the thoroughly statutory nature of the jurisdiction provides opportunities to teach fundamental skills of statutory interpretation, the constitutional role of the court as interpreter of parliamentary rules, and an understanding of the relative authority and status of court decisions. In these ways, there is a distinctive pedagogy in the Australian Griffith Code jurisdictions. Having explored the distinctiveness, however, and in light of the fundamental equivalence of *all* statutes, codes and consolidation Acts included, we have suggested that some of the distinctive teaching practices in a Griffith Code jurisdiction relating to statutory interpretation may well be relevant in all Australian criminal law jurisdictions.

References

Cadoppi, A. and Cullinane, K. (2000) 'The Zanardelli Code and Codification in the Countries of the Common law' *James Cook University Law Review*, vol. 7, p116.

Council of Australian Law Deans (2015) *Council of Australian Law Deans Good Practice Guide to Teaching Statutory Interpretation*.

Edwards, E., Harding, R. and Campbell, I. (1992) *The Criminal Codes: Commentary and Materials*, 4th ed., Lawbook Co.

Finn, P. (1992) 'Statutes and the Common Law' *University of Western Australia Law Review*, vol. 22, p7.

Gagelar, S. (2011) 'Common law Statutes and Judicial Legislation: Statutory Interpretation as a Common law Process' *Monash University Law Review*, vol. 37, p1.

Goode, M. (2002) 'Constructing Criminal Law Reform and the Model Criminal Code' *Criminal Law Journal*, vol. 26, p152.

Griffith, S. (1897) *An Explanatory Letter to the Honourable Attorney-General*.

Tarrant, S. (2013) 'Building Bridges in Australian Criminal Law: Codification and the Common Law' *Monash University Law Review*, vol. 39, p838.

Whitney, K., Flynn, M. and Moyle, P. (2000) *The Criminal Codes: Commentary and Materials*, 5th ed., Lawbook Co.

Wright, B. (2008) 'Criminal Law Codification and Imperial Projects: The Self-Governing Jurisdiction Codes of the 1890's' *Legal History*, vol. 12, p19.

Zimmermann, R. (1995) 'Codification: History and Present Significance of an Idea' *European Review of Private Law*, vol. 3, p5.

Chapter 8

Teaching criminal law as statutory interpretation

Jeremy Gans

As Gledhill and Livings observe in Chapter 1, the dominant model of teaching criminal law involves violence and property offences. This is not so with the Criminal Law and Procedure course at Melbourne Law School. Indeed, since the launch of the school's new Juris Doctor course in 2008, either all (in 2009–2010 & 2014) or half (in 2011–2013 and 2015) of all students have been taught criminal law without closely studying the staple crimes of murder, manslaughter, rape, assault, theft, or fraud.

Instead, students have been taught a generalised course on statutory offences, systematically working through how all such offences are read, enforced, and subject to general principles of criminal responsibility, as well as focus units on topics such as offence seriousness, incorporation of community standards, incorporation of regulatory discretion, statutory exceptions, and the role of victims and states in the substantive criminal law. Over 12 weeks (i.e. a single semester course), students examine over a dozen examples of offence types, including public order offences, driving offences, pollution offences, drug trafficking, occupational health offences, and money laundering. The core course teaches both the general law for reading all statutes and special rules for reading criminal offence provisions, drawn from both the common law and federal *Criminal Code* provisions applicable in the state of Victoria. Since 2012, the course has used a new text, *Modern Criminal Law of Australia* (Gans 2012), which was purposely written to teach all Australian criminal law as statutory interpretation. The end-of-course assessment, as well as mid-course group feedback assessment, requires students to examine statutory offences that they have not studied and that have often never been the subject of case analysis or secondary literature.

The heart of the course is the proposition that statutory interpretation is the core skill required to study contemporary criminal law. The rationale for and methodology of this approach is explored in this chapter.

Why teach criminal law as statutory interpretation?

The case for teaching criminal law as statutory interpretation (and specifically teaching it the way it is taught at Melbourne Law School) involves the following propositions. First, the key skill that criminal lawyers need is to be able determine the meaning of the thousands of criminal offences, which involves understanding that the text setting out the offence may interact with the general rules of criminal law. Crucially, this involves teaching the general rules as an aspect of the core task of interpreting a statutory offence provision rather than as a separate set of principles. The meaning of a difficult word in an offence provision may be resolved (or highlighted) by the application of a relevant rule of responsibility to that word (for example, a word requiring the court to make a moral judgment, such as indecency, or dishonesty, or exploitation, is less problematic if the accompanying fault element requires an awareness of the possibility of that moral judgment). Likewise, the question of how to apply a general concept of criminal responsibility to a difficult offence provision may involve considering whether the offence provision should be interpreted so as to be receptive (or non-receptive) to the application of that concept (for example, the application of the rule that liability for omissions depends on a legal duty to act may influence how a word that potentially carries an open-ended obligation to act is read.) The result is that students are taught that the criminal law is a marriage between the substantive law (as set out in offences throughout the statute book) and core concepts (as set out in common law or in a criminal code) and that, like all marriages, it often requires effort to make it work. This is consistent with the approach outlined in Chapter 2 by Donson and O'Sullivan, who argue that the core concepts of actus reus and mens rea should not be taught separately from the substantive law, but rather holistically alongside offences and should emphasise the uncertain application of these core concepts to many substantive offences.

Second, element analysis provides an essential and accessible framework for studying statutory offences. Contemporary element analysis is central to the course at Melbourne Law School, with three early weeks spent working through the three core physical elements of conduct, results, and circumstances and the general rules of criminal responsibility applicable to each. In each week, the course uses running examples (driving, pollution, and trafficking) to identify a range of different statutory offences that illustrate both the utility of these core concepts and rules and also the occasions when they are less useful by normalising both the utility and vulnerability of these foundational elements for the course's students. As well, the first week of the second half of the course is spent analysing offences that incorporate judgments or standards to be made by the court (e.g. danger, dishonesty, indecency, offensiveness, reasonableness, etc.) and the many (and, in Australia, often incoherent) ways that criminal responsibility is assigned to such elements. This fits with the approach favoured in Chapter 3 by Child, who argues that the pedagogical utility of element analysis can be muddied by courses that focus on particular offences or doctrines where formal analysis is routinely sidelined. To the extent that this muddying arises in the study of common law offences, or offences such as manslaughter and theft that have historical origins that precede contemporary norms of criminal responsibility and are heavily reliant on appellate exegesis, a course that focuses on statutory interpretation avoids some of these missteps

Third, focusing on the interpretation of statutory offences – a common feature across all criminal jurisdictions – is a counterweight to the fracturing of rules of criminal responsibility across Australia described by Crofts and Tarrant in Chapter 7. The meaning of the words of the offences themselves can be understood, at least initially, independently of the applicable general rules. As well, as Crofts and Tarrant note, the codes can provide an excellent introduction to statutory interpretation (just as statutory interpretation can provide an excellent entrée to the codes). All Australian jurisdictions face the relatively new complication of a different, more contemporary code applying to federal offences in that jurisdiction, which has been enacted in recent decades. Indeed, the new federal code – to a large degree, a written version of Australia's common law – also provides an excellent way of teaching the otherwise amorphous unwritten law (and, more controversially, in identifying common features between the common law and the older codes).

Fourth, regulatory offences are considered alongside more serious crimes and also as components of more complex regulatory schemes that combine a variety of crime types alongside civil and administrative rules. Not only does a statutory interpretation approach readily allow coverage of the range of modern criminal offences – the Melbourne Law School course addresses such important regimes as public order offences, driving offences, pollution offences, customs offences and taxation offences, not merely as passing mentions or extension topics but as core examples – but it also permits the ready teaching and assessment of little-studied aspects of criminal regulation, such as the incorporation of regulatory decision making (e.g. licensing or classification decisions) into the definition of criminal offences and regulatory defences such as reasonable excuse, lawful excuse, and due diligence. Indeed, the final week of the course examines the role of states in criminal justice, including potentially authorising criminal actions, committing crimes, and combining the roles of regulator, prosecutor, victim, and judge. A course that focuses on statutory interpretation naturally addresses Kilcommins *et al.*'s familiar but vital argument in Chapter 17 that traditional criminal law teaching largely ignores regulatory crime.

Finally, the course text uses running offence examples – 12, one for each component of the course: public order, public places, driving, pollution, drugs, sexual offences, slavery, endangerment, money laundering, abortion, domestic violence, and land use – and the course materials supplement these examples with alternative offence types (e.g. social security, people smuggling, grooming, homicide). This arguably satisfies Gledhill's call in Chapter 16 for course infrastructure to allow individual lecturers to choose which offences illustrate basic principles. In such a course, all statutory offences are potential examples, and there is certainly little or no reason to cover any particular offence type, although focus is also important at times. On the other hand, the sheer number of examples covered in the course textbook and materials also limits that flexibility to an extent, because the number of running examples potentially crowds out other options. Introducing further examples of interest to a particular teacher takes valuable lecture time (and imposes fresh reading on students), but may not illustrate the same general principles (or do so as effectively) as the ones covered in the text. In 2015, the course trialled a modified structure that dropped some of the book chapters to allow individual teachers to focus on offences of interest to them, including both other regulatory regimes (e.g. tax offences) and more traditional crimes (murder, theft).

To sum up, teaching criminal law as statutory interpretation helps to counter a number of recognised problems in traditional criminal law pedagogy: the siloing of general and special parts of the criminal law, the isolated or muddied teaching of element analysis, sidelining of codes and/or common law in particular jurisdictions, ignoring regulatory crimes, and lack of flexibility to permit individual teachers to teach offences that interest them. A more general pedagogical benefit to teaching criminal law this way is that focussing on skills of statutory interpretation in at least one compulsory subject is an important counterweight to the otherwise inappropriate emphasis given to case analysis in many law degrees. Indeed, in recent years, various stakeholders have pushed for Australian law schools to introduce dedicated compulsory subjects on statutory interpretation (Law Admissions Consultative Committee 2009). Melbourne Law School, citing its criminal law course, has instead argued that this goal is achievable within the existing compulsory curriculum. This approach is surely preferable, avoiding what would otherwise become an isolated (and, potentially, disliked) subject on statutes.

None of this means that all criminal law courses, or any of them, ought to be taught in this way. Indeed, other chapters in this collection suggest a number of reasons not to teach criminal law as statutory interpretation. Livings argues (Chapter 12) that criminal law should not be isolated from situational concerns; while some of these concerns (e.g. statutory civil and administrative provisions that accompany criminal ones) can be accommodated in a statutory interpretation model, others (e.g. social context and common law procedures) are not a natural fit. Steel's argument (Chapter 9) for introducing students to criminal law politics is accommodated in a statutory interpretation model to some extent (particularly in the range of offences that the model readily covers), but a focus on the skill of reading statutes risks ignoring or downplaying consideration of the development, reform, and critique of those statutes unless considerable care is taken. Likewise, a focus on reading statutes, while increasing the emphasis on statutory context (including parliament's role in the criminal law), de-emphasises non-statutory contexts (including the common law, public perceptions, and non-government stakeholders). Perhaps the starkest problem with this model is demonstrated in the chapters (Chapters 14 and 15) by Quince and Tolmie on minority and indigenous and feminist perspectives on criminal law. A course full of statutes and the law on reading them sidelines the traditional sources for exploring these perspectives (e.g. key judgments, critical literature, diverse viewpoints), while the focus on breadth in criminal offences leaves little room for the in-depth treatment of topics such as rape law reform, the partial defence of provocation, and the criminalisation of intoxication that are traditional mainstays of criminal law pedagogy on these perspectives. In the past, the statutory interpretation focus has accommodated lecturers who wished to teach criminal law in the traditional way (e.g. drawing the main principles from appellate cases on homicide and rape), although I'm not convinced that that level of divergence in teaching approaches was fair to students (as the case focus may leave such students ill prepared for an exam that requires them to confront a statute they haven't studied before, without the assistance of case analysis).

Doubtless, some courses that focus on homicide, rape, and theft do so without incorporating much context, critique, or alternative perspectives, particularly as courses become semesterised and the body of key cases grows. Many criminal law teachers have become adept at planting such material within the traditional structure, particularly the fertile fields of homicide defences and rape law reform. The Melbourne Law School course aims to achieve similar ends in less obvious fields, such as exploring social control through the law on discretion; poverty law through the law of omissions; environmental law through the law of results; feminism through the law on sentencing, slavery, and abortion; and indigenous perspectives through the law on sentencing and land use. At least some aspects of the politics of criminal justice are at the forefront of the course through the study of the content and background of statutory offences, providing a ready and continuing example of over-criminalisation and democratic deficiencies. Nevertheless, a choice to teach criminal law as statutory interpretation clearly involves some compromise of other criminal law pedagogy goals.

How to teach criminal law as statutory interpretation

Simply adding some statutory interpretation skills to a traditional criminal law course is straightforward. Most traditional courses already cover some statutory interpretation when they teach students how to tell if an offence is strict liability or not, and perhaps also cover the interpretation of any particular statutory offences taught. Adding more (for example, more interpretation issues, or simply more offences) demands some moderately difficult decisions about compressing or dropping other aspects of the course, as well as broadening the focus of assessment – the stuff of incremental curriculum development.

At Melbourne Law School, an opportunity to switch from a traditional course to a statutory interpretation format in a single step presented itself when the entire law school (and, indeed, the university) made a dramatic change in 2008 from teaching law and other professional degrees to undergraduates in combination with other degrees, to teaching professional degrees exclusively as graduate subjects. For law, this meant not only a new degree (a Juris Doctor) but also a temporary drop in student numbers as we waited for the new potential enrolees from our own university to finish their new broad-based undergraduate degrees. For compulsory subjects, this meant a year or two when each course was taught by just one teacher to only one or two classes. My decision to take a fresh start with criminal law in 2009 was informed by my involvement in an earlier equally dramatic change to the core subject on evidence, which shifted the course's focus from legal rules and appellate decisions to fact analysis and trial documents.

As was the case with evidence law (Palmer 2011), the key step in developing the new criminal law curriculum was a change in assessment. Students were told that the end-of-semester exam would be exclusively about a statutory offence that students had *not* studied. This puts a core claim of criminal law teaching – that studying criminal law teaches students skills that can be transferred to any other crime – literally to the test. This step could only work along with other changes to assessment practices. The offence that would be tested would be a real offence from the statute book – drafting a hypothetical statutory offence for testing purposes would be both bizarre and dreary for staff and students alike and also unnecessary given the thousands of real statutory offences on offer. To enable the students to do the research aspects of statutory interpretation (reading a lengthy statute, finding relevant definitions, researching comparable provisions, locating explanatory material, finding any relevant cases), the exam was a take-home, set over a weekend. And to ensure that students engage deeply with the statute – something unlikely with either a convoluted hypothetical fact matrix that would only test a narrow aspect of the provision or a broad-based essay that would only require surface consideration – students were given a very brief and hopefully realistic motivational query by a client seeking advice on future events.

End-of-year exams to date have used offences of piracy, people smuggling, official secrets, mass copyright infringements, stalking, and taxi licensing. The fact scenarios have all been drawn from recent events, e.g. a commercial fleet owner developing employee protocols for piracy off the Horn of Africa, a refugee council advising new immigrants on how to fund relatives to be smuggled to Australia, a newspaper editor hoping to publish Wikipedia leaks, a copyright agency wanting to prosecute ISPs for their customers' torrents, a social media company concerned about liability for cyberbullying, a taxi regulator hoping to prosecute Uber, etc. In addition to its benefits in testing statutory interpretation, this model also introduces students to an aspect of legal professional life that traditional law assessment neglects: proactively advising clients about planned actions. Clients in exam and syndicate exercise scenarios include political activists, regulators, insurance companies, and a variety of corporations. For the majority of students who do not intend to practice criminal law, the assessment underlines how criminal law can be important to commercial, governmental, and community-sector legal practices.

With the new assessment in place, all that remained was to fill 12 weeks of classes with statutory interpretation of criminal offences. The approach taken in Melbourne Law School is one that I developed ad hoc in early 2009. The first step was to divide the course into two halves, with the first six weeks devoted to a general approach for reading criminal offences and the second to variations on that approach. One motivation for this division was to facilitate the feedback exercises, which could test the entire 'general' approach halfway through the course. However, the split approach had at least one downside: the course became quite difficult in its second half, which took students (and some lecturers) by surprise and allowed little time for formal revision. Recent years have revealed an upside, with the split nature of the course naturally allowing room for more experimentation in its second half, including a partial return to somewhat more traditional styles of teaching to accommodate other lecturers' preferences.

The 'general approach to reading criminal offences' comprises three related parts: general statutory interpretation, the role of discretion in offence statutes, and element analysis. Most law teachers are familiar with (and may well have taught in introductory courses) contemporary statutory interpretation, with its trinity of language, context, and purpose. In Australia (and, I expect, elsewhere), there are useful judicial treatments of these approaches in the context of criminal offences, notably during constitutional challenges to certain offences. Australia's meagre constitutional rights regime means that many of those challenges involve free speech challenges to public order offences, which became the running example for the introduction to the course. In a pattern followed in subsequent weeks, the cases in this example are taught alongside new offences that had received little or no judicial discussion, such as upskirting and revenge porn offences. The classes also consider interpretative approaches with particular relevance to criminal offences: the strict construction of penal provisions and the reluctance to read provisions as reducing common law rights (the so-called principle of legality).

Most law teachers recognise the need to emphasise the role of discretion in criminal justice. That treatment is a natural adjunct to statutory interpretation, given the role of prosecutorial and sentencing discretion in particular as ameliorating some of the overbreadth and vagueness that characterises many criminal offences. The approach taken at Melbourne Law School is to focus on how discretions alter the scope and impact of statutory offences – for example, through the public interest aspect of prosecutorial discretion (with its concern for whether an offence is technical, obsolete, detrimental to public confidence and the like) and the broad focus of sentencing discretion (which can negate statutory reforms, for better or worse, and which requires a painful ranking of specific instances of offences). In addition, the course examines the way that policing discretions (arrest, move on powers, etc.) and administrative discretions (licensing, classification, etc.) can interact with, and at times expand or contract, the scope of criminal offences. Again, there is an overlap with constitutional law in Australia, which also regulates the extent to which criminal justice processes can be outsourced to the executive.

Completing this modern 'marriage' between statute readers and criminal justice decision-makers is a third partner: the general rules of criminal responsibility. Here the course tracks the three types of physical elements (recognised in, amongst other places, Australia's federal criminal code): conduct, results, and circumstances (or, for the more alliteratively inclined, conduct, consequences, and context). In successive weeks, each of these element types is scrutinised at two levels: first, how to determine the meaning of a particular instance of physical element and second, the particular rules of criminal responsibility applicable to that type of physical element. While this discussion tracks some of the analysis of matters such as intent, recklessness, causation, and strict liability offered in traditional courses, it does so in a way that both emphasises the system that underlies criminal responsibility and in the ways that the system can fail. Particular issues that come to the fore in such an approach include the problem of status offences, the difficulties of applying a requirement of voluntariness to some offences (e.g. driving offences) the law of omissions (recently the subject of repeated litigation in Australia's High Court in the context of social security fraud), the varying requirements of causation (e.g. the contrast between homicide and pollution offences), and an emergent question of whether subjective fault elements require knowledge, not only of the underlying facts but also their legal character (e.g. the character of possession in a slavery offence, the nationality of obscure islands in a people smuggling case). The latter issue is consolidated in the first week of the second half of the course, which focuses on the role of standards such as danger, dishonesty, and indecency in criminal offences.

Teaching such general material requires a careful use of examples, which must be varied enough to cover the general concepts robustly, but narrow enough to not overwhelm students. At Melbourne Law School, the approach focuses on offence types, with public order offences studied in the early classes on interpretation and (non-sentencing) discretion and then driving offences, pollution offences, and drug trafficking as the key examples for conduct, results, and circumstance elements. In each week, the classes pick apart one or two detailed examples from the case law: a law student protesting speech regulation in a regional pedestrian mall, a failed prosecution of protesters at a semi-public shopping centre, a drunk passenger who managed to accidentally start a car moving, a lackadaisical latex delivery person who polluted a creek, a widely discussed death by drug overdose on a cruise ship, a bog standard airport drug smuggling case, a slavery case at an otherwise lawful brothel. The statutory focus means that these studies are not confined to local jurisdictions: the class can and does study driving cases from South Australia, pollution cases from Canada, and pornography cases from the United States, including comparing and contrasting distant statutory offences and rules of responsibility to Victorian ones.

The early versions of the course took advantage of smaller (and fewer) classes and worked from case and legislative extracts that students needed to be guided carefully through during, before, and after class. This allowed time to write a textbook for the course, following a timely and flexible commissioning by Cambridge University Press, and also doubling as a treatise on the law of statutory offences in Australia. Once published, the textbook provided students with a detailed analysis of many individual statutory offences set out the way traditional casebooks set out case extracts. The textbook also consolidated the more difficult material in the second half of the course, including coverage of inchoate offences using a detailed chapter-length tracking of the criminality of a single instance of drug importation (and associated money laundering) and original research on statutory defences and the role of victims and states in offence definitions. By covering the essential statutory and case analysis, the textbook allowed for more flexibility in the class materials, which could readily focus on recent controversies, such as terrorism, grooming, and the criminal law response to natural disasters.

In a review of *Modern Criminal Law of Australia* (O'Leary & Greene 2012), two Queensland academics observed,

> For us, it fulfilled its promise of inter-jurisdictional application. Wearing our practitioner hats, we were interested to learn about other jurisdiction's systems and found gems of knowledge that seem otherwise ignored in many criminal law texts ... However, wearing our academic mortarboards, we are not convinced of the utility of this approach for teaching. We found it a little convoluted in terms of accessing the applicable law. Gans may have provided the fishing rod but it was difficult to know where to cast the line. We anticipate difficulty in content-delivery and would be interested in hearing more about Gans' way of confronting this problem.

The authors were right to anticipate difficulty. Students find the new course challenging, as do its teachers. Significant changes to the course have been made on each of the seven times it's been taught to date, and doubtless the same is true of the other law school that uses the text (at Sydney's Macquarie University). These difficulties need to be balanced against the course's pedagogical rewards. I, for one, couldn't now imagine teaching criminal law any other way.

Any major change to assessment and curriculum requires keeping multiple stakeholders onside. For the law school (concerned amongst other things by the prospect of plagiarism or collusion in a take-home exam), the novelty and depth of the new criminal law take-home exam was a selling point, especially given the need to establish the new JD's bona fides as a graduate degree and the success of the similar take-home exam used to teach evidence law. For law students (concerned amongst other things about a test that required quite different study habits and writing style to other law subjects), the answer, especially in the early years, was extensive (assessable but redeemable) formative exercises (done as groups, with highly detailed feedback accessible to all), which doubled as teaching opportunities; at times, I set up as many as eight such tasks a semester, which were readily achievable given the thousands of actual offences available. For other law teachers (who gradually came on board from the second offering onwards), the early hook was that the assessment model still worked with traditional teaching focused on homicide and the like (which, after all, is supposed to teach skills transferrable to the rest of the criminal law); more recently (and more realistically), traditional teaching has been accommodated by dropping some of the later units on specialised aspects of statutory interpretation (e.g. reasonable excuse, the victim rule, shield of the crown) in favour of a deep-dive consideration of two offence types chosen by individual lecturers (tested by a traditional essay question alongside the statutory interpretation question in the take-home).

A further stakeholder to accommodate is the profession, who can be a force for both inertia and change in law teaching. The switch to statutory interpretation prompted enthusiasm from some professionals (e.g. specialists in statutory criminal law, such as work safety or liquidation offences, who asked me to teach specialised versions of the course to their graduate staff) and headshaking from many others (including some judges) who could not conceive of a criminal law course without homicide. A seemingly more significant barrier was Australia's detailed (and recently nationally adopted) academic requirements for admission to legal practice that specifies a list of nine criminal law topics to teach, including 'homicide and offences', which inconveniently requires coverage of Victoria's two common law offences of murder and manslaughter' (see *Legal Profession Uniform Admission Rules 2015* (NSW), Schedule 1). Fortunately, these requirements' drafters improbably provided a far-sighted alternative that only mandates study of two much broader offence classes:

> The topics should provide knowledge of the general doctrines of the criminal law and, in particular, examination of both offences against the person and against property. Selective treatment should also be given to various defences and to elements of criminal procedure.

More fortunately, the profession in 2011 began to actively push for statutory interpretation to be added to the list of mandatory academic subjects and, in particular, to be specifically assessed (Law Admissions Consultative Committee 2009). Australian law schools' push back was to argue that statutory interpretation skills were already being taught within the existing curriculum. At Melbourne Law School (at least), this claim was clearly demonstrable, thanks largely to criminal law and its assessment. The result was something of a reversal in pressures on criminal law curriculum development; any changes to criminal law are now vetted by the law school to ensure that statutory interpretation remained the focus.

In short, in the space of five years, teaching criminal law as statutory interpretation at Melbourne Law School went from being the product of a fortuitous opportunity arising from external changes to the wider university, to being entrenched by a fortuitous new movement arising from broader legal pedagogy pursued by non-university stakeholders. Whether this is coincidence, arbitrariness, or synergy is for others to judge.

References

Gans, Jeremy, *Modern Criminal Law of Australia*, Cambridge UP, Melbourne, 2012.

Law Admissions Consultative Committee, *Approaches to Interpretation*, Law Council of Australia, 2009 available at: <http://www1.lawcouncil.asn.au/LACC/images/pdfs/ApproachestoInterpretationLawSchools.pdf>.

O'Leary, Jodie & Greene, Elizabeth, 'Book Review: Modern Criminal Law of Australia' (2012) 24 *Bond Law Review* 178.

Palmer, Andrew, 'Why and How to Teach Proof' (2011) 33 *Sydney Law Review* 563.

Chapter 9

Shaking the foundations
Criminal law as a means of critiquing the assumptions of the centrality of doctrine in law

Alex Steel

Criminal law is a course that students generally take early in their degree and as such it is seen as a foundational course that not only has the role of teaching criminal law but also a range of more general legal skills. Because of this, students need a course with clear structure that produces a sense that they "understand" something. That structure tends to revolve around classes on general principles followed by classes on the core offences and how they apply the principles. This gives students the chance to learn how to break down offences into their elements and how to use judicial statements to interpret the scope of those elements. However, without a critical approach to the general principles, students can develop an overly simplified understanding of how criminal law is applied in practice and an uncritical acceptance of claims of doctrinal clarity.

The structural separation of criminal law

This structure of 'general principles applied to core offences' is deeply embedded in the legal curriculum. It has a long history. As a result of the efforts of academic writers in the late nineteenth century to see law as a science (Simpson 1981), treatises on specific areas of law that described defined doctrinal areas became predominant and influenced how courses evolved. For example, the development of separate texts on torts (e.g. Pollock on Torts) and on contracts (e.g. Chitty on Contracts) paralleled the creation of separate courses in universities: a course on "civil obligations" blending contract and tort remains exotic.

Similarly criminal law has long been seen as a separate doctrinal area. Practitioner admitting bodies routinely require law schools to teach a separately defined area of law known as "criminal law".

This is not the case in the statute book. Although there is generally a *Crimes Act* or *Criminal Code*, there are often individual Acts dealing with subsets of criminal law (e.g. theft, public order offences, drugs), and there are whole statutory regimes that contain criminal sanctions (e.g. copyright, corporations law, traffic rules, land law). Even though statutory regimes regularly contain both civil and criminal regulation, courses dealing with those regimes rarely give sufficient time to the criminal aspects. Courses in corporation law, intellectual property, etc., tend to downplay the criminal elements of their doctrinal area because of this textbook/curriculum-led separation. Rarely is the question of whether such regulatory offences are part of some overarching notion of criminal law principles considered. Criminal law courses too tend to gloss over connections to other areas of law (a point Ben Livings makes in chapter 12). This again because of the way the textbook writers have defined the core of criminal law.

The structuring role of the textbook

As noted in chapter 1, modern textbooks typically divide criminal law into a series of clear-cut chapters arranged by doctrinal areas: General Principles, Murder/Manslaughter, Assault/Sexual Assault, Theft/Fraud, Extensions of Liability, Defences. This is presented as an ahistorical, timeless, and logical division. But that is misleading, as can be shown by a comparison with the past. William Blackstone's 1769 *Commentaries on the Laws of England* (which emerged from Blackstone's Oxford lecture notes) order criminal law very differently. Blackstone's division of law into private and public led him to arrange his commentaries as follows:

> I shall . . . proceed to distribute the several offenses, which are either directly or by consequence injurious to civil society, and therefore punishable by the laws of England, under the following general heads: first, those which are more immediately injurious to God and his holy religion; secondly, such as violate and transgress the law of nations; thirdly, such as more especially affect the sovereign executive power of the state, or the king and his government; fourthly, such as more directly infringe the rights of the public or common wealth; and, lastly, such as derogate from those rights and duties, which are owing to particular individuals, and in the preservation and vindication of which community is deeply interested.
>
> (Blackstone 1979, 42)

After chapters on capacity and accessories, the Commentaries thus has chapters on offences against God and Religion (25pp), Law of Nations (8pp), Treason (20pp), Felonies injurious to the King's Prerogative (8pp), Praemunire (17pp), Misprision and Contempt (8pp), Public Justice (15pp), Public Peace (12pp), Public Trade (7pp), Public Health and the Economy (15pp), Homicide (29pp), the Person (15pp), Habitations (9pp), and Private Property (19pp). The length of treatment of each area reflects the extent to which Blackstone wished to make a political point; for example, the chapter on Praemunire is largely an extensive diatribe about the evils of Papery.

Significantly, Blackstone's arrangement was the first to attempt to systematise into an overall framework both common law crimes and the growing number of statutory offences. He rates crimes against the sovereign of most importance, then interference with the market and violence against individuals, and, finally, interference with individual property interests. This also has an overtly political aim to demonstrate the underlying genius of the common law and critique the mass of badly drafted statutory offences.

Thus in his introduction to Book IV he argues:

> In proportion to the importance of the criminal law, ought also to be the care and attention of the legislature in properly forming and enforcing it. It should be founded upon principles that are permanent, uniform, and universal; and always conformable to the dictates of truth and justice, the feelings of humanity, and the indelible rights of mankind: though it sometimes (provided there be no transgression of these eternal boundaries) may be modified, narrowed, or enlarged, according to the local or occasional necessities of the state which it is meant to govern. And yet, either from a want of attention to these principles in the first concoction of the laws, and adopting in their stead the impetuous dictates of avarice, ambition, and revenge ; from retaining the discordant political regulations, which successive conquerors or factions have established, in the various revolutions of government ; from giving a lasting efficacy to sanctions that were intended to be temporary, and made (as Lord Bacon expresses it) merely upon the spur of the occasion ; or from, lastly, too hastily employing such means as are greatly disproportionate to their end, in order to check the progress of some very prevalent offence ; from, or from all, of these causes it hath happened, that the criminal law is in every country of Europe more rude and imperfect than the civil.
>
> (Blackstone 1979, 2–3)

As examples of this imperfection he notes,

> And surely equal precaution is necessary, when laws are to be established, which may affect the property, liberty, and perhaps even lives, of thousands. Had such a reference taken place, it is impossible that in the eighteenth century it could ever have been made a capital crime, to break down (however maliciously) the mound of a fishpond, whereby any fish shall escape; or cut down a cherry tree in an orchard. Were even a committee appointed but once in an hundred years to revise the criminal law, it could not have continued to this hour a felony without benefit of clergy, to be seen for one month in the company of persons who call themselves, or are called, Egyptians.
>
> (Blackstone 1979, 4; see also Kennedy 1978; Stern 2013; cf. Watson 1988)

Little appears to have changed in the academic view of law and order politics since the eighteenth century, though textbook critiques have become more muted.

Blackstone's systemisation redrew the mass of pleas of the crown into a seemingly logical order, not apparent on the face of the various Acts and common law judgments. This effort to idealise the law into a rational system is the beginning of the structure of criminal law doctrine we have today.

That process was then continued by influential English writers, including Jeremy Bentham, Edward Hyde East, James Fitzjames Stephens, William Russell, Glanville Williams, and Andrew Ashworth. Each writer seeks to re-organise and further rationalise the corpus of criminal law. Some emphasise the rights of the individual, some individual property rights. Some downplay the significance of the role of defences to liability, some increase it. Over time, the idea of mental elements and general principles becomes important. Significantly, each writer has an agenda.

Contemporaneously, Ashworth and Horder, in Chapters 2 and 3 of *Principles of Criminal Law* (Ashworth and Horder 2013) go so far as to formulate a comprehensive set of principles for criminal law. These chapters are remarkable for the way in which they encapsulate the liberal ideal of a criminal law and how the chapters are largely devoid of any judicial or legislative authority for the principles. They are arguably the high-point of the academic project in textbooks to redefine criminal law as a logical and just legal regime.

Such sets of principles, being normative and based on philosophical positions are highly political and invite students to judge existing criminal law negatively against them. This indeed may be the purpose of higher education – to equip students with a set of tools of critique – and they are critical grist to the mill of academic commentary on the current state of the criminal law. But it is important to also make sure when we teach criminal law that students understand that few politicians and few judges in lower courts pay any heed to such normative positions when developing or applying the law. The principles will help you in an essay, but not with representing a client. As academics, we hope such principles will influence law making and shore up principled law reform commission reports, but they are regularly trashed by politicians responding to community concerns about crime (cf. Ashworth 2000; Brown 2013).

This normative approach in traditional textbooks also implies the boundaries to be placed around what is, and what is not, criminal law and around what is important to study (cf. Husak 2003). In practice, doctrinal niceties of voluntariness and intention are rarely in issue – the most pressing issues are identifying which charge is appropriate, what acts are required to be proved, and whether there is evidence to convince a magistrate or judge. Yet textbooks routinely take up significant numbers of pages on detailed analysis of higher court decisions about the general principles and then rush over complex statutory offences that are often prosecuted – if they mention them at all. Blackstone's bias against statutory criminal law lives on in many texts.

The combination of a textbook concentration on 'core' offences and the analysis of those offences through emphasis of the underlying 'rules' acts to reinforce an academic, ahistorical view of criminal law. That view is an important one. It is the dominant way in which higher courts describe the criminal law, and it is an important heuristic learning scaffold for students. But any criminal law practitioner knows that such 'law in the books' cuts little ice with everyday legal practice when dealing with law enforcement or the lower courts.

That is not to say all criminal law textbooks are so arranged, nor that all writers are unaware of this abstracting doctrinal process. In the vanguard of the modern move away from such an approach are books such as *Criminal Laws: Materials and Commentary on Criminal Process and Procedure in New South Wales* (Brown et al. 2015) and *Reconstructing Criminal Law* (Wells and Quick 2010), both first published in 1990. More radically, Jeremy Gans's *Modern Criminal Law of Australia* dispenses entirely with the traditional general principles/ serious offences approach. His book structures criminal law as Words, Choices, Conduct, Results, Circumstances, Sentences, Standards, Groups, Failures, Exceptions, Victims, States (Gans 2011). The alien appearance of this categorisation underlines the strength of the way textbooks have tightly defined criminal law doctrine.

Criminal Laws (of which I am now a co-author) grew out of the criminal law courses taught at the University of New South Wales since the 1980s. It places the doctrinal reification of criminal law into its broader cultural and political environment to demonstrate that there is in fact not one criminal law, but as the book's title suggests, "a collection of diverse 'criminal laws'" (Brown et al. 2015, 1) and that these are open to critique. As the introductory chapter to *Criminal Laws* notes:

> Under the traditional approach to the study of criminal law, the object of inquiry is not seen to be problematic. Everybody is assumed to know and accept what criminal law "is". The prophecy is a self-fulfilling one. The result is a considerable degree of consensus about what it is appropriate to cover, but this consensus is taken for granted and has rarely been the subject of reflection. [By concentrating on common law offences with long histories] . . . [t]he resulting picture is of a criminal law which possesses a sense of inevitability; its effective limits are not seen to be in issue.
>
> It is a picture which is based on unspoken assumptions about some perceived essence of Criminal Law, one which conceals crucial questions about what criminal law is – its potential and limits . . . It is a legal insider's view of criminal law; the task in hand is seen as being, at most, one of law reform requiring the expertise of criminal lawyers, rather than social policy-making necessitating contributions from a much broader range of experts and community representatives.
>
> (Brown et al. 2015, 2)

Alan Norrie has argued that there is a link between this abstracted sense of general principles and the agenda of eighteenth century text writers and reformers, who were determined to build a legal system which could support the middle-class market economy. These reformers ignored the social origins of crime and very real conflicts over the role of markets and the law. Instead they created an abstracted ideal of 'economic man' or 'juridical man': "abstractions from real people emphasising one side of human life – the ability to reason and calculate – at the expense of every social circumstance that actually brings individuals to reason and calculate in particular ways" (Norrie 2014, 26–7).

Consequently, in teaching criminal law, we need to be aware of the way appeal court decisions use general principle to abstract away from the real lives of offenders and victims. We need to find ways to bring back into the classroom the political dimension of much of criminal law. Partly this is achieved by emphasising the broader context within which criminal law is taught (Steel 2013), the real-life facts of the parties (Mertz 2007), and the competing visions of how behaviour should be recognised and regulated. Other chapters in the volume explore the importance of context: see Loughnan, Quince, and Tolmie (Chapters 13–15). Melanie Schwartz and I have also discussed this elsewhere (Steel and Schwartz 2013)

Putting this into effect

What follows is an account of how a course can be structured so as to de-centre the 'core offences' in favour of a more realistic approach to the way criminal law is encountered. The UNSW criminal law courses (Crime and the Criminal Process and Criminal Laws) allow students to study the general principles within a broader critical environment and with a series of juxtapositions. The order in which offences and issues are dealt with is designed to counter the abstracting tendency.

Process, police, and principles

Crime and the Criminal Process begins with classes on criminalisation and penalty (theoretical, historical, and colonial, with emphasis on indigenous over-imprisonment) and then takes students through pre-trial and trial processes. Emphasis is placed on the extent of summary justice and on-the-spot fine notices and their contrast to the elaborated forms of indictable justice found in the appeal judgments. The rhetoric of the presumption of innocence, the right to a fair trial, and no punishment without trial are contrasted with the ubiquity of prosecutorial discretion, the recent highly political interventions into bail, legal aid, and the role of the jury. NSW bail law in particular has been amended frequently and increasingly punitively (Brown and Quilter 2014; Steel 2009) – demonstrating highly political and erratic, but speedy and dramatic, changes to criminal law.

Attention then turns to the role of the police, in particular, the high degrees of practically unreviewable discretion and the variability of policing on different populations – especially indigenous populations. The importance of foregrounding police discretion is to demonstrate their gatekeeper role in defining crime (Dixon 1997) – definitions that can be at odds with parliamentary and court understandings. Changes to legislation in this area can also demonstrate the significant political control police exert over their discretion (Sentas and McMahon 2013). Students also often have had their own dealings with police and having students consider the practical ability they have to question police behaviour can be engaging. Students also spend three days observing criminal courts where they see the justice system in action and can contextualise their understanding of the role of the key actors.

At this point, the components of criminal law said to be generally applicable are introduced – capacity and liability, actus reus and what amounts to an act, mens rea and how states of mind are separated from circumstances, onus of proof, and the 'golden thread'. The common law concepts are also examined in light of courts' attempts to create principled approaches to implying mens rea into statutory offences and the widespread use of strict liability (*Sweet v Parsley* [1970] AC 132; *He Kaw Teh* (1985) 157 CLR 523 and *B v DPP* [2000] 2 AC 428). Placing this discussion after process and court visits means that when students come to these principles, they already have a nuanced understanding of the reality of criminal justice and can assess the extent to which the principles structure or fail to structure everyday justice. They can judge the abstracted ideals against the gritty reality (cf. Norrie 2014).

Applying the principles to offences

Traditionally, discussion of the components of criminal law is then demonstrated by a detailed analysis of homicide. This reinforces the centrality of those principles. But homicide is largely atypical (Brown *et al.* 2015, 744). Key concepts are common law based, there is an extensive history of philosophically based judicial development of the approach to liability, and there are a number of defences not available to other offences.

Accordingly, Crime and the Criminal Process instead first examines two statutory criminal regimes, the NSW *Drug Misuse and Trafficking Act* 1985 and the *Summary Offences Act 1988*. Both Acts are obviously controversial and political, account for a significant amount of prosecutions in local courts, and criminalise behaviours that are within the experience of most students. There is emphasis in the surrounding commentary on the health and social impacts of the laws and their enforcement (cf. Steel and Schwartz 2013). But the Acts themselves are also highly useful tools for demonstrating the limited reach of the general principles.

The *Drug Act* is a complex statutory regime containing a range of offences from summary to indictable offences with life imprisonment. It represents an excellent opportunity to ask students to read an Act as a whole and to experience some of their first criminal laws as statutory rather than common law based, given the absence of any corresponding common law history. Most importantly, the approach of deeming certain weights of drugs to be evidence of an intention to deal in them represents a deliberate choice by the Parliament to create offences that are as serious as any other offence in the criminal calendar but which fail to adhere to the fundamental general principles of judgments such as *He Kaw Teh* and *Woolmington* [1935] AC 462. The extension of liability to those 'taking part' or possessing precursors also demonstrates the alacrity with which parliaments are willing to criminalise highly inchoate behaviours that predate the actus reus of the main offences. This underlines the precarious position of the general principles in the face of strong political desire for convictions.

The *Summary Offences Act* is also a statutory regime students can be asked to read as a whole. By contrast to drug offences, these offences have very long histories as police discretionary offences. Discussion of these offences in light of the previous discussion of police powers can demonstrate the ease with which they can be abused and used against particular populations – often indigenous.

Public order offences represent a very clear example of the inconsistent application of the 'general principles'. The physical elements of the offences are often highly subjective and based on community reaction. The decided cases allow students to see, for example, the way in which courts inconsistently can assume what the community considers 'offensive'. Further, despite High Court statements as to presumptions of mens rea, there is little law on the mental elements of these offences or their scope (cf. *Coleman v Power* [2004] 220 CLR 1; *Morse* [2011] NZSC 45). This allows students to debate what the appropriate mental elements of the offences should be. It also highlights the inconsistent attention courts give to supposedly serious and non-serious offences. Analysing summary offences in the same way that serious indictable offences are analysed can be a provocative and interesting exercise (see e.g. McNamara and Quilter 2015; Quilter and McNamara 2013).

Approaches to violence

In the second UNSW course, Criminal Laws, the 'core offences' are dealt with, but with a strong emphasis on how politically constructed they are. Continuing the de-centring of homicide as the stereotypical crime, as of 2016, common assault is examined first. The elements of assault are examined through the prism of male violence and the exceptions for consent to sporting violence (cf. Standen 2009) but not for sado-masochistic violence by considering *Brown* [1994] 1 AC 212 with its strong suggestions of homophobia (Bibbings and Alldridge 1993).

The emphasis on avoiding unnecessary convictions by broader consent exceptions and an emphasis on mens rea is then contrasted with sexual assault. The struggle for appropriate laws to recognise sexual violence and the tension between feminist and traditional liberal notions of proof and consent is highlighted. The classes are used to demonstrate the artificiality of any notion of general principles of liability, and instead the need to recognise that approaches to liability are very much a product of the form of behaviour prohibited. Julia Tolmie discusses these issues in more detail (Chapter 15).

Homicide is then examined, followed by defences, theft and fraud, and complicity.

Problematising homicide

While homicide is often taught as the fulcrum of the general principles of criminal law, there is much about this that is problematic. Despite the historic case law development of a requirement of full intentional mens rea for serious offences, homicide remains deeply compromised by the statutory preservation of felony (or constructive) murder and modern interventions such as the Australian one-punch killing laws (Quilter 2015). Highly gendered histories behind concepts of reasonable people for manslaughter- and murder-specific defences also expose the highly political backgrounds to ostensibly abstract doctrines. The way in which the law seeks to define responsibility for omissions is also instructive. In *Stone and Dobinson* [1977] 1 QB 354, the emphasis on the duty of care of the defendants masks the broader scandal of a failure of welfare services. How liability for drug-related deaths is constructed suggests moral underpinnings to doctrine (cf. *Evans* [2009] 1 WLR 1999 and *Burns* [2012] 246 CLR 334). Contrasting the approach to killings by individuals with those by corporations also highlights policy considerations in determining liability.

Defences – political limits of exculpation

The limitations of claims of non-political general principles are possibly at their most obvious in criminal defences. First, it is arguable that the mental defences are only available to indictable rather than summary offences (NSWLRC 2013, 43) – an availability based on form not substance. Second, the defences are inconsistent in where the onus of proof lies. Some defences are only available for a subset of offences or only for murder. The defences are deeply implicated by out-dated views of the mind (see Arlie Loughnan, Chapter 13) and sexist, gendered attitudes (Crofts and Loughnan 2013). Yet despite the alacrity with which Parliaments create new offences and remove assumed requirements of proof, there has been an extraordinary reluctance to modernise and re-consider defences. It can be argued that this is because defences are a direct challenge to the abstracted 'juridical man' of the eighteenth century reformers.

Theft and fraud – protecting property interests

Property offences are deeply political and the case law demonstrates strongly held judicial beliefs as to the role of the law. Theft laws were deeply implicated in the reforming role of the eighteenth century with George Fletcher famously highlighting the way larceny moved from an offence of public order to one protecting property interests (Fletcher 2000). The complexity of the offence of larceny highlights the long struggle of the courts to continue to extend protection to property owners across increasingly complex social arrangements (Steel 2008). The English *Theft Act*'s redrawing of those boundaries and the enthusiasm of the courts to uphold dubiously framed prosecutions (e.g. *Hinks* [2001] 2 AC 241) – even at the expense of destroying liberal principles of criminal law – is also a strong example of the variability with which principle is applied in criminal law.

The increasingly generally drawn fraud and dishonesty offences also demonstrate the modern move to reliance on apparent mental states for liability and provide a segue to complicity.

Complicity – politics and fear

Finally, ending the course on an analysis of conspiracy and other forms of complicity is a powerful way of demonstrating the tension between notions of liberal core principles and the political drive to protect the community against the perceived risk of criminal groups (McNamara 2014) and to accept that risk of future wrongdoing can justify association-based offences. Links can be drawn through the historical development of consorting offences to terrorism offences (McSherry 2004).

Conclusion

Because of the early position of criminal law in the curriculum, structure is important for students, and the idea of general principles remains a key way of providing that structure. Students need a pre-determined logical framework to help them make sense of the mass of laws. This process of abstraction and re-categorisation is a fundamental element of critical thinking – a key graduate attribute. And the statutory offences, while often antithetical to the general principles, are drafted and interpreted in light of them. But it is possible, while providing that framework, to do so in a critical manner and to problematise the abstracting tendencies of criminal law principle.

References

Ashworth, Andrew. 2000. "Is the Criminal Law a Lost Cause?" *Law Quarterly Review* 116 (2): 225–56.

Ashworth, Andrew, and Jeremy Horder. 2013. *Principles of Criminal Law*. Oxford University Press.

Bibbings, Lois, and Peter Alldridge. 1993. "Sexual Expression, Body Alteration, and the Defence of Consent." *Journal of Law and Society* 20: 356.

Blackstone, William. 1979. *Commentaries on the Laws of England*. Chicago: University of Chicago Press.

Brown, David. 2013. "Criminalisation and Normative Theory." *Current Issues in Criminal Justice* 25: 605.

Brown, David, David Farrier, Luke McNamara, Alex Steel, Michael Grewcock, Julia Quilter, and Melanie Schwartz. 2015. *Criminal Laws: Materials and Commentary on Criminal Law and Process of New South Wales*. Federation Press.

Brown, David, and Julia Quilter. 2014. "Speaking Too Soon: The Sabotage of Bail Reform in New South Wales." *International Journal For Crime, Justice and Social Democracy*, 3: 4.

Crofts, Thomas, and Arlie Loughnan. 2013. "Provocation: The Good, the Bad and the Ugly." *Criminal Law Journal* 37: 23.

Dixon, David. 1997. *Law in Policing: Legal Regulation and Police Practices*. Vol. 239. Clarendon Press Oxford.

Fletcher, George P. 2000. *Rethinking Criminal Law*. Oxford University Press.

Gans, Jeremy. 2011. *Modern Criminal Law of Australia*. Cambridge University Press.

Husak, Douglas. 2003. "Crimes Outside the Core." *Tulsa Law Review* 39: 755.

Kennedy, Duncan. 1978. "Structure of Blackstone's Commentaries, The." *Buffalo Law Review* 28: 205.

McNamara, Luke. 2014. "A Judicial Contribution to Over-Criminalisation?: Extended Joint Criminal Enterprise Liability for Murder." *Criminal Law Journal* 58: 104.

McNamara, Luke, and Quilter, Julia. 2015. "Public Intoxication in NSW: The Contours of Criminalisation." *Sydney Law Review* 37: 1.

McSherry, Bernadette. 2004. "Terrorism Offences in the Criminal Code: Broadening the Boundaries of Australian Criminal Laws." *University of New South Wales Law Journal* 27: 354.

Mertz, Elizabeth. 2007. *The Language of Law School: Learning to 'Think Like a Lawyer.'* New York: Oxford University Press.

Norrie, Alan. 2014. *Crime, Reason and History: A Critical Introduction to Criminal Law*. Cambridge University Press.

NSWLRC. 2013. "People with Cognitive and Mental Health Impairments in the Criminal Justice System: Criminal Responsibility and Consequences." 138. New South Wales Law Reform Commission.

Quilter, Julia. 2015. "Assault Causing Death Crimes as a Response to 'One Punch' and 'Alcohol Fuelled' Violence: A Critical Examination of Australian Laws." In Thomas Crofts, Arlie Loughnan (ed) Criminalisation and Criminal Responsibility in Australia, Oxford University Press. http://ro.uow.edu.au/lhapapers/2012/.

Quilter, Julia, and Luke McNamara. 2013. "Time to Define the Cornerstone of Public Order Legislation: The Elements of Offensive Conduct and Language under the Summary Offences Act 1988 (NSW)." *University of New South Wales Law Journal* 36: 534.

Sentas, Vicki, and Rebecca McMahon. 2013. "Changes to Police Powers of Arrest in New South Wales." *Current Issues in Criminal Justice* 25: 785.

Simpson, A. W. B. 1981. "The Rise and Fall of the Legal Treatise: Legal Principles and the Forms of Legal Literature." *The University of Chicago Law Review* 48 (3): 632–79. doi:10.2307/1599330.

Standen, Jeffrey. 2009. "The Manly Sports: The Problematic Use of Criminal Law to Regulate Sports Violence." *The Journal of Criminal Law and Criminology*, 99: 619–42.

Steel, Alex. 2008. "Taking Possession: The Defining Element in Theft." *Melbourne University Law Review* 32: 1030–64.

———. 2009. "Bail in Australia: Legislative Introduction and Amendment Since 1970." *Australia & New Zealand Critical Criminology Conference 2009: Conference Proceedings*, 228.

———. 2013. "Good Practice Guide (Bachelor of Laws) Law in Broader Contexts." *Legal Education Associate Deans' Network Website*. http://lawteachnetwork.org/resources.html.

Steel, Alex, and Melanie Schwartz. 2013. "Broader Social Context as a Lens for Learning: Teaching Criminal Law." In *Disciplines: The Lenses of Learning*, edited by Kathryn Coleman and Adele Flood. Common Ground Publishing. http://works.bepress.com/alex_steel/40.

Stern, Simon. 2013. *William Blackstone, Commentaries on the Laws of England*, Vol. 4 (1769). SSRN Scholarly Paper ID 2296451. Rochester, NY: Social Science Research Network. http://papers.ssrn.com/abstract=2296451.

Watson, Alan. 1988. "The Structure of Blackstone's Commentaries." *Yale Law Journal* 97 (1998), 795–821.

Wells, Celia, and Oliver Quick. 2010. *Lacey, Wells and Quick Reconstructing Criminal Law: Text and Materials*. Cambridge University Press.

Chapter 10

The challenges and benefits of integrating criminal law, litigation and evidence

Adam Jackson and Kevin Kerrigan

Introduction

Criminal law is often delivered as a first-year subject in English law degrees. Notwithstanding the conceptual challenges of the underpinning principles and the complexity of some offences, criminal law is an attractive subject for new law students for a variety of educational and cultural reasons. Since broad themes of criminal law and criminal justice pervade popular culture through literature, film, television, and gaming, there is a ready appeal for students, general accessibility, and an often misplaced confidence that they already know how the law operates.

As has been outlined by Gledhill and Livings in the Introduction to this collection, first law degrees tend to focus on substantive criminal law. Many will offer the law of evidence as an optional subject, often in year three, and it is quite rare to find criminal process covered in the undergraduate curriculum, so most students do not encounter this unless and until they complete the Legal Practice or Bar course.

This chapter outlines an ambitious project to integrate criminal law, litigation and evidence as a single package in the first year of Northumbria Law School's Exempting Law Degree. It outlines the principle of integrating substantive law, skills, and process to offer a rounded picture of the criminal justice system. It also notes the difficulties of making such a large and complex module work for first-year law students and provides some practical guidance on how this approach may be implemented in other programmes.

The context – integrating theory and practice

The LLB (Hons) Exempting degree was first validated at Northumbria University in 1992 as part of Northumbria Law School's response to the training review that led to the establishment of the first Legal Practice Course which replaced the old Law Society Finals. Uniquely at the time, the Exempting degree combined the 'academic' stage of legal education with the 'vocational' stage. It was thus a qualifying law degree for the purposes of the Joint Statement and exempted graduates from completing a Legal Practice Course. In 1998, a barrister version of the Exempting degree was introduced, which followed the same model but exempted graduates from the Bar Vocational Course then in existence.

Rather than following a linear approach, whereby knowledge and practice areas followed sequentially, the Exempting degree adopted an integrated philosophy which sought to combine the study of theory and substance with the practice of skills and process. In this way, the degree was intended to more authentically represent the way legal issues and legal disputes arose in the real world.

In some ways, the Exempting law degree was pushing at the boundaries of public policy and legal regulation in the early 1990s. The new Legal Practice Course had introduced high-quality skills training into the vocational stage and moved away from the rigid rote learning and turgid centralised assessments required by the Law Society Finals, but it did nothing to better connect with the undergraduate law degree and preserved the staged approach towards qualification as a solicitor.

In the mid-1990s, the Lord Chancellor's Advisory Committee on Legal Education and Conduct (ACLEC) recognised and promoted the value of integration as promoting student learning:

> A liberal and humane legal education implies that students are engaged in active rather than passive learning . . . and that the teaching of appropriate and defined skills is undertaken in a way which combines practical knowledge with theoretical understanding . . . the rigid demarcation between the "academic" and "vocational" stages needs to disappear.
> (ACLEC 1996, para. 2.2.)

The ACLEC report highlighted the Northumbria model as a way in which legal education providers could connect the academic and vocational stage: "We have extolled the virtues of integrated education and training . . . as exemplified at present by the Northumbria exempting degree" (ACLEC 1996, para. 5.19).

Just over ten years later, in the US context, the *Carnegie Report* offered a similar exhortation:

> We are convinced that this is a propitious moment for uniting, in a single educational framework, the two sides of legal knowledge: (1) formal knowledge and (2) the experience of practice. We therefore attempt in this report to imagine a more capacious, yet more integrated, legal education.
> (Sullivan *et al.* 2007, p12)

Exempting degrees remain relatively rare in England and Wales with only six such courses currently listed on the UK's University and College Admissions Service course register. One reason for the dearth of such programmes is that most law schools do not have the mix of academically and professionally qualified staff to deliver an integrated curriculum. As will be seen, the knowledge and skills mix required in the integrated crime, litigation and evidence module almost inevitably requires qualified solicitors or barristers as part of the teaching team.

In 2009, Northumbria developed its Exempting Law Degree into an Integrated Master's Degree, the M Law, which offered sufficient higher-level dissertation and clinical legal education modules to justify the award of a masters-level qualification. This still operates, with an annual intake of around 250 students. From 2009–2014, as part of a pilot with the Solicitors' Regulation Authority, the School also offered the M Law (Solicitor) degree, a five-year programme which included all three stages of qualification (i.e. including the training stage) by utilising placement in practice and in-house clinical legal education through the Student Law Office, the Law School's free legal advice and representation service.

The pedagogic approach behind these degrees has always been integration of theory and practice: students are more engaged and develop deeper understanding when they learn of the social context in which the abstract legal rules operate and the way those rules are applied in the legal system. Dickerson suggests:

> It is essential that law schools teach students about the role of law and lawyers in society. Many of our students enter law school without a strong background in history and government, without any information about legal jurisprudence, and with inaccurate presumptions about lawyers' roles in society . . . Such lack of understanding – and misunderstanding – inhibits our students' ability to truly master both doctrine and skills.
>
> (2007, p54)

Indeed, Barry *et al.* suggest,

> [l]aw schools should teach all of the lawyering skills and values that students will need in practice . . . as a commitment to teaching law as a complex relationship between lawyer, client and the societal obligations that both must consider.
>
> (2000, p73)

Most modules on the M Law programme adopt an approach that enable students to explore the social or practical implications of the law but a 'spine' of fully integrated modules offer students a challenging experience of putting themselves in the position of legal practitioners, representing simulated or real clients and in so doing gaining a realistic insight into the impact of the law whilst at the same time developing high-level legal skills.

The fully integrated M Law modules are Crime, Litigation and Evidence (year 1), Tort, Litigation and Evidence (year 2), Property Law and Practice (year 3), Law of Business Associations (year 3), and Student Law Office (years 3 and 4). The intention is that students' knowledge and skills are developed progressively across the four years of the programme so that in the final year they are operating as proto-professionals. Crime, Litigation, and Evidence (CLE) is the starting point for this progressive journey, and it is thus vitally important as a step into a different way of learning for students.

At the time of this writing, a further redesign project is being undertaken to revamp the Exempting degree in response to the profession's training review (Gaymer et al. 2013), and as part of this, the integrated modules are being reviewed. Later in the chapter, we will explore the lessons about the operation of the existing CLE module that will inform the new approach.

The integrated crime, litigation, and evidence module

The current iteration of the CLE module is a compulsory, 40-credit, 'year-long' module which runs in semesters one and two (September–December and January–March) of the first year of the M Law programme. The module follows a relatively standard teaching delivery pattern of three 50 minute lectures per week and ten fortnightly 1 hour and 50 minute workshops (small-group sessions for around 16 students). The lectures are shared between the three subject groups roughly in the ratio 50% substantive criminal law, 25% litigation (criminal procedure), and 25% evidence. The workshops are fully integrated between the three subjects and, whilst the amount of each individual subject area covered varies per workshop, the workshop programme broadly reflects a similar ratio to the lectures. Lectures are delivered by a subject specialist in each area, while the workshop sessions are facilitated by tutors who are familiar with all three subject areas (for example, due to experience as criminal practitioners or academics with cross-field research interests). Lectures begin one week in advance of the workshops and, in addition, during that week, all students on the module undertake a one-hour introductory seminar. The introductory seminar requires only limited preparation and is designed to introduce students to the basic principles of criminal law, criminal procedure, and evidence.

Students are provided with extensive materials at the beginning of the module, comprising a detailed course handbook, workshop materials, and a 'Scenario Booklet' containing four detailed case studies. Each case study comprises materials that broadly reflect the materials that would be available in practice, including witness statements, interview transcripts, disclosure schedules, expert reports, proofs of evidence, etc. These materials form the basis of the workshop questions and students are expected to have detailed knowledge of each case study in advance of its use in the workshops.

The workshops are largely structured around the litigation (criminal procedure) element of the module so that students can follow a logical progression through the criminal process. The module, therefore, starts with a consideration of police station procedure and progresses through the pre-trial process (including dealing with funding, bail, allocation, disclosure, etc.), trial, sentencing, and appeals. Each scenario deals with a different aspect of the criminal law and evidential issues are dealt with as they arise. For example, confessions and inferences from silence are considered in the context of the police station interview, whereas witness handling, special measures directions, hostile witnesses, hearsay, etc., are dealt with largely in the context of the trial. The workshops combine a range of skills requiring the students to engage in group work, undertake practical legal research, deliver presentations, and engage in advocacy.

The original assessment model for the CLE module has undergone significant restructuring over time, and a great deal of work has been undertaken to ensure that the module is effectively "constructively aligned" (Biggs 2003). Initially, as the module comprised part of the criminal procedure and evidence assessments for the purposes of the Bar Vocational Course (BVC), a large part of the assessment was prescribed by the Bar Standards Board, primarily the need to assess a large breadth of content via multiple-choice questions. The move to centralised assessments on the Bar Professional Training Course (BPTC) has removed this constraint.

Currently, students on the CLE module are summatively assessed by:

- a reflective Court Visit Report, submitted at the beginning of semester two and marked on a pass/fail basis; and
- examination at the end of the module

The examination element of the assessment is relatively complex, owing primarily to the fact that it is assessing three distinct knowledge areas, but closely reflects the approach taken in workshops, i.e. a problem-type scenario presented in the form of realistic documents (usually a witness statement and other material).

The examination itself is split into two papers. Paper 1 is three hours in length and comprises two parts. Part 1 requires the students to identify relevant offences and defences which may arise from a given factual scenario. Students are given 1 hour and 30 minutes to complete part 1 after which they hand in their answers. They are then given additional material and have a further 1 hour and 30 minutes to complete written litigation questions and litigation and evidence multiple-choice questions all linked to the scenario. Paper 2 is a one-hour, multiple-choice paper which assesses a broader range of substantive knowledge. In advance of the summative assessment, all students are given the opportunity to complete a formative, "mid-sessional" mock examination on which they receive written feedback and which forms the basis of a workshop discussion.

The rationale for an integrated learning package

Many traditional models of teaching criminal law rely heavily on the knowledge transmission model and extensive use of the case method. As far back as 1942, the Association of American Law Schools committee commented,

> Under the case method students were not only to derive the holdings from the cases but were critically to appraise the application of the legal principles

involved... we realise now that much of this theory of the case method has not in practice been realised. Actually, students too often regard the cases as authoritative solutions which they need only read and absorb; each case becomes an end in itself, and the educative process stops at the very threshold of its most significant stage (Committee on Teaching and Examination Methods, Handbook of the Association of American Law Schools).

(1942, pp85, 87–88)

Criticism of transmission models of learning has continued to grow, both in respect of the effectiveness of the model as a means of conveying relevant information and in respect of its ability to engage students with the subject matter that they are learning. As Kember and Gow suggest:

> The knowledge transmission model orientation appears to assume that what is transmitted is received as sent, an assumption that teaching models do not seem to accept. The student appears to be neglected in the information transmission process by being regarded as a passive receiver.
>
> (1994, p66)

Furthermore they conclude that "... in departments where the predominant orientation is toward knowledge transmission, the students' use of deep approach is likely to decline through the period of the course of study" (1994, p67).

The CLE module is designed expressly to encourage students to take the step towards the aforementioned "significant" stage of learning towards a deep approach to understanding both the substantive law and the procedural context in which it operates. The goal is to move the student beyond simply learning a set of rules or precedents so that they become someone who "is capable of relating to a concept or topic in a way that an expert in that subject does." (Ramsden 2003, p41). Whilst, as noted earlier, the CLE module does not depart entirely from use of the transmission model of learning, deploying as it does large-group lectures in each of the three subject areas, it incorporates the model as simply one of a number of pedagogic tools.

The CLE module is designed to introduce students to a mode of experiential learning with "experiential" defined and understood in the following terms:

> Experiential education uses students' experiences in the roles of lawyers or their observations of practicing lawyers and judges to guide their learning. Experiential education integrates theory and practice by combining academic inquiry with actual experience.
>
> (Stuckey 2006, p811)

Through engagement with a range of realistic scenarios, practical activities, problem questions, and court visits (see earlier in the chapter) students are provided with an opportunity to experience an integrated, experiential mode of learning at the very beginning of their undergraduate studies which, amongst other things, is intended to engage them with their studies and begins to prepare them for the more varied experiential learning opportunities (including clinic and PBL) that they will experience later in the programme. The CLE module is therefore designed to encourage the development of a range of academic skills synonymous with Bloom's 'Taxonomy of Learning in Action' (1956).

It therefore becomes vitally important that the practical and experiential elements of the module engage students to do more than just learn the procedural rules in order to avoid becoming merely a form-filling exercise. As Biggs suggests,

> Knowing facts and how to carry out operations may well be part of the means for understanding and interpreting the world, but the quantitative conception stops at the facts and skills. A quantitative change in knowledge does not of itself change understanding.
>
> (1989, p10)

Part of the challenge of an integrated model such as CLE is ensuring that students perceive the relevance of the tasks that they are asked to undertake. Ramsden suggests that a failure to perceive relevance is associated with a surface approach to learning, while interest in a subject (and a perception of the relevance of a task) is associated with a deeper approach (2003, p43). According to Tang,

> Students engaging a deep approach have an intrinsic motivation of felt need based on interest in the task. The strategies thus adopted are task specific and aim at seeking and understanding the meaning of what is being learnt. Not only do these students relate the different aspects of the information with one another, they also relate them to their previous learning and their personal experiences.
>
> (1994, p1)

The CLE module provides an opportunity to build on students' intrinsic motivations, which often include interest in the subject matter and the desire to gain insight into the practice of law so as to promote a deeper approach to learning. This in turn should encourage a decompartmentalisation whereby students are encouraged to think both about the interlinking nature of doctrinal law and procedural rules and the relevance of pervasive skills (problem solving, legal research, advocacy, etc.) to a range of subject areas.

Practical issues and resources

In order to be able to successfully operate an integrated curriculum, careful attention must be paid to the learning resources and staffing available. In the criminal context, the need for a connection between the substantive offence and the legal process also require a strategic approach towards the running order of the curriculum. Some of these logistical issues will be explored in this section.

Human resources – although it is clearly possible for a 'law and society' approach to be adopted using a traditional, non-practitioner teaching base, if a module is to include realistic legal process and legal practice issues, it is essential to have input from solicitors or barristers on the design and teaching team. The CLE team has always involved a mix of academically and professionally qualified colleagues to construct the package of learning materials and deliver the teaching sessions.

Case studies – the core learning vehicle in CLE is the case study. These are now familiar learning resources in many law schools, and the key to success is to ensure they are:

- Realistic – so that students can believe in the scenario, the context, and the characters and so that the module will be relevant and useful as a preparation for real practice.
- Engaging – so that student imaginations are captured and they are willing to participate in the various role plays and other activities.
- Multifaceted – the case study needs to be sufficiently complex to enable a range of substantive and procedural issues to arise.
- Sustainable – given the extensive time and resources put into creating case studies, they need to be capable of being recycled in future years so designers should avoid time-specific content where possible.

Documentation and other resources – as has been seen, the CLE module works on the basis of realistic case files. These will typically include documentation from a criminal case, such as Police log, Witness statements, Custody record, Police interview transcript, Identification records, Disclosure report, Unused material log, and Defence statement. The key practical difference from traditional materials is that the case file uses real or facsimile forms. There is typically no narrative account, so the students have to find out what happened by reading across documents. They also have to learn that what they are reading may be a partial, mistaken, or false view of what took place and that there may be major gaps in the facts as presented. In this way, the students develop basic fact management skills.

It is possible to add colour and drama to a case file by using other media such as voice or video recording (e.g. simulated police interviews, 999 calls, or CCTV images) or even real artefacts (such as alleged stolen property, fingerprint lifts, or weapons). Clearly, these cannot be included in the file but can make an excellent focal point to a teaching session – handing around a "blood-soaked brick" in a lecture theatre really grabs students' attention.

Legal facilities and premises – It is not absolutely essential to have bespoke courtrooms or interview rooms for an integrated CLE module, but the Exempting degree has benefited from a donated Victorian magistrates' court which has been adapted to also accommodate a jury box for conversion to a Crown Court. This is equipped with CCTV for recording and feedback plus live link into interview rooms for realistic vulnerable witness testimony and into lecture theatres for large-group viewing. A suite of civil courtrooms and client interview rooms with CCTV facilities have been built around the criminal court to make up a large legal skills centre which is used for the Exempting degree and the free-standing professional programmes.

Legal practice texts – Many law schools have specialist law libraries on site. The Law Practice Collection at Northumbria Law School enables Exempting degree students to access a wide range of practitioner texts alongside more traditional law reports, journals, and texts. CLE students work from the outset with the heavyweight professional tomes such as *Archbold, Blackstone's*, and *Stone's*.

External facilities – It is important to note that in most major towns and cities there are criminal courts, either magistrates' courts or Crown Courts, albeit recently diminished by a major closure programme. The vast majority of criminal hearings are open to the public, including students. As mentioned, the CLE module takes extensive advantage of this, requiring every student to undertake an observation visit and reflective report as part of the seminar programme. This helps students better appreciate how the criminal justice system really operates and to observe prosecutors, solicitors, barristers, and judges in their working environment.

Integrated assessments – It is self-evident that if students learn criminal law, litigation, and evidence in an integrated manner, they should be assessed in this way too. This throws up its own challenges in that assessments must be constructed so as to test students' knowledge, skills and practice awareness, while reducing unnecessary complexity that could unfairly undermine student performance in the pressure of the exam room. While retaining an unseen examination assessment, the CLE module has adopted a mini-case file approach which gives rise to issues relating to substantive criminal law, procedure, and the law of evidence plus additional substantive areas addressed by multiple-choice questions.

Reflection, lessons learned, and future development

The development of a fully integrated CLE module has involved a process of evolution both in respect of the module itself and the programmes on which it has been delivered. Overall, we are satisfied that the integrated CLE module has been a success. The module is interesting and engaging, with strong student satisfaction levels and consistently positive student feedback in module reviews. It provides students with an opportunity to see the bigger picture of how the substantive law and legal rules that they are learning operate in a 'real world' practical context and despite the challenging nature of the module, student performance remains consistently strong. The module balances simulated activity and exposure to the reality of practice, encouraging students to understand the context in which they are learning and helping them to develop a range of vital skills.

Identifying these successes does not mean that we are blind to the challenges of running a module such as CLE. There are clear practical difficulties, which include sequencing a module of this kind so that topics are dealt with in a way and at a time that feels natural to the students, staffing a large module with tutors who are confident enough to teach across three subject areas, and trying to avoid creating a module that is overly complex and inappropriate for the level at which it is delivered whilst at the same time avoiding superficiality.

The risk of superficiality in some ways reflects the realities of criminal practice in that the process-driven imperatives of the criminal justice system can tend to dominate to the detriment of deeper engagement with the substantive criminal law. The challenge was to encourage students to think beyond the tasks in hand and to address more normative questions about how and why the system is constructed in the way it is. There is no doubt that a fully integrated CLE module is a challenge for first-year students, in particular in trying to incorporate the litigation and evidence elements of the module, which are traditionally-taught either later in a degree programme, or at a postgraduate level. In addition, having a year 1 module based on realistic materials and dealing with challenging issues such as sexual offences, offences of violence against the person, and homicide can prove emotionally taxing for some students.

Despite the complex nature of the module, student performance remains consistently strong. However, part of the success of the CLE module has been our ability to learn from past experiences and adapt accordingly. As previously discussed, at the time of writing, the M Law programme is undergoing a process of revalidation. The revalidated programme will include a new version of the CLE module that stops short of full integration. This new formulation will include a 20-credit criminal law module in semester one followed by a 20-credit criminal trial process module (litigation and evidence) in semester two. Although separated temporally, the modules will retain the use of a common set of realistic materials, the use of experiential learning methods, and a focus on the integration of theory and practice. As well as covering the qualifying law degree elements of criminal law, the semester one crime module will provide a foundation for the semester two trial process module. It is hoped that by presenting both modules as part of an overall whole we can retain the benefits of integration whilst removing some of the inherent complexity associated with requiring students to engage with three complex subjects from day one of their undergraduate study.

The new modules essentially accept that trying to address three subjects at the same time in the first year of a law degree is over ambitious. The partial decoupling of the substantive from the procedural and proof elements enables more focused attention on the fundamental rules and concepts while retaining the benefits of integration such as reinforcement of theory in a practical context and an appreciation of the real-world application of the criminal law.

Conclusion

This chapter has offered an insight into the aspiration of Northumbria Law School to create a fully integrated curriculum and methodology for learning criminal law, criminal process, and proof. The CLE module, as part of both the Exempting Law Degree and M Law Degree programmes, has pioneered an ambitious pedagogy that mixes didactic, experiential, observational, reflective, and participatory approaches. Student satisfaction and engagement has been high and in many ways the module has been a great success.

Nevertheless, the desire for holistic realism stretches students' capacities for concentration, organisation, and evaluation, particularly given that this is a first-year module. There is a risk that the structural and factual complexity of the module obscures the essential learning, particularly for weaker students. As the integrated package has been developed and refined, it has become an end in itself that on reflection risks prioritising form over function. In light of this, future development will pull back on complete integration for the sake of simplicity and focus, while retaining the connection between substance and process deemed essential for student engagement and overall understanding.

References

ACLEC (the Lord Chancellor's Advisory Committee on Legal Education) (April 1996) 1st Report, London.

Barrows, H.S. and Tamblyn, R.M. (1980) *Problem-Based Learning: An Approach to Medical Education*, New York: Springer Publishing.

Barry, M. et al., Clinical Education for this Millennium; The Third Wave, (2000) 7 *Clinical Law Review*, 1.

Biggs, J. (2003) *Teaching for Quality Learning at University – What the Student Does*, 2nd Edition, Buckingham: SRHE / Open University Press.

Bloom, B. (1956) *Taxonomy of Educational Objectives: Handbook 1: Cognitive Domain*, New York: David McKay Company.

Committee on Teaching and Examination Methods (1942) *Handbook of the Association of American Law Schools*.

Dickerson, D., Building Bridges: A Call for Greater Collaboration Between Legal Writing and Clinical Professors, (2007) 4 *Journal of the Association of Legal Writing Directors*, 45–55.

Gaymer, J. and Potter, M.(2013) *The Future of Legal Services Education and Training Regulation in England and Wales*, report of the Legal Education and Training Review.

Kember, D. and Gow, L., Orientations to Teaching and Their Effect on the Quality of Student Learning, (1994) 65 (1) *The Journal of Higher Education*, 58–74.

Law Society and General Council of the Bar (1999) *A Joint Statement Issued by the Law Society and the General Council of the Bar on the Completion of the Initial or Academic Stage of Training by Obtaining an Undergraduate Degree*.

Ramsden, P. (2003) *Learning to Teach in Higher Education*, London: Routledge.

Stuckey, R. (2006) *Best Practices for Legal Education: A Vision and a Road Map*, Columbia, SC: University of South Carolina.

Sullivan, W. et al. (2007), *Educating Lawyers–Preparation for the Profession of Law*, report of the Carnegie Foundation for the Advancement of Teaching, (USA) Jossey-Bass.

Tang, C. (1994) Assessment and student learning: Effects of modes of assessment on students' preparation strategies. In G. Gibbs (Ed.) *Improving Student Learning: Theory and Practice*. (pp151–170). Oxford: Oxford Brookes University, The Oxford Centre for Staff Development.

Chapter 11

'Crime and the criminal process'

Challenging traditions, breaking boundaries

Phil Scraton and John Stannard

Introduction

A criticism frequently levelled at traditional Criminal Law courses is that, in content and presentation, they over-emphasise black-letter doctrine while failing to engage with the broader context in which criminal law operates. In 2007, following a review of the undergraduate law syllabus at Queen's University, Belfast, a new compulsory Year One module was introduced: *Crime and the Criminal Process*. The first semester module, taught by doctrinal criminal lawyers and critical criminologists, was designed to provide a contextual understanding of 'crime' and the criminal justice process. Before students grappled with Criminal Law and its institutions, it was considered essential that they were encouraged to question misconceptions about 'crime', 'deviance', and 'conflict' within advanced democratic societies. Critical criminological analysis offered the lens through which the definitions of 'crime', the process of criminalisation, and the administration of criminal justice could be viewed and questioned. Taught in two distinct but related halves, and delivered through 24 lectures supported by weekly themed tutorials, the module proved highly popular with students. It was offered for six years: 2007–2013. Despite its popularity with tutors and students, in 2014, it was abandoned by the school to facilitate a further syllabus revision. This article traces its development and consolidation as an innovative, unique, and challenging module and demonstrates that in paving the way for teaching undergraduate law core subjects, it remains important to ground students' learning in critical analysis.

Background

In 2006, as part of the review of the undergraduate Law and Masters in Legal Science programmes, it was decided to offer a compulsory year one, semester one module, *Crime and the Criminal Process*. The rationale was that prior to engaging with the 'function of the criminal law' in 'set[ting] the parameters within which the criminal justice system operates' (Allen 2011, p2), students should be introduced to the contested terrain of what constitutes 'crime' at any given moment in any given jurisdiction. In developing the module, the coordinating tutors fused their distinct but related fields – critical criminology (PS) and doctrinal criminal law (JS).

In its previous incarnation, the undergraduate law degree had offered students a second-year optional module, *Criminology: Theory and Practice*. A popular module, it was chosen by approximately half of the year group. Reorganisation of the degree removed this option, and it was agreed by the course development team that 'core' conceptual and theoretical elements should be introduced earlier to all students. In 2006, JS initiated a successful extra-mural course, *An Introduction to the Criminal Justice System*. It provided students with an outline of criminal procedure that focused on the 'nature' and aetiology of crime, key issues in substantive criminal law and evidence, and an outline of the workings of the sentencing system. It provided a 'dry run', in part, for the planned undergraduate module. Although successful, feedback from the extra-mural course pointed towards further development of criminological analysis.

The withdrawal of second-year Criminology and the helpful student evaluations of the extra-mural course together provided a significant opportunity to initiate a module combining an introduction to critical criminological analysis with an introduction to the criminal justice system. *Crime and the Criminal Process* would be a precursor to a second-semester compulsory module in Criminal Law. Its development brought together lawyers and criminologists. (The School of Law was, and remains, home to the Institute of Criminology and Criminal Justice.)

Teaching criminal law – challenging traditions?

In 1990, Peter Alldridge wrote a trenchant article in *Legal Studies* entitled 'What's Wrong with the Traditional Criminal Law Course?' In his critique of undergraduate Criminal Law, he argued that black-letter law courses focused primarily on the application of statutes and reported cases, confined by the medium of the 'problem question'. Significant contributions from within applied social sciences, and the potential of empirical critiques, were ignored. Their philosophical underpinning, invariable and unquestioning, relied on liberal individualism. Within this narrow framework, emphasis was restricted to attribution, neglecting legal procedure, law enforcement, and sentencing. It introduced students to a system based on designation, while underplaying procedural discretion and coercion. Consequently, Criminal Law was presented as a "sealed, self-authenticating unity", encouraging the view that the "All England Reports" constituted "a mirror of life" (Alldridge 1990, pp38–41).

Highlighting three issues, Alldridge's critique extended to the underlying philosophy of the traditional Criminal Law course. First, he explored why Criminal Law courses concentrated on responsibility or attribution to the exclusion of other elements. He listed several factors: the influence of analytical legal philosophy, academic preoccupation with codification, and, not least, the "discipline-oriented assumption that contextual and empirical issues regarding Criminal Law were the province of Criminology or Penology" (Alldridge 1990, pp42–47). Second, he proposed that the prevalent concept of responsibility was "profoundly and immutably individualistic". The pre-eminent New Right proposition that "society" did not exist, he argued, was one "to which the criminal law has long been wedded" (Alldridge 1990, pp47–49). Finally, he sought redress to this imbalance by drawing on work within philosophy, psychology, and ethics.

Alldridge's critique appears counter-intuitive to those outside the traditional law school curriculum, not least because Criminal Law has the potential, in content and analysis, to be uniquely enjoyable, capturing the "rich tapestry of human life" (Farmer 1996, p57). For many students, however, Farmer notes the experience is quite different. Possibly fired by a passion for justice, by an enthusiasm for famous trials and by a commitment to strong advocacy, they arrive in their first class to be told that the most fundamental principle in Criminal Law is *actus non facit reum nisi mens sit rea* (an act does not make a defendant guilty without a guilty mind). They may be taught that it is essential to determine whether or not elements of a crime, such as 'possession', are to be classified as part of *mens rea* (awareness of and intention to commit an unlawful act) or as mental elements in the *actus reus* (the commission of the act).

Taken aback by the durability of Latin, students are then confronted with the question of whether or not a person can be considered reckless without conscious advertence to the consequences and whether such advertence could take place at the back of a mind as well as the front! Nor should one forget the earth-shattering problem of the man who leaves 'his club', and takes an umbrella from the stand thinking it belongs to someone else. In a state of absent-mindedness, he has taken his own umbrella. Does this constitute attempted theft? It is sobering to contemplate the bottles of academic ink that have been spilled on this issue – some, it is confessed, by one of the authors of this chapter. While this account of the traditional Criminal Law course is something of a caricature, it gives a flavour of the grandly defended traditional approach.

It is disappointing that Alldridge's call for a significant reappraisal of Criminal Law teaching has not led to significant change. A cursory glance at contemporary courses and texts bears this out. Allen (2011, p4) recognises that the "criminal law represents the rules of social control within a society" and raises the obvious questions of how "the rules are determined" and if there is "an essential criterion which determines which behaviour merits criminal sanction". His responses are instructive: "criminal law is a reflection of corporate or societal morality" and "the wrongdoing" it "seeks to punish is that which threatens the fundamental values upon which society is founded". "Harm" done to the individual through crime also "threatens the security and well-being" of "society". Thus the consequent "criminal sanction operates as a form of social control both punishing the offender and reasserting the mores of that society". The focus, then, shifts from the seemingly straightforward terrain of *actus reus* and *mens rea* to the more complex issues of what constitutes a 'society', how its 'mores' are determined and what constitutes 'well-being'. Further, 'social control' is presented as unproblematic when, in fact, processes of control and regulation are imposed and administered through state institutions.

Similarly, Heaton and de Than (2011, p2) discuss the quest for "the Holy Grail of a general definition of a 'crime' which identifies the quality of an act or omission which makes it an offence". They conclude that the diversity and complexity of criminal acts are such that the search for "essential characteristics . . . based on moral criteria or otherwise, have proved fruitless". Inevitably, therefore, an act transforms into a crime only because it progresses through criminal proceedings. Consequently, 'crime' is entirely processual, its status determined by successful prosecution through the courts. Herring (2009a, p4) notes the 'circularity' of the proposition: "criminal law" is "that part of the law which uses criminal procedures" and "criminal procedures" are those "which apply to the criminal law". He suggests that the 'distinctive role' of the criminal law is as a deterrent from "doing acts that harm others in society", establishing "conditions" for the application of punishments and providing "guidance on the kinds of behaviour which are seen by society as acceptable". The process is an "established state response to crime". Harm, causation, and censure are the touchstones. Quoting Ashworth, Herring concludes that "criminal liability is the strongest formal condemnation that society can inflict".

'Crime' and the process of criminalisation

> Acts are not, they *become*. So also with crime. Crime does not exist. Crime is created. First there are acts. There follows a long process of giving meaning to these acts.
> (Christie 1998, p121)

Taught primarily as a first point of entry into the legal profession, it is inevitable that undergraduate Law courses are structured around vocational priorities. Yet, in Britain and Northern Ireland, only a quarter of undergraduate Law students register as trainee solicitors, although a significant cohort gains employment in other related professions (see AGCAS 2015). Those who enter legal practice, as other trained professionals, retain a degree of personal discretion in their day-to-day work, but their autonomy or agency is relative, delimited by institutional and ideological controls. State funding of professional courses is predicated on their prescribed utility and their function in maintaining and supporting the status quo. As Nils Christie (1994, p58) astutely observed in his analysis of "crime control as industry", the "invasion" of "management ideology" and vocational "correspondence" have responded to the expectation that students receive "useful knowledge" to service the professions (see Scraton 2007 for a more developed discussion of 'correspondence'). Yet despite such pressures, there should be scope to enable and encourage students in the development of knowledge and skills beyond the confines of professional training. Their future employment and their interventionist work will not occur in a vacuum. It is essential, therefore, that their studies include a critical introduction to the social, cultural, political, and economic climate in which the profession operates. As Morrison (2009, p7) affirms, if a criminal act is considered solely as a violation of the criminal law, then the only 'common element' between crimes is that each is a procedural violation.

Nils Christie's earlier assertion is apposite, given that a crime, in definition, commission, policing, and punishment is the consequence of a process through which meaning is ascribed to an act. This applies also to 'deviance', usually defined as acts that do not necessarily contravene the criminal law but, in some way, depart from socially acceptable behaviour. In his highly influential text, *Outsiders*, Howard Becker (1963, p9) states, "deviance is not a quality of the act" committed "but the consequence of the application by others of the rules and sanctions to an 'offender' . . . deviant behaviour is behaviour that people so label". Such rules and sanctions, when administered by the State through criminal law become defined as 'crimes'. As Crowther (2007, p125) notes, "the criminal justice process cannot be understood in isolation from the many complex and consequences of, and responses to, crime".

Muncie and McLaughlin (1996, p7) consider that defining crime as an unlawful act, punishable through the application of the due process of the Law, appears "straightforward and uncontroversial". In considering the 'act' committed and the 'process' applied, however, "some understanding of criminal law, social mores and social order" is required. Addressing this apparently self-evident issue at the outset of a Law degree requires consideration of the situational dynamics of 'crime' and 'deviance' within an interpretive analysis that traces how acts are defined through social construction, ideological imperatives, and political priorities. This necessitates exploration of the ideological framework through which certain acts, individuals, and/or groups become criminalised and revealing and reflecting historical changes in the social and political order within a jurisdiction at any particular moment.

In conceptualising *Crime and the Criminal Process*, the priority was to reveal and engage with common-sense assumptions held by first-year students regarding 'crime', 'deviance', and 'the Law'. As discussed earlier, asserting that crime is a criminal law violation is as unhelpful as it is self-evident. This extends also to affirming that a deviant act is a norm infraction. In introducing the module, using recent media coverage of well-known cases, students were invited to consider the circumstances under which the 'Law' should intervene in personal life. Following this, they were given 11 examples of unlawful behaviour and asked to keep a running total of when they 'last broke the Law' (e.g. buying goods 'off the back of a lorry', smoking dope/under-age drinking, keeping money found in the street, false/exaggerated insurance claim, using a handheld mobile phone while driving). A show of hands of three hundred students demonstrated that all had broken the Law in the previous 12 months and most had committed over half of the crimes listed. This pattern was consistent throughout the life of the module.

While most of the unlawful acts listed appeared to be 'minor' offences, their potential outcomes were not, raising the question: 'Petty or serious, who decides?' To keep change from £20 when only a £10 note had been offered might be justified by the happy recipient as a minor redistribution of profits from a large supermarket chain, but it was the low-paid cashier who had the £10 balance taken from her/his pay packet. Reminiscing of his time as an undergraduate, PS recounted buying pipe tobacco that had been swept from the floor by a worker at a well-known tobacco manufacturers in Liverpool. After repackaging the tobacco into four-ounce plastic bags, he sold it on to his lecturers and professors at University. Dubbed the 'Great St Bruno Tobacco Heist' students were asked to consider what might happen if this scam had been uncovered. The worker would have lost his job and possibly been prosecuted as a deterrent to others. PS would have been cautioned – but what would have been the fate of the professors?

These anecdotes were used to explore the relationship between *context, circumstances*, and *consequences* in defining crime, formulating laws, and prosecuting acts. Exploring assumptions about what constitutes 'vandalism', not in name a criminal offence, students soon were debating the significance of social construction and political ideology. Also in the mix, particularly regarding circumstances, were issues of motive, meaning, and mitigation. 'Crime' was defined as an act or acts in contravention of the properly constituted laws of a state jurisdiction or federated jurisdiction and subject to prosecution as an offence/offences through due process of the courts. 'Deviance' was defined as an act, acts, or a way of life that breaks with socially and culturally accepted conventions within a group, class, religion, and/or society – subject to exclusion, exiling, and ostracism. Yet their seemingly objective application already was challenged by the subjectivity of their occurrence.

The ideological construction of criminal or deviant acts and the differential 'meaning' attributed to them extends beyond personal and social interaction. It is deeply institutionalised and provides the justification for social marginalisation, differential policing, and harsh punishments. From this foundation, students were introduced to the relationship between agency, the experiential social circumstances of action, interaction and reaction, and structure, as well as the less apparent confining context of class, 'race', sectarianism, gender, and age. Against this backdrop, 'crime' and 'harm', punishment and proportionality, and the implicit tensions between retributive and restorative outcomes were discussed.

Moving on from this initial conceptual discussion, the module was structured to respond to Nils Christie's invocation to consider how 'meaning' is ascribed to 'acts' that come to be defined as 'crimes'. After the introductory sessions that involved engaging students personally as well as academically in questioning assumptions about crime being essentially *beyond* their personal behaviour, and found only in the actions of *others*, the issues were fleshed out in five sessions. The first, *Measuring 'Crime'*, questioned Margaret Thatcher's infamous comment, "a crime is a crime is a crime". It covered notions of the 'gravity' or perceived seriousness of crime and how different crimes are measured and recorded, tracing the multi-agency discretionary path between an offence being committed and conviction.

Further, it considered alternative forms of accounting and the significant impact of *harmful* behaviours not defined as crimes but accepted and tolerated. For example, all students could relate to their own direct or indirect experiences of bullying, which raised further key issues of familial and gendered assaults. Contrasting "crimes of the powerful" with "crimes of the poor", it concluded that reconceptualising "crime as *harm* opens up the possibility of dealing with pain, suffering and injury as conflicts and troubles deserving negotiation, mediation and arbitration rather than as *criminal* events deserving guilt, punishment and exclusion" (Muncie 2000, p223).

Having established the implicit relativism at the heart of calibrating 'seriousness' the *Reporting 'Crime'* session focused on the media as the key vehicle in the social construction of crime. Using contemporary examples, it addressed the imperatives of newsworthiness, including how 'crime news' is mediated through a well-defined process of 'news manufacture'. It introduced the key concepts first explored by Stan Cohen (1972) of "folk devils" and "moral panics", focusing on how the latter embodies "heightened emotion, fear, dread, anxiety and a strong sense of righteousness" resulting in "strengthening the social control apparatus of society – tougher or renewed rules, more intense public hostility and condemnation, more laws, longer sentences, more police, more arrests and more prison cells" (Goode and Ben-Yehuda 1994, p31).

Reflecting on the nineteenth century development of contemporary criminal justice, 'new' policing and 'new' forms of imprisonment, *Targeting 'Crime'*, traced the 'Victorian legacy' founded on 'disciplining the masses', regulating the 'threat' of a criminal, pathological 'underclass' and the rise of the social reform movement. This regulatory legacy was considered with regard to contemporary studies and local policy initiatives. 'Soft' (e.g. housing departments) and 'hard' (e.g. zero-tolerance policing) State interventions directed towards 'problem' families and communities were addressed, including the use of new technology to target 'crime' and 'anti-social behaviour (e.g. dispersal zones, CCTV, drones, thermal imaging, 'mosquito' devices).

Having introduced students to the 'path' travelled from 'act' to 'crime', and the significance of external factors (historical, social, cultural, political) to the determinations associated with definition, seriousness, and regulation, the final session in this section considered punishment. *Punishing 'Crime'* addressed the third priority of the *context, circumstances*, and *consequences* triptych. Students were introduced to the Weberian proposition that within its jurisdiction the State alone claims the 'monopoly' on the use of physical force – the power to punish. This involved consideration of the dynamics of punishment, retribution, and deterrence, including the principles of 'just deserts', proportionality, and consistency. The focus moved from the dungeon-like bridewells and prison hulks to the development of the so-called new prison and its commitment to 'disciplining the subject'. Finally, claims made for rehabilitation and desistance from crime within current penal studies were examined.

In scope and content, the first five sessions covered considerable ground. Yet, supported by focused readings and thematic tutorial workshops, students were engaged in a topic – 'crime' – with which they were familiar in their everyday lives. Mobilising their curiosity, triggered by news, television and film, was never difficult. Lecture and tutorial attendances remained high. Having achieved their engagement, the module moved to four introductory lectures on the main 'theoretical traditions' within criminological analysis. This was not intended as a comprehensive review of criminological theory but an introduction to the importance of theoretical context.

The four sessions were *Biologies and Personalities* (biological/physiological determinism, eugenics, personality theories, individual pathology), *Cultures and Environments* (social disorganisation as social pathology; strain, subcultural, and differential association theories; urbanisation), *Labels and Reactions* (identity and reputation; labelling, social, and societal reaction; social exclusion and 'outsider status'), and *Power and Context* (critical social research, historical and contemporary materialism, structural relations and social conflict, the politics of criminalisation, 'crimes' of the 'powerless'/'powerful').

Introducing the social and political construction of 'crime', the process of 'criminalisation' and the breadth of theoretical analyses, the lectures were supported by five tutorial workshops conducted in small groups. Registration remained consistent at approximately three hundred undergraduate and postgraduate (MLegSci) students. To ensure consistency across such a large cohort, tutorial workshops were prescribed, which combined discussion themes, set readings, and key questions. Reflecting the lecture content, the five tutorial topics were *'Crime', Representation, and the Media*; *Children, Young People, and Moral Panics*; *'Crime' and Pathology*; *Gender, 'Crime', and Criminal Justice*; and *'Crimes' of the Powerful*. In addition to 'core readings' (the 'set text' was Scraton 2007), other academic, policy, and media readings were archived on the module's dedicated online site. Tutorials were complemented by an online discussion forum with topics initiated by tutors and students. Detailed instructions and guidance regarding assignment preparation and writing were also available online.

Introduction to the criminal justice system

Having established foundational debates and dilemmas within academic and popular discourses concerning the context, circumstances, and consequences of 'crime' and criminal justice, the module's second distinct element introduced students to the operation of the criminal justice system. Its significance was not to provide a full introduction to the criminal law, which would come later in a separate module, but to provide an initial grounding in *process* to students unfamiliar with the progression of a criminal case from arrest through to judgement, sentencing, and appeal. Broadly speaking, this part of the module fell into four sections.

In the first section, intended as a bridge between the two halves of the module, the criminal justice system – both in the sense of the relevant institutions and in the sense of the rules and principles applied by these institutions (Hudson 2006) – was characterised as a response by the State, though by no means the only response, to the problem of 'crime'. Other key issues highlighted in this section were the objectives of the criminal justice system, the 'crime control' and 'due process' models of criminal justice as outlined by Packer (1964), and the different branches of the criminal justice system (substantive criminal law, criminal procedure, evidence, and sentencing).

In the second section, the focus was on understanding how the criminal justice system operated, including the rules relating to arrest and summons, police investigation, charging, and prosecution of offences. These rules provided a good introduction to the classic skills of legal analysis and problem solving, in particular, by using scenarios in which students were asked to identify irregularities in the process. Complaints that the law was difficult to understand were met with the observation that these were rules which every police officer has to fully understand if he or she is not going to get into trouble!

In the third section, the opportunity was taken to diverge from criminal procedure by exploring selected topics from substantive criminal law (non-fatal offences against the person, self-defence and the prevention of crime, and intoxication) and evidence (the rules relating to 'bad character' and the burden and standard of proof in criminal cases). In this way, students were given a taste of other aspects of the criminal justice system. The final section of this part, and of the module as a whole, dealt with the processes of trial, sentencing, and appeal so that upon completing the module, students had a flavour of the criminal justice system in all its aspects.

In general, the reaction of students to this part, and to the module as a whole, was very positive. Subsequently, many indicated that it had provided them with a solid introduction to modules such as Criminal Law, Evidence, and Sentencing. One problem, however, was that ten lectures, delivered over five weeks, did not provide sufficient time to introduce the criminal justice process. Another issue, that remained unresolved, was the linkage between the two halves of the module. While 'Crime' and 'Criminal Process' were successful as discrete elements, their relationship required further development. This was the task in hand when the module was withdrawn.

Conclusion

Crime and the Criminal Process was taught successfully for six years. Its lectures, twice weekly, received highly positive formal and informal evaluations from the six cohorts of undergraduate, postgraduate, and international students, as well as from the diverse range of tutors who led the workshops. Evaluations and tutorial team discussions resulted in adaptations throughout the module's life and plans were afoot to develop the module into a 'second phase' when, regrettably, in 2012, the decision was taken to revamp the undergraduate first year, which involved sacrificing its most successful module for a more traditional professional legal skills foundation. The intended restructure focused on a more radical approach to integrating the two distinct elements by using the case material introduced in the first element; for example, taking topical or well-known cases beyond media representation, political discourse, and policy implications and tracing their progress as illustrative of black-letter law. While there would be difficulties to surmount, particularly in forgoing a general introduction to the criminal justice system, the prospect of using well-known cases as an introduction to the potential and dilemmas of litigation, both in domestic courts and in the European Court of Human Rights, pedagogically was engaging and exciting.

The decision to withdraw *Crime and the Criminal Process* without evaluating its innovatory contribution, specifically to the learning and development of over 1,800 students and more generally to Criminal Law pedagogy, was disappointing. As stated in the introduction, it has been a quarter of a century since Peter Alldridge presented his scathing critiques of the 'traditional' Law course yet, as this collection demonstrates, in many institutions the teaching of Criminal Law remains locked into an approach dictated by pedagogical convention and professional expectation. This case example demonstrates that an uneasy relationship persists between academic law and the professions. Placed in the context of 'what a law school is for', this phenomenon is not new (see: Birks 1994; Bradney 1998, 2003; Cownie 2004; Twining 1994). Indeed, it has been argued that the 'traditional' law school is a twentieth-century phenomenon, and it is questionable whether it can be sustained in its present form (Stannard 2011).

Introducing his 'great debates in law' text on criminal law, Herring (2009b, vi) engages with the issues raised in the introduction to this article. He notes the "dangers" implicit in teaching and learning criminal law as "a set of rules and developing the skills to apply the rules to different scenarios". While this is 'useful', he proposes a different approach based on why particular laws are introduced and prevail, how the law applies to "novel situations" and whether it "reflect[s] prejudices". He begins with a discussion of "criminalization" and the intensity of "political and academic debate" about what acts should be defined as illegal and what "principles" should be privileged "in making criminalization decisions" (Herring 2009b, p1). Inevitably, this leads to consideration of the 'harm principle', and the role and function of law in reducing and preventing harm. Herring's engagement with the meaning of harm, its scope (harm to self/harm to others/harm to the 'public interest'/indirect harms) and the role of the State in defining, policing, and criminalising harm returns the debate to the foci on which *Crime and the Criminal Process* was founded.

This connects directly to the critical analysis of 'crime', 'deviance', 'harm', and 'punishment' central to the module. While identifying individuals' agency in committing 'acts', it also recognises the determining contexts of structural relations (class, 'race', gender, sexuality, age, and so on) in which such acts occur. Criminal Law, and the process of criminalization, from the outlawing of certain acts through to their regulation and punishment, cannot assume ascendancy above the maelstrom of everyday life by claiming some form of quasi-divine, doctrinal intervention administered by robed high priests of Law's temple. They reflect, and are reflective of, the status quo derived in the traditions of the society in which they originate. Introducing students to the shifting ground on which the Criminal Law stands; to the social, political, economic, and ideological contexts in which it adjudicates; to the complex circumstances of criminalization that obtain; and to the often punitive consequences it generates, are essential ingredients of critical pedagogy.

Bibliography

AGCAS (2015) 'What do law graduates do?' http://www.prospects.ac.uk/options_law.htm London: Association of Graduate Careers Advisory Services, accessed 19 October 2015.

Alldridge, P. (1990) 'What's wrong with the traditional criminal law course?' *Legal Studies* Vol 10, No 1, pp 38–62.

Allen, M. (2011) *Textbook on Criminal Law* Oxford: Oxford University Press (11th Edn).

Becker, H. (1963) *Outsiders: Studies in the Sociology of Deviance* New York: Free Press.

Birks, P. (1994) *Reviewing Legal Education* Oxford: Oxford University Press.

Bradney, A. (1998) 'Law as a parasitic discipline' *Journal of Law and Society* Vol 25, No 1, pp 71–84.

Bradney, A. (2003) *Conversations, Choices and Chances: The Liberal Law School in the Twenty-First Century* London: Bloomsbury Publishing.

Christie, N. (1994) *Crime Control as Industry* London: Routledge (2nd Edn).

Christie, N. (1998) 'Between civility and the state' in V. Ruggiero, N. South, and I. Taylor [eds] *The New European Criminology: Crime and Social Order in Europe* London: Routledge pp 119–124.

Cohen, S. (1972) *Folk Devils and Moral Panics* London: MacGibbon and Kee.

Cownie, F. (2004) *Legal Academics: Culture and Identities* Oxford: Hart Publishing.

Crowther, C. (2007) *An Introduction to Criminology and Criminal Justice* Houndmills: Palgrave Macmillan.

Farmer, L. (1996) 'The obsession with definition: The nature of crime and critical legal theory' *Social and Legal Studies* Vol 5, pp 57–73.

Goode, E. and Ben-Yehuda, N. (1994) *Moral Panics: The Social Construction of Deviance* Cambridge, USA: Blackwell.

Heaton, R. and de Than, C. (2011) *Criminal Law* Oxford: Oxford University Press (3rd Edn).

Herring, J. (2009a) *Criminal Law* Houndmills: Palgrave Macmillan (6th Edn).

Herring, J. (2009b) *Criminal Law: Great Debates* Houndmills: Palgrave Macmillan.

Hudson, B. (2006) 'The criminal justice system' in E. McLaughlin, and J Muncie [eds] *Sage Dictionary of Criminology* London: Sage (2nd Edn).

Morrison, W. (2009) 'What is crime? Contrasting definitions and perspectives' in C. Hale *et al.* [eds] *Criminology* Oxford: Oxford University Press (2nd Edn) pp 3–22.

Muncie, J. (2000) 'Decriminalising Criminology' in G. Mair, and R. Tarling [eds] *British Criminology Conference: Selected Proceedings*, britsoccrim.org/volume3/010.pdf accessed 20 August 2015.

Muncie, J. and McLaughlin, E. (1996) *The Problem of Crime* London: Sage.
Packer, H. (1964) 'Two Models of the Criminal Process' *University of Pennsylvania Law Review* Vol 113:, pp 1.
Scraton, P. (2007) *Power, Conflict and Criminalisation* London: Routledge.
Stannard, J. (2011) 'Thirty years on: Reflections of an outsider' in T. Mohr, and J. Schweppe [eds] *Thirty Years of Legal Scholarship: The Irish Association of Law Teachers* Dublin: Round Hall pp 335–339.
Twining, W. (1994) *Blackstone's Tower: The English Law School* London: Stevens and Sons/Sweet and Maxwell.

Chapter 12

Context and connection

Ben Livings

Introduction

Over a quarter of a century ago, Alldridge criticised the dominant approach to teaching criminal law, in large part due to its narrowly doctrinal focus (1990; see also Farmer 1995). In the years since, pedagogy in law schools has been influenced by a more widespread awareness and acceptance of educational theory and an increasing attention on the quality of university teaching (Norton *et al.* 2013). The aspirations, and in many cases the practice, of teaching have progressed beyond the simple conveying of legal doctrine to passive learners (James 2004; *cf.* Johnstone 1992). James (2004) points to a phenomenon that he terms 'pedagogicalism'; an orthodoxy that has built up in recent decades around the nature of what constitutes 'good teaching', and the development of institutional auditing methods by which to encourage or enforce its adoption in law schools.

Notwithstanding these developments, much of the substance of Alldridge's criticism still pertains. Contributions to this book point to the continued hold of the traditional model of criminal law teaching and numerous ways in which it is inadequate. Conversely, these also comprise evidence of a desire and willingness for a more progressive approach; several present a compelling case for a large-scale re-imagination of the criminal law course, either in the way in which it is delivered (Fitzpatrick, ch 5; Boylan-Kemp and Huxley-Binns, ch 6), the topics covered (Gledhill, ch 16), or both (Gans, ch 8). In this chapter, I suggest that a major failing of the doctrinal approach lies in the lack of attention paid to the social and institutional context in which the criminal law operates.

The demand for a contextualised understanding of the law in legal education is, of course, not new, and dates back at least as far as Blackstone (Hepple 1996). In this chapter, I advocate the provision and incorporation of context by reference to materials with cross-curricular relevance. This is an expeditious and convenient means by which to enliven and contextualise the criminal law course and can also lead to a better understanding of the way in which the sub-disciplines of academic legal education fit together and interact. The thoughts set out are born of my experiences in university law schools in England and Wales (hereafter abbreviated to 'England') and New South Wales (NSW), Australia. This has included teaching traditionally-modelled substantive criminal law courses; courses which focus on broader aspects of criminal process, evidence and sentencing; and, importantly for the purposes of this chapter, medical law and sports law.

The chapter first explores some of the forces that shape the content of the modern law degree and the particular pressures that might inhibit a contextual approach on the criminal law course. Cohen writes, "Criminal law should be seen as both a unique and important subject as well as part of a larger integrated curriculum with articulated goals and complementary components" (2004, p1195), and this correlates with research suggesting that students want to connect their academic understanding of the law with 'real life' – to see how the law fits together across sub-disciplinary boundaries and applies to the world (Rubin Henderson 2003; Townes O'Brien 2014). Twining has written of the introspective tendencies of academic law and its institutions, and this is often true of its sub-disciplines (1994); a sense of 'the law' as involving a more or less integrated whole is often lost when it is considered and experienced in terms of discrete 'modules' or 'units' of study. There have been attempts to achieve better coherence across the curriculum through the use of 'capstone' courses, which seek to '"bring together" students' fragmented knowledge' (Kift *et al.* 2008; see also Blackshields *et al.* 2014), but this can also be achieved as part of the study of the individual components of the degree. A corollary of a more coherent understanding of the role of the criminal law itself is a better appreciation of its importance across the curriculum and how it feeds into a broader conception of law and the legal system.

The forces that shape

Perhaps the paramount influence shaping the curriculum of the law degree derives from the stipulations of the relevant accreditation bodies (see Gledhill and Livings, ch 1), which must be met in order for a law degree to satisfy the demands of academic legal training in the respective jurisdictions. Insofar as their requirements must be met, these bodies are potentially powerful forces, but their stipulations do not have much to say about the pedagogy of the criminal law course, and their existence and content cannot explain the widespread adherence to the traditional model, except perhaps insofar as a lack of specificity may feed a complacency or an unwillingness to do something that might prove controversial (*cf.* Gans, ch 8). It should also be noted that these accreditation bodies may perpetuate a fragmented approach to legal education by prescribing content according to traditionally accepted sub-disciplinary subject boundaries. In these respects, the influence of the accreditation bodies may be disproportionate to the reality of their demands (Sanders 2014).

Another potentially powerful influence on contemporary law teaching is an embedded sense of its own pedagogical tradition. This is manifested in, and perpetuated by, the available textbooks. No doubt many academics produce their own detailed study guides or student resources, and some may even produce a textbook to meet the needs of their students (see Gans, ch 8). This latter avenue is not necessarily open to, or desired by, all teachers of criminal law in light of work schedules or a wish to write in other areas. The use of an existing textbook is therefore likely to be an important pedagogical tool for the majority, and their teaching will be influenced by the approach and coverage offered in the chosen text.

The titles and content of these texts further the view of sub-disciplinary boundaries, with the format of most doing little to suggest the potential connections across subject areas. Some criminal law textbooks have a history stretching back over many editions (see Gledhill and Livings, ch 1; Donson and O'Sullivan, ch 2). They tend to conform to the traditional approach alluded to earlier, according to which the philosophical, societal, and institutional issues that underlie the operation of the criminal law are marginalised (although *cf.* Brown *et al.* 2015; Wells and Quick 2010). These contextualising factors are usually addressed briefly in the opening chapter/s, but, as Farmer notes, the substantive coverage is confined to positivistic exposition and analysis: "The criminal-law textbook embodies the supreme positivism of the law. The moral, political and social dimensions of the law are tantalizingly raised and dismissed in a single movement in favour of grinding technical discussions of legal minutiae" (Farmer 1996, p57).

Aside from the influence of accreditation bodies and textbooks, a variety of institutional pressures may help to shape the teaching in law schools. The "integrated curriculum with articulated goals and complementary components" that Cohen advocates (2004, p1195) is a laudable aim, but developments in law degrees are not perfectly co-ordinated. They take place in response to a range of stimuli and circumstances, each of which may manifest conflicting demands. Absent the opportunity or necessity for a concerted and harmonised effort, such as the inauguration of a new programme, the 'revalidation' of an existing programme, or even the coming together of a new law school, the content and approaches of individual subjects ('modules' or 'units') are only sporadically considered from the point of view of their contribution to the broader curriculum, and then usually from a perspective that does not look much beyond the frequently generic claims of bureaucratised 'learning outcomes' and 'graduate attributes'. Even where these infrequent opportunities for diversification do arise, it appears that innovation in relation to criminal law teaching is relatively rare; as Gledhill and Livings note (ch 1), the potential for diversity across jurisdictions and as a result of a significant expansion in legal education over recent decades has not, in the majority of cases, led to a substantial divergence in practice.

Another potential influence on a criminal law course is the priorities of a particular institution, which might be formed in part by relevant 'stakeholders', including academics, students, and potential employers. The priorities within and across these groups may conflict. To be noted in this context are long-standing disagreements over the aims of academic legal education (Twining 1996); Wilson and Morris have noted that "no global 'purpose' has been articulated for the law degree" (1994, p102). For example, some might believe that the law degree should be judged chiefly in terms of its value as a step in the inexorable move to legal practice. The corollary of this would be a criminal law course tailored to the preparation for practice of those who are to be involved in the day-to-day administration of criminal justice. Whether this is best served by the dominant approach is an assumption that is challenged at numerous points throughout this volume: see, for instance, Gledhill (ch 16) on the absence of prevalent offences such as drugs and driving offences from the curriculum and Kilcommins *et al.* (ch 17) on the need to teach more regulatory crime.

A broader view of the degree as preparation for more varied avenues of employment points to the acquisition of knowledge and learning of transferrable skills that could be of use across a range of prospective careers. This has led to a recent trend (and particularly in England) for traditionally defined legal subjects to incorporate a 'skills' element (advocacy is a common choice in criminal law), which is included in order to embed a heightened level of 'employability' on the part of the student (Newbery-Jones 2015).

For others, the law degree should prioritise the development of critical thinking as part of a liberal education (see, for example, Bradney 2003). From this perspective, what is interesting and valuable about the criminal law might be the irrupting conflicts that arise from its historical and politically conflicted context, or the inevitable problems and tensions that inhere when trying to reduce normative aims to legal rules (see, for example, Farmer 1997; Norrie 2014).

Those who devise the criminal law course might plan to satisfy one or all of such aims (Oliver 1994). Despite the divergent approaches they suggest (Twining 1996), the priorities outlined earlier might converge around a general consensus in relation to teaching students to 'think like lawyers', although there is plenty of scope for disagreement over what precisely this means (Rubin Henderson 2003). When it comes to the criminal law, Child (ch 3) and Gans (ch 8) suggest that teaching students to 'think like lawyers' when it comes to the criminal law means equipping them with the tools to extrapolate from the limited set of offences studied and apply the knowledge and skills acquired to the broader spectrum of possible criminal liability. The particularism of an increasingly statute-based criminal law means that this is arguably best achieved by examining criminal law in the context of criminalisation and enforcement practices. Indeed, each of the aims referred to earlier benefits from an understanding of the context in which the criminal law operates. This is evidently true for those who pursue a liberal approach; Bradney suggests that "focusing solely on technical information produces graduates who are nothing more than semi-intelligent dictionaries" (2003, p97). It is equally important when it comes to inculcating transferrable skills and is fundamental to understanding the practice of law. As Easteal writes, "effective legal practice . . . requires an understanding of the societal context in which the law is practised, and such an understanding is not easily imparted by the traditional approach to teaching law" (2008, p163).

Missed context, missed opportunity

The external and intra-institutional pressures described earlier may help to explain an apparent pedagogical inertia when it comes to teaching criminal law. Intellectual movements such as 'law and society' and 'critical legal studies' have fuelled an appreciation of the possibilities that exist in a broader and more inclusive approach to the criminal law, but this has not led to an abandonment of the traditional approach. In 1998, Bradney described the "academic doctrinal project which has dominated United Kingdom university law schools for most of their history, the attempt to explain law solely through the internal evidence offered by judgements and statutes", as "entering its final death throes" (p71). But it is far from clear that this will occur in the near future; Loughnan points to a resurgence of traditional teaching methods as a result of political, logistical, and financial pressures (ch 13).

Alldridge noted that "the uncertainty of the real world leads the traditional course to seek refuge in the security of formalism", and attributed this paucity of ambition to "conservatism and indolence" (1990, p40). It might also be symptomatic of an academically constrained 'comfort zone' on the part of those who teach criminal law; in charting what he termed the "decline of law as an autonomous discipline", Posner points to "the decline of lawyers' self-confidence . . . due partly to the rise of other disciplines to positions where they can rival the law's claim to privileged insight into its subject matter" (1987, p769). Retreating into a narrow doctrinal interpretation of the criminal law, therefore, brings a sense of security created through the construal of "a discipline whose boundaries are clear and narrow", whereby "[n]ew information can easily be slotted into the existing framework. Students can be confronted by omniscience" (Alldridge 1990, p46). The 'omniscience' of Alldridge's caricature is of course illusory, whichever learning outcome is sought; a more productive approach to learning "involves seeing law as a phenomenon located in society and history, interconnected with other political and cultural institutions and the subject of philosophical theories and debates" (Johnstone 1992, p22).

The abstraction of the traditional model is evident in the treatment of its source material. According to the doctrinal approach, appellate judgments are the principal lens through which the rule system of the criminal law is viewed and constructed. This can present a distorted view when it comes to criminal law regimes that are either increasingly codified, or at least derive largely from statute (see Crofts and Tarrant, ch 7; Gans, ch 8; Leeming 2013), but an examination of cases remains axiomatic to the study of the criminal law in jurisdictions such as England and NSW (though *cf.* the views of Walker 2009). They are used in order to generate a (more or less universalisable) rule in respect of the elements of particular offences; many examples could be offered: the line of cases culminating in *R v Woollin* [1999] AC 82 demonstrates the potential scope of 'intention', the alternative versions of recklessness previously offered under *R v Cunningham* [1957] 2 QB 396 and *R v Caldwell* [1982] AC 341 are now seemingly resolved in favour of the subjective formulation employed by the House of Lords in *R v G* [2003] UKHL 50, *R v Ghosh* [1982] QB 1053 provides a pragmatic but complex test for dishonesty in theft/larceny, and *Royall v R* [1991] HCA 27 stands as authority for the alternative tests for causation. Alldridge (1990) points to such cases as constituting 'the canon' when it comes to criminal law, and from their various rationes decidendi, rules are derived and schemata of the respective offences constructed.

Under this approach, the enquiry relies upon a positivistic conception of the criminal law that overstates its coherence and political neutrality, and anything that can challenge this is excluded in order that the criminal law can be "presented to the student as a sealed, self-authenticating unity" (Alldridge 1990, p41). The inherent artificiality of the picture that results is reflected in the 'problem questions' that are typically central to criminal law teaching and assessment, which must be drafted in such a way as to isolate the legal issues under examination from their broader operational and institutional context. It can be argued that this approach inculcates an analytical way of thinking and encourages the student to 'think like a lawyer' in piecing together the various technical requirements that need to be fulfilled in order to establish liability, but attempting to confer and develop an understanding of the criminal law solely by reference to an assemblage of stated rules harvested from a range of appellate judgments presents a myopic and somewhat abstract view of its operation.

This approach to parsing appellate judgments potentially has a number of deleterious effects. Criminal law is often taught as an early part of a law degree; the subject is seen as accessible and interesting and a good means by which to stimulate discussion and harness the enthusiasm of newly enrolled law students (see Fitzpatrick, ch 5; Jackson and Kerrigan, ch 10). The textbooks, and indeed those involved in teaching the subject, are likely to make the point that the criminal law is a pervasive influence in social life, which hints at a contextualisation that may provide a useful vehicle for introducing legal method and analysis. The accessibility of the subject means that it may also be perceived as 'easier' than some of the supposedly drier topics found on the degree. As Farmer (1995) implies, however, the 'grinding' doctrinal approach impoverishes the syllabus, since it presents an unrealistic picture. This is bound to inhibit learning, as students cannot harness their own intuition and experience of the organisation of the world to understand the peculiar doctrinal and institutional arrangements of the criminal law; as Twining points out, much learning about law takes place away from the law school (1995). The abstract nature of the approach may lead to a dissonance in the learning experience of those students who also study what might reasonably be seen as complementary disciplines, such as the social sciences (the pairing of law and criminology, for example, is relatively common in NSW). It also fails to capitalise on the intuitive appeal of the subject matter; for Bradney, "there can be little doubt that the essential aridity of doctrinal study has a disabling effect on most of those who are subject to it" (1998, p76; see also Scraton and Stannard, ch 11).

Perhaps more importantly, this abstraction detaches the study of criminal law from some of the more pressing and interesting aspects of its operational actuality. For example, a *'Woollin* direction' is a rare event, and when it comes to the question of how to construe intention, the criminal justice system more usually proceeds in the shadow of evidential difficulties. Similarly, consideration of those partial defences which have their roots in 'provocation' (now known as 'loss of control' and 'extreme provocation' in England and NSW, respectively) lends itself to analysis and critique according to their historical role as 'concessions to human frailty' (see, for example, Horder 1992), but they tend to be examined chiefly in terms of the internal arrangement of subjective and objective requirements.

This narrow focus excludes consideration of important policy questions, such as the way in which the criminal law should respond to vulnerability or social marginalisation on the part of victims and/or perpetrators (see Tolmie, ch 15). It also ignores institutional arrangements, such as the requirement for the prosecution to be able to build a case that can discharge its proof burden, the range of alternative legal or regulatory mechanisms that might be preferable to the use of the criminal law, or manifold other considerations that must be borne in mind when the application of the criminal law is considered in its broader context. For instance, understanding the social and institutional backdrop against which sexual offences are committed and then processed through the criminal justice system, from complaint through to disposal and offender-management, is essential to understanding the criminal law's response to them. Although the practicalities of policing and the question of evidential inadequacy, for example, may come up in discussion when it comes to the apparently over-broad technical application of the dishonest appropriation ('asportation' in NSW) standard employed in theft (larceny in NSW), the role of case examination is not usually to site the criminal law in any context beyond that needed in order to demonstrate the black-letter operation of the rule in question.

Context and connection

Given the importance of context to a realistic portrayal of the criminal law, the question becomes how best to incorporate it. An expansive, contextualised vision of the criminal law might be hampered by competing demands for space on the curriculum. There is a temptation to surrender to the 'tyranny of coverage', an internalised pressure to cover as much of the substantive law as is possible (O'Shea 2004). In his advocation of law as a liberal education, however, Bradney notes:

> [time] in a curriculum is finite. If the students are to both acquire a technical learning and an awareness of values and structures they will have to learn less technical information than they would have done if they had just focused on that.
>
> (2003, p97)

Heeding Bradney's advice is perhaps inevitable to a degree, but not succumbing to the 'tyranny of coverage' is only part of the solution. As well as the available space, pragmatic limitations may come from the resistance of some students, who just want to 'know the law' (see Crowe 2011), or who are not already familiar enough with a particular theoretical perspective to understand its potential value; this might precipitate what Crowe terms a "descent into nihilism" (2011, p67).

The rich and diverse history of 'law in context' scholarship engenders a degree of ambiguity when the term is used to characterise an approach to teaching (see Loughnan, ch 13). It can connote a pedagogy whereby the 'context' derives from a range of sources, such as the use of politico-philosophical theory, empirical social science data, or an understanding of the institutional backdrop against which the law operates. In this chapter, I suggest that making connections with other sub-disciplinary areas can provide an intuitive and straightforward sense of context for the criminal law. In advocating this relatively modest means by which to appraise the function of the criminal law, I do not wish to undervalue the importance of 'deeper' perspectives. Law has been described as a 'parasitic discipline' (Bradney 1998); it is, and should be, open to examination from a range of theoretical and interdisciplinary perspectives. The examination of criminal law from the standpoint of a developed and coherent theoretical lens (for example, feminism) has much to offer in deconstructing and challenging the criminal law's claims to neutrality, but each perspective can only provide a partial account. The criminal law is the product of multiple and competing socio-political forces. Whilst the traditional approach is undoubtedly susceptible to criticism on the basis that it is intellectually or contextually incomplete, those who adopt alternative approaches need to be wary of also not providing partial accounts, especially in light of the constraints imposed by the available space on the curriculum.

Numerous areas of the legal curriculum, both substantive and procedural, can provide material pertinent to the study of criminal law and augment the traditional criminal law course so as to provide students with a less abstract way of viewing the role and function of the criminal law. Here I offer the example of the criminal law's treatment of violence on the sports field, as seen through the English Court of Appeal case of *R v Barnes* [2004] 1 WLR 910, which concerned an appeal on the part of a footballer convicted of an offence under s 20 of the Offences Against the Person Act 1861. This case is likely to receive extended treatment on a sports law course, where it serves as a statement of the law in relation to consensual harm and thus the lawfulness of contact sports. At a deeper level, it illustrates the way in which legal rules are interpreted so as to accommodate sports practices, against the backdrop of a sophisticated system of rules and regulation; what some have termed a 'lex sportiva' (Beloff 2005).

In this short judgment, a number of issues central to the criminal law, and to the administration of criminal justice, are raised. At its heart, the *Barnes* judgment is a simple policy declaration that certain sports in which there is a risk of injury are lawful notwithstanding this, and therefore those who participate in 'legitimate sport' are not acting unlawfully. The way in which this is expressed doctrinally is by way of an offence/defence paradigm according to which prima facie offences of violence are vitiated where the defence of consent is available and applicable (following the House of Lords judgment in *R v Brown* [1994] 1 AC 212). As such, the case is useful to a criminal law course on a number of levels. These include a demonstration of a number of aspects of substantive criminal law, particularly as they relate to offences against the person: mens rea principles (particularly recklessness), causation, and the defence of consent, including the influence of policy reasoning.

Understanding the criminal law in areas which depend heavily upon public policy considerations can present a challenge to students. Midson (2010) emphasises the importance of context in order to negotiate the 'invisible factors' that underpin the articulation of the principles of causation, and this is also true when it comes to the lawfulness of consensual harm. In examining the availability and limits of consent in relation to offences against the person, the focus in textbooks and in criminal law teaching is likely to be on the leading case of *Brown*, which derived from the prosecution of a number of men engaged in sado-masochism: the House of Lords held that consent was a defence to (sometimes serious) harm, where it was during the course of 'lawful activities' such as surgery, tattooing and piercing, and contact sports.

The judgment in *Brown* stretches to over 60 pages and encompasses conflicted opinions on the part of the five Law Lords that can take a long time to dissemble. In some respects, the salacious subject matter might be considered ideal for engaging students, but it can polarise opinion and some may be uncomfortable offering personal views on sexual matters. These visceral responses are potentially valuable and may help prepare students for the realities of legal practice (Townes O'Brien 2014, p61), but, as Brown and Murray (ch 4) note, they can also hold students back. By contrast, *Barnes* is a more concise judgment (12 pages), given by Lord Woolf alone, and is concerned with the commission of an activity (football) the existence of which few would consider controversial. These factors make profitable discussion of the way in which the doctrines of the criminal law are made to serve the normative demands of public policy much easier.

Aside from its usefulness in illustrating doctrine, and particularly the public policy rationale behind the availability and operation of the defence of consent, *Barnes* presents an opportunity for a consideration of the broader social and institutional context in which the criminal law is played out, as it takes place against the well-developed ethical and regulatory framework of competitive sport. Giving judgment, Lord Woolf considered the "heart of the question" to be "when it is appropriate for criminal proceedings to be instituted after an injury is caused to one player by another player in the course of a sporting event" (p912). In addressing this, Lord Woolf held:

> the starting point is the fact that most organised sports have their own disciplinary procedures for enforcing their particular rules and standards of

conduct. As a result, in the majority of situations there is not only no need for criminal proceedings, it is undesirable that there should be any criminal proceedings. Further, in addition to a criminal prosecution, there is the possibility of an injured player obtaining damages in a civil action from another player, if that other player caused him injuries through negligence or an assault . . . a criminal prosecution should be reserved for those situations where the conduct is sufficiently grave to be properly categorised as criminal.

(pp912–13)

The judgment therefore acknowledges the pluralistic legal context in which the criminal law here operates and the tortious and regulatory alternatives that inform the decision as to whether prosecution is appropriate.

The particular ethical and regulatory framework of sport provides a useful setting against which to examine the criminal law, but there are a number of other areas which also provide fertile territory. For instance, the practice of medicine is underpinned by the fundamental principles of medical ethics (usually described as involving a balance of autonomy, beneficence, nonmaleficence, and justice; Gillon 1994) and a similarly well-developed regulatory system. Assisted dying is another area that can enable cross-curricular contextualisation of a subject that naturally invokes consideration of the underlying ethical and sociopolitical issues. The House of Lords case of *R (Purdy) v DPP* [2009] UKHL 45 comprises a particularly useful resource and highlights the importance of prosecutorial discretion to the operation of the criminal law. There are also promising possibilities to be explored in the area of white-collar crime and the regulation of corporations.

Conclusion

An enduring adherence to the traditional doctrinal approach criticised by Alldridge over 25 years ago may be attributed to a number of causes. The requirements of the accreditation bodies that mandate the study of criminal law as a justifiably important part of the law degree are not particularly prescriptive in terms of content, but they do little to encourage divergence or imagination in teaching. Beyond this, a number of other, more or less subtle factors may also feed a degree of pedagogical inertia and serve to reify an accepted way of doing things, such as the expectations and demands of the various 'stakeholders', the centripetal force exerted by the criminal law texts, and an innate conservatism amongst those who teach criminal law. This might stem from a Langdellian belief in a legal science that can be isolated from its social and political context (Chase 1979), or a desire to construe a narrow field of enquiry as a means of excluding potentially limitless material that could take the academic outside of his or her 'comfort zone'.

In this chapter, I have argued that context is a vital means by which to enliven criminal law and enable a more thorough understanding of the subject. A straightforward means by which to introduce this is by harnessing topics that cross ostensible subject boundaries, such as those that might more readily be associated with sports, medical, or corporate law. As well as enhancing student understanding of the criminal law itself, this appreciation of its role and function also helps to facilitate an understanding of its connections with other parts of the legal curriculum. For instance, an examination of the *Barnes* judgment can provide a focus for considerations of the structural elements of the substantive criminal law, as well as acting as a discussion point for the legitimate scope of criminalisation against a pluralistic regulatory and legal backdrop.

References

Alldridge, P, 'What's Wrong with the Traditional Criminal Law Course?' (1990) 10 *Legal Studies* 38.
Beloff, M, 'Is There a Lex Sportiva?' (2005) 5 *International Sports Law Review* 49.
Blackshields, D et al. (eds), *Integrative Learning: International Research and Practice* (Routledge, 2014).
Bradney, A, 'Law as a Parasitic Discipline' (1998) 25 *Journal of Law and Society* 71.
Bradney, A, *Conversation, Choices and Chances: The Liberal Law School in the Twenty-First Century* (Hart, 2003).
Brown, D et al., *Criminal Laws: Materials and Commentary on Criminal Law and Process of New South Wales* (The Federation Press, 2015).
Chase, A, 'The Birth of the Modern Law School' (1979) 23 *The American Journal of Legal History* 329.
Cohen, NP, 'Teaching Criminal Law: Curing the Disconnect' (2004) 48 *St Louis University Law Journal* 1195.
Crowe, J, 'Reasoning from the Ground Up: Some Strategies for Teaching Theory to Law Students' (2011) 21 *Legal Education Review* 49.
Easteal, P, 'Teaching about the Nexus between Law and Society: From Pedagogy to Andragogy' (2008) 18 *Legal Education Review* 163.
Farmer, L, 'The Obsession with Definition: The Nature of Crime and Critical Legal Theory' (1996) 5 *Social and Legal Studies* 57.
Farmer, L, *Criminal Law, Tradition and Legal Order – Crime and the Genius of Scots Law 1747 to the Present* (Cambridge University Press, 1997).
Gillon, R, 'Medical Ethics: Four Principles Plus Attention to Scope' (1994) 309 (6948) *British Medical Journal* 184.
Hepple, B, 'The Renewal of the Liberal Law Degree' (1996) 55 *Cambridge Law Journal* 470.
James, N, 'The Good Law Teacher: The Propagation of Pedagogicalism in Australian Legal Education' (2004) 27 (1) *University of New South Wales Law Journal* 147.
Johnstone, R, 'Rethinking the Teaching of Law' (1992) 3 (1) *Legal Education Review* 17.
Kift, S, Field, R and Wells, I, 'Promoting Sustainable Professional Futures for Law Graduates through Curriculum Renewal in Legal Education: A Final Year Experience (FYE2)' (2008) 15 (2) *eLaw Journal* 145.
Leeming, M, 'Theories and Principles Underlying the Development of the Common Law – The Statutory Elephant in the Room' (2013) 36 *University of New South Wales Law Journal* 1002.
Midson, B, 'Teaching Causation in Criminal Law: Learning to Think Like Policy Analysts' (2010) 20 *Legal Education Review* 109.

Newbery-Jones, C, 'Trying to Do the Right Thing: Experiential Learning, e-Learning and Employability Skills in Modern Legal Education' (2015) 6 (1) *European Journal of Law and Technology*.

Norrie, A, *Crime, Reason and History* (3rd edn, Cambridge University Press, 2014).

Norton, A, Sonnemann, J and Cherastidtham, I, *Taking University Teaching Seriously* (Grattan Institute, 2013).

Oliver, D, 'Teaching and Learning Law: Pressures on the Liberal Law Degree' in P Birks (ed), *Reviewing Legal Education* (OUP, 1994).

O'Shea, P, 'The Complete Law School – Avoiding the Production of Half-Lawyers' (2004) 29 *Alternative Law Journal* 272.

Rubin Henderson, B, 'Asking the Lost Question: What Is the Purpose of Law School?' (2003) 53 *Journal of Legal Education* 48.

Sanders, A, 'Poor Thinking, Poor Outcome? The Future of the Law Degree after the Legal Education and Training Review and the Case for Socio-Legalism' in H Sommerlad others (eds), *The Futures of Legal Education and the Legal Profession* (Bloomsbury, 2014).

Twining, W, *Blackstone's Tower: The English Law School* (Sweet & Maxwell, 1994).

Twining, W, 'What Are Law Schools For?' (1995) 46 *Northern Ireland Legal Quarterly* 291.

Twining, W, 'Bureaucratic Rationalism and the Quiet (R)evolution' (1996) 7 *Legal Education Review* 291.

Walker, A, 'The Anti-Case Method: Herbert Wechsler and the Political History of the Criminal Law Course' (2009) 7 *Ohio State Journal of Criminal Law* 217.

Wells, C and Quick, O, *Lacey, Wells and Quick: Reconstructing Criminal Law* (4th edn, Cambridge University Press, 2010).

Wilson, W and Morris, G, 'The Future of the Academic Law Degree' in P Birks (ed), *Reviewing Legal Education* (OUP, 1994).

Chapter 13

Teaching and learning criminal law 'in context'

Taking 'context' seriously

Arlie Loughnan

Introduction

An informal survey of foundational criminal law courses taught in Australian law schools shows that a number of institutions state that they teach criminal law 'in context'. To take the University of Sydney as an example, our course handbook states that the criminal law course is "designed to introduce the general principles of criminal law in NSW, and to critically analyse these in their contemporary social and political context" (University of Sydney 2015). The popularity of the descriptor 'law in context' in current criminal law courses suggests that the term has positive associations, but it is not clear that all references to teaching 'in context' mean the same thing: adoption of the 'in context' mantle ranges from the casual, even rhetorical, to a more self-conscious reference to a particular pedagogical tradition. As a description of the way in which criminal law courses are taught, the 'in context' tag is capable of capturing a range of different styles and approaches (more or less reflective) to the practice of teaching law.

What is meant by 'law in context'? It is hard to pin down this evocative and talismanic term, and a review of the pedagogical and scholarly literature suggests that various terms (such as 'law and society') are used to convey similar ideas. For the purposes of this chapter, a 'law in context' approach revolves around the idea that law can only be properly or fully understood if studied *in context*, or, put another way, a 'law in context' approach entails *fidelity to context* (Selznick 2003, p181). As Chris Tomlins argues, an approach to law as 'law in context' views law not as a domain in relation to other, extrinsic domains of social life, but as constituted or defined by 'context' (Tomlins 2013, p149). While 'context' might have different meanings, I take it to convey the idea of the place or location, understood broadly to encompass the historical, cultural, political, economic, and other dimensions of a social system. The imperative to take context as constitutive or definitional in this approach extends to thinking, researching, and writing about law, as well as law teaching, and, thus, 'law in context' connotes an intellectual and/or pedagogical disposition. However, given external constraints, this disposition might be only imperfectly or incompletely realised in a particular scholarly or teaching setting.

In this chapter, I seek to make a modest contribution to ongoing and multi-faceted efforts to develop our understanding and practice of teaching criminal law 'in context'. While there is a rich array of socio-legal and other research that may be harnessed to the task of learning law, frameworks for the incorporation of that material into law curricula or law teaching have remained somewhat elusive (Steel 2013, p24). Based on a review of the pedagogical and scholarly literature, I suggest that there are four hallmarks of a pedagogical approach to criminal law that takes the idea of 'law in context' seriously. Of course, there is a range of ways in which a commitment to 'law in context' might manifest itself, and the discussion offered in this chapter is not intended to be prescriptive. Rather, it is intended to aid reflective teaching practice and to assist those criminal law lecturers, tutors, and professionals who aim to take the idea of teaching 'law in context' seriously.

The development of 'law in context' teaching in Australia

'Law in context' approaches in Australia developed against a background of the traditional 'black-letter' teaching and learning methods which featured in Australian law schools until the 1970s. In this era, although formally incorporated into the academy, legal education had not fully separated from its origins as an apprenticeship and reflected a "trade school" ethos (Steel and Schwartz 2013, p9). In Australia, law was taught primarily by practitioners offering their services while pursuing full-time careers at the bar or on the bench (Thornton 2011, p61). The theory of legal education subtending this system worked on a model of the 'transmission of frozen knowledge' – an instructor presented an expository lecture and students committed rules to memory and regurgitated them in examinations (Thornton 2011, p85) – with law treated as objective, authoritative, and stable, relatively speaking (Duncanson 1996, p80). As Ross Cranston has written, in this tradition, the typical, if unstated, context for the teaching of most areas of law extended no further than a general idea about the lawyer in the service of government or business, and the 'well-heeled John Doe' as his or her client (1978, p67).

The advent of 'law in context' teaching in Australian law schools shook this tradition and the narrow and limited idea of 'context' associated with it. The appearance of 'law in context' teaching in Australia is closely tied to the influence of the 'law and society' (also known as socio-legal studies) intellectual movement and the subsequent critical legal studies movement. The impact of these movements, which profoundly influenced both legal research and legal pedagogy, can be detected in Australia from the 1970s. Developing in different strands in the United States and United Kingdom, the law and society movement challenged law's claims to autonomy (Tomlins 2013), with an emphasis on the social, political, and economic environment in which legal principles and practices operate (Cranston 1978, p64). As Margaret Thornton writes about the 'social' in a socio-legal approach to law, it eschews "the artificial line of demarcation" between law and other spheres of life (2006, p5). The later critical legal studies movement, which advanced a view of social life as "legally – which is to say linguistically or discursively – constituted" (Tomlins 2013, pp141–42), was more avowedly critical, promoting deeper theoretical engagement and the use of interdisciplinary materials in teaching and learning law (Davies 2013). The take up of this intellectual movement has been less enthusiastic than that of law and society, but, in broad terms, it fed into the then emergent popularity of a 'law in context' approach to teaching.

The story of the development of 'law in context' teaching in Australia is also the story of the 'new' universities, such as La Trobe University and Macquarie University, which were established in the 1960s and 1970s. For example, the Legal Studies Department at La Trobe, which was created in 1972 and subsumed into a Law School in 1994, was heavily influenced by both the socio-legal studies and the critical legal studies movements (Davies 2013; Thornton 2006; Tomlins 2013). These movements were attractive in that they connected with the demands of activists and reformers in Australia, as elsewhere, who had begun to agitate for profound legal change in order to achieve social change (Davies 2008). This commitment to 'law in context' in research and teaching dovetailed closely with progressive imperatives. The 'new' law departments and schools adopted subjects reflecting social rather than legal phenomena (Cranston 1978, p66) and embraced innovative methods of teaching law (Davies 2013, pp53–5). Specific initiatives included clinical legal education as well as methods to embrace 'student-centred learning' and encourage critique, reflection, and dialogue between teacher and students in small interactive seminars (Davies 2008; Thornton 2011).

The move to 'student-centred learning' renewed emphasis on contextual or social dimensions of law studies. Around the time the Commonwealth Tertiary Education Commission report (the Pearce Report) into legal education in Australia was published in 1987, "broader social perspectives" were regular features of the curriculum (Steel 2013, p9). Nonetheless, the Pearce Report concluded that Australian law schools were too narrow and rule-oriented, and it recommended that all law schools consider the attention they paid to theoretical and critical perspectives on law (Pearce, Campbell and Harding 1987, p57). While, it seems that, by critique, the Report meant critical thinking as one aspect of 'thinking like a lawyer' rather than a broader "sociopolitical form of critique" (James 2004a, p384), it is clear that a wider view of law teaching and legal education had come to the fore. By the last decade of the twentieth century, legal education in Australia combined doctrine, practical skills classes, and academic approaches to law (Thornton 2011, p62). This period has been described as the era of the 'liberal law degree' – in which critical interdisciplinary perspectives and insights from the humanities and social sciences were embedded in legal pedagogy to encourage "the development of well-rounded lawyers" (Thornton 2011, p63).

The formulation in 1992 of the 'Priestley 11', and its gradual implementation across the law curriculum, as a national accreditation standard for law graduates, represented a step away from the liberal approach described above. The 'Priestley 11', now incorporated into the *Legal Profession Uniform Admission Rules 2015* (Rule 5 (1)(c)), emphasises legal *content*, not context, and, in effect, structures the law curriculum as a set of discrete doctrinal areas. The focus is on traditional areas of knowledge, not on graduate attributes or skills (Keyes and Johnstone 2004, p544). Although the method of teaching law remains open, method must serve content, and it is notable that, as evidenced by the 'Priestley 11', the legal profession exercises a profound and perhaps growing influence over the law curriculum (Keyes and Johnstone 2004, p555).

At the same time as the 'Priestley 11' has been bedded down in Australian law schools, the tertiary sector has undergone radical change. The last two decades has seen the rise of the neo-liberal university in Australia, according to which universities are increasingly corporatised and managerialist and run along business lines (Thornton 2011). This has altered the cast of legal research and education (Bartie 2014). Pursuant to policies of deregulation and removal of public funding, the number of law schools in Australia, the number of law students enrolled in them, and the fees those students are paying, has burgeoned. Within law schools, there has been a shift away from "radical critique and the social" in favour of "the technocratic and the applied" (Thornton 2011, p80). Renewed emphasis has been given to vocational training for legal practice. This change has coincided with a return to the 'passive pedagogy' – lectures and exams – of the past, as pressures of student numbers and academic research productivity requirements make multiple small-group seminars a luxury (Thornton 2006, p14; Thornton 2011, pp86–87).

These conditions have placed pressure on institutional commitments to a 'law in context' approach to teaching. The popularity of the descriptor in current criminal law course syllabus and law school marketing materials suggests that the term continues to have positive associations, but it is clear that it does not denote a particular approach to teaching criminal law. Indeed, as a descriptor, 'law in context' moves between different associations – the applied study of criminal law principles on one hand, or a critical approach to criminal legal doctrine on the other hand (or perhaps even a more diffuse idea of *über* law – law *plus* context, more bang for the law student buck). Under current conditions, the ambiguity about the ethos of 'law in context' teaching – whether it connotes a critical or a practical emphasis – seems to have ensured its survival. A focus on practical learning as well as applied knowledge and skills is in ascendancy in the current era and underscores the idea that law schools should serve the practising profession (Thornton 2011, p81). In part based on the ambiguity about the ethos of 'law in context' teaching, recognition of 'law in context' teaching persists, even if only at the level of rhetoric.

Taking teaching and learning criminal law 'in context' seriously

What does it mean to take the teaching of criminal law 'in context' seriously? Just as there are different methods and analytical techniques that inform 'law in context' research (Charlesworth 2007), so there are different ways of embracing a 'law in context' approach to teaching. As mentioned above, commitment to a 'law in context' approach is an intellectual and/or pedagogical disposition. Without adopting an overly prescriptive approach to teaching criminal law 'in context' (Steel 2013), it is possible to sketch out the hallmarks of such an approach. Based on a review of the pedagogical and scholarly literature, I suggest that there are four hallmarks of this approach: providing students with a conceptual apparatus for critically assessing legal principles and practices, demonstrating a historical sensibility, taking into account criminal law's institutional framework (encompassing but extending beyond criminal procedure and evidence), and including multidisciplinary perspectives on legal topics. I examine each of these in turn.

First, the foundation of a 'law in context' approach to criminal law teaching is the introduction of a conceptual apparatus that permits students to develop a language to critically assess legal principles and practices (Havemann 1995, p143). This language might encompass concepts of class, race or ethnicity, Indigeneity, and gender and ability, as well as social institutions, such as the economy and the family (Havemann 1995, p143). It is this language that permits students to understand the significance of context(s). As Alex Steel writes in his 2013 Good Practice Guide, prepared for the *Australian Learning and Teaching Council* (ALTC), there are multiple 'contexts' relevant to the study of law. These include 'commercial/business', 'cultural and linguistic', 'Indigenous', 'political', 'law reform', 'environment/sustainability', and 'disability/impairment' (Steel 2013, pp14–6). A conceptual apparatus ensures that students do not merely 'add' 'context' to the study of law, or assume 'contexts' are determinative of particular legal arrangements (Selznick 2003, p180). Further, developing a conceptual apparatus for critical study fosters reflexivity. Law students are not only empowered to 'read' the social order but also to understand their own role in it (Havemann 1995, pp138–39).

Demonstrating a historical sensibility is the second hallmark of a 'law in context' approach. It is a truism that law is a historicised practice, but, with the pressures generated by external factors, such as semesterisation, this awareness may reduce to a rough chronology of case law and statute. While criminal law textbooks typically begin with the definition of crime, crime is not something that is fixed (Farmer 1996). As Lindsay Farmer argues, when viewed historically, crime was defined by the development of stricter procedural rules, with jurisdiction coming to be determined not according to geographic space but according to procedure (1996, p65). The introduction of material to demonstrate historical sensibility assists students in appreciating change over time, and, when combined with use of extra-legal sources such as films, invites students to engage with law on an emotional as well as cognitive level (Miller and DiMatteo 2012, p164). In Australia (and elsewhere), a crucial part of historical sensibility is attention to the reality of colonisation and the post-colonial nature of settler societies (Havemann 1995, p148–49; Steel and Schwartz 2013, pp19–20), as well as the effects of the criminal justice system on Indigenous people. In relation to criminal law, this aspect of 'context' is essential for a 'located' or 'placed' grasp of the law.

A considered regard for the law's institutional framework constitutes the third hallmark of a 'law in context' approach. In relation to criminal law, this involves taking into account rules of evidence and procedure that determine how particular laws operate (Brown *et al.* 2015, p4) and appreciating the role of factors such as the discretion exercised by police and prosecution prior to trial (Brown *et al.* 2015, v), as well as considering penal practices governing punishment post-conviction. However, taking the criminal law's institutional framework into account requires looking beyond the bounds of the criminal justice system. Positive law – rules, regulations, cases and statutes, typically assumed to be 'real' law – is only part of the larger and less unified 'legal order' – "positive law plus its premises, institutions and sustaining culture" – that comes into view when a 'law in context' approach is taken seriously (Selznick 2003, pp178–79). Here relevant considerations might include the existence of professionalised legal practitioners, an independent judiciary, and principles of public justice. In already full criminal law curricula, it is not possible to incorporate all aspects of the criminal law's institutional framework, but sketching it out will go a significant way towards 'contextualising' criminal law principles and practices.

Use of materials from other disciplines is the fourth and final hallmark of a 'law in context' approach. Materials from different disciplines permit law students to develop a theory of relevant context(s) for instance, of the interaction of different spheres of social life. Research in criminology, sociology, and psychology, for example, can inform a richer and more nuanced understanding of the operation of criminal law and criminal justice institutions (Brown *et al.* 2015, p6). In addition, social scientific disciplinary material informs a 'deep' approach to criminal law, enabling students to appreciate the social policy implications of law and legal change and to develop analytical skills (Miller and DiMatteo 2012, p160). More broadly, materials from other disciplines are vital in facilitating students' appreciation of the way in which legal principles (such as the rule of law or the presumption of innocence) are inflected by extant power imbalances and social inequalities. Just as importantly, these materials assist students in recognising the situated nature of knowledge and the limits of legal ways of thinking about the world.

Taken together, these four hallmarks of a 'law in context' approach to teaching criminal law provide a safeguard against inculcating an overly narrow and limited understanding of criminal law among law students. Such a narrow understanding would be characterised by a relatively abstract and abstracted consideration of legal principle, with exceptions to such principles (such as strict liability offences in the context of the primacy of subjectivism) being marginalised or even disregarded altogether. This sort of approach is problematic in that it comes to represent and feed into a Whiggish treatment of the development of the criminal law as an ever-greater refinement of conceptually coherent guiding principles for judges and legislators. The criminal law is not a wholly rational enterprise (Farmer 1996), and it is not possible to fully grasp it if it is approached in an abstract way, as something like a practical application of liberal political philosophy (Lacey 2013). A 'law in context' approach promises a more sophisticated treatment of criminal law principles and practices by taking into account change and contingency and allowing for incoherence and inconsistency across the field (or fields) and at any one point in time.

Case study: 'Contextualising' mental incapacity in criminal law

By comparison with offences (such as homicide and sexual assault) and defences (such as provocation), mental incapacity is not typically subject to a significant degree of 'contextualisation' in foundational criminal law courses, although that context is crucially important in understanding the development, rationale, and operation of this area of criminal law. Recognising the need to develop material that provides frameworks for teaching law 'in context' (Steel 2013, p24), this case study applies the four hallmarks of a 'law in context' approach, outlined previously, to the insanity/mental illness defence.

As mentioned above, 'law in context' demands the introduction of a conceptual apparatus that permits students to develop a language to critically assess legal principles and practices. In relation to mental incapacity, the key concepts are hybrid medical, legal, and social concepts (such as disease, disorder, incapacity, and ability/disability). In criminal law, 'mental incapacity' refers to an impairment in the cognitive, moral, and volitional capacities that criminal law assumes and requires (see Loughnan 2012). It is generally thought about as a subset of defences (with procedural provisions such as unfitness to plead included alongside insanity/mental illness, for instance), but we can query whether the concept of defence – something that is assumed to be in the accused's interest to raise – is the most apt concept here. Recognising the various roles of mental incapacity provisions in criminal law – including, I suggest, an inculpatory role (that is, a role in enabling individuals to be convicted of criminal offences) – may lead us to question the seductive story that the development of this area of the law has been a concession to the needs of people with mental disorders and other conditions (Loughnan 2012). The language used in this area of criminal law – in particular, the stigmatising language of 'insanity' – and the legal and popular assumptions made about the relations between mental illness and crime demands a careful and reflective approach in the criminal law classroom.

Another hallmark of a 'law in context' approach involves demonstrating an historical sensibility. This is particularly significant when it comes to mental incapacity – an arena marked by a long-standing common law defence (insanity/mental illness) and only recent statutory additions (such as diminished responsibility/substantial impairment). In NSW, the insanity defence was renamed the defence of mental illness in the 1990s (see Mental Health (Forensic Provisions) Act 1990 NSW). Behind the complex web of statutory provisions now governing the operational and procedural aspects of the defence, the substantive 'test' for insanity continues to be governed by the common law, and, specifically, the *M'Naghten Rules*, formulated in 1843 (*M'Naghten's Case* (1843) 10 Cl & Fin 200). These *Rules* provide a three-part test: that an individual suffer from a "defect of reason", which is caused by a "disease of the mind", and result in he or she not knowing the "nature and quality" of the act or that it was wrong. How is it possible that this rather ancient case still determines the test for insanity, given the myriad of legal and medical advances in the period since then? Elsewhere, I argue that the combination of three factors – the manner in which the *Rules* were created, the use of terms of art within the *Rules*, and their dependency on the special verdict which ties successful use of the insanity defence to disposition – together with a lack of political will to enact reform – explain the durability of *M'Naghten*, despite its well-recognised limitations (Loughnan 2016).

Taking into account the institutional framework of law is the third hallmark of a 'law in context' approach. Here, this framework is dominated by the historical practice of subjecting people with mental incapacity who were alleged to have committed criminal offences to indefinite detention, either in prisons or hospitals. As is well known, in Australian jurisdictions (and elsewhere), the forensic mentally ill, also known as 'criminal lunatics' or the 'criminally insane', have long been subject to detention following the successful use of the insanity/mental illness defence. The development of a particular procedural device – the special verdict, 'not guilty by reason of insanity' – reflects a policy concern with marking out those defendants who are to be subject to the special coercive powers of the state from those who are either to be acquitted or convicted through the normal processes of the criminal law (Mackay 1995). Indefinite detention was based on remarkably durable beliefs about the 'dangerousness' and 'abnormality' of mentally disordered people charged with criminal offences. More recently, detention has been complemented by other disposal options that provide for coercion short of a denial of liberty, but a notion of 'dangerousness' subsists. As the NSW Law Reform Commission recognises, "the modern defence of mental illness" is grounded in "recognition of impaired mental functioning as an excuse from criminal responsibility" and "protection of the community through detention of those, who, because of their mental illness, pose a threat to themselves or others" (NSW Law Reform Commission 2010, CP 6 [3.5]).

The institutional framework for insanity/mental illness has influenced legal developments. In part because of the restricted disposal consequences of a successful insanity/mental illness verdict, historically, the defence has been more likely to be raised in serious criminal trials, such as homicide trials. This has meant that the jurisprudence of the mental illness defence has developed in the context of such trials, skewing the legal profile of claims to exculpation on the basis of mental illness and influencing the kind of issues that form part of legal inquiry (for example, whether a particular clinical condition is "prone to reoccur" and thus likely to constitute a "disease of the mind" per the *M'Naughten Rules*). In addition, in part in response to the problems with the defence of mental illness, a partial defence of diminished responsibility (now called substantial impairment) was introduced into NSW. After reformulation in the 1990s (via the Crimes Amendment (Diminished Responsibility) Act 1997), the NSW law of substantial impairment provides that a person who would otherwise be guilty of murder will not be convicted of it if, at the time of the killing, his or her capacity to understand events, or judge whether actions are right or wrong, or control himself or herself was "substantially impaired" by an "abnormality of mind" arising from an "underlying condition" (s23A(1)(a) Crimes Act 1900 NSW). But this defence has had its own problems – particularly around the pathologisation of what might otherwise be regarded as rational behavior (such as responding to domestic violence) – that track not only varying police and prosecution practices, but also, more broadly, changing social attitudes to violence.

The fourth and final hallmark of a 'law in context' approach is the overlay of multidisciplinary perspectives on legal topics. In relation to mental incapacity, a medical *Weltanschauung* or worldview is one such important perspective. The hybrid nature of the key concepts in this part of the criminal law terrain, mentioned earlier, hints at the significance of expert medical knowledge (and especially psychiatric and psychological knowledge). Expert medical perspectives– on the clinical features of particular conditions, and on prognoses and treatment options, for instance – loom large over criminal law and its procedural and penal analogues. Yet this dominance has been subject to challenge. The rise of disability activism and disability studies has encouraged the growth of new perspectives on mental illness and other conditions as they play out in criminal law and practice (see Steele and Thomas 2014). These perspectives add critical voices to those of feminist scholars and activists, who have critiqued the way in which women defendants are constructed through this part of criminal law (see e.g. Allen 1987). Looking forward, it is likely that the insanity/mental illness defence, and the *M'Naghten Rules* in particular, will have to be amended in light of developments in international human rights law – in particular Article 12 of the United Nations *Convention on the Rights of Persons with Disabilities*, which guarantees equal protection before the law, and problematises disability-specific criminal laws (Bartlett 2012). It is this area of law that will guide the future development of the law of insanity and mental incapacity more broadly.

Conclusion

In the era of the neo-liberal university, it is easy to feel despondent about the exciting, even radical, potential of a 'law in context' approach to teaching. 'Law in context' is not an innocent idea (Selznick 2003, p178), but, under current conditions, it seems vulnerable to an evacuation of all substantive meaning. Legal education in Australia is now structured across multiple different discourses, including doctrinalism, corporatism, and vocationalism (James 2004a). It is not possible (nor perhaps desirable) to subordinate all to a 'law in context' approach, howsoever interpreted. But, recognising the limits of already full curricula, and the constraints of the 'Priestley 11', it is still possible to take the notion of teaching criminal law 'in context' seriously. The enhancement to student learning gained from 'in context' teaching of criminal law principles makes a serious effort towards doing so imperative. Reinvigorating descriptors commonly given to foundational criminal law courses – ensuring the label 'in context' genuinely means something – is a step in the right direction.

References

Allen, H 1987 *Justice Unbalanced: Gender, Psychiatry and Judicial Decisions* Open University Press, Milton Keynes, Philadelphia, England.

Bartie, S 2014 'Towards a History of Law as an Academic Discipline', *Melbourne University Law Review* vol. 38, no. 2, pp444–481.

Bartlett, P 2012 'The United Nations Convention on the Rights of Persons with Disabilities and Mental Health Law', *The Modern Law Review*, vol. 75, no. 5, pp752–778.

Brown, D, Farrier, D, McNamara, L, Steel, A, Grewcock, M, Quilter, J & Schwarz, M 2015 *Criminal Laws: Materials and Commentary on Criminal Law and Process of New South Wales*, 6th edn, The Federation Press, Annandale, NSW.

Charlesworth, L 2007 'On Historical Contextualisation: Some Critical Socio-Legal Reflections', *Crimes and Misdemeanours*, vol. 1, no. 1, pp1–40.

Cranston, R 1978 'Law and Society: A Different Approach to Legal Education', *Monash University Law Review*, vol. 5, no. 1, pp54–69.

Davies, S 2008 'Better Off Not Knowing? Power, Knowledge and the Limits of Legal Education', *Australian Journal of Gender and Law*, vol. 1, no. 1, pp1–13.

Davies, S 2013 'From Law to "Legal Consciousness": A Socio-Legal Pedagogical Expedition', *Law in Context*, vol. 29, no. 2, pp42–58.

Duncanson, I 1996 'Degrees of Law: Interdisciplinarity in the Law Discipline', *Griffith Law Review*, vol. 7, pp77–103.

Farmer, L 1996 'The Obsession with Definition: The Nature of Crime and Critical Legal Theory', *Social and Legal Studies*, vol. 5, pp57–73.

Havemann, P 1995 ' "Law in Context": Taking Context Seriously', *Waikato Law Review*, vol. 3, pp137–162.

James, N 2004a 'Australian Legal Education and the Instability of Critique', *Melbourne University Law Review*, vol. 28, no. 2, pp375–405.

James, N 2004b 'Marginalisation of Radical Discourses in Australian Legal Education', *Legal Education Review*, vol. 16, pp55–74.

Keyes, M & Johnstone, R 2004 'Changing Legal Education: Rhetoric, Realty, and Prospects for the Future', *Sydney Law Review*, vol. 26, p537.

Lacey, N 2013 'Institutionalising Responsibility: Implications for Jurisprudence', *Jurisprudence*, vol. 4, no. 1, pp1–19.

Loughnan, A 2012, *Manifest Madness: Mental Incapacity in Criminal Law*, Oxford University Press, Oxford.

Loughnan, A 2016, 'M'Naghten's Case (1843)' in Philip Handler, Henry Mares and Ian Williams (eds.) *Landmark Cases: Criminal Law*, Hart Publishing, Oxford.

Mackay, R 1995 *Mental Condition Defences in Criminal Law*, Clarendon Press, Oxford.

Miller, S & DiMatteo, L 2012, 'Law in Context: Teaching Legal Studies Through the Lens of Extra-Legal Sources', *Journal of Legal Studies Education*, vol. 29, no. 2, pp155–189.

NSW Law Reform Commission 2010 *People with Cognitive and Mental Health Impairments in the Criminal Justice System*, (Consultation Papers 1–6), New South Wales Law Reform Commission, Sydney, NSW.

Pearce, D, Campbell, E & Harding, D 1987 *Australian Law Schools: A Discipline Assessment for the Commonwealth Tertiary Education Committee*, Australian Government Publishing Service, Canberra.

Selznick, P 2003 ' "Law in Context" Revisited', *Journal of Law and Society*, vol. 30, no. 2, pp177–186.

Steel, A 2013 *Good Practice Guide (Bachelor of Laws): Law in Broader Contexts*, Australian Learning and Teaching Council Threshold Learning Outcomes Good Practice Guides.

Steel, A & Schwartz, M 2013, 'Broader Social Context as a Lens for Learning: Teaching Criminal Law' in K Coleman and A Flood (eds.) *Disciplines: The Lenses of Learning*, Common Ground, Champaign, IL.

Steele, L & Thomas, S 2014 'Disability at the Periphery: Legal Theory, Disability and Criminal Law', *Griffith Law Review*, vol. 23, no. 3, pp357–369.

Thornton, M 2006 'The Dissolution of the Social in the Legal Academy', *Australian Feminist Law Journal*, vol. 25, no. 1, pp3–18.

Thornton, M 2011, *Privatising the Public University: The Case of Law*, Routledge, London.

Tomlins, C 2013 'Law "and", Law "in", Law "as": The Definition, Rejection and Recuperation of the Socio-Legal Enterprise', *Law in Context*, vol. 29, no. 2, pp137–163.

University of Sydney, Course Handbook, Faculty of Law 2015 http://sydney.edu.au/handbooks/law/undergraduate/units_of_study/compulsory_descriptions.shtml

Chapter 14

Teaching indigenous and minority students and perspectives in criminal law

Khylee Quince

> I am always the subject
> Never the artist
> Forever the antagonist
> Cos it's not even our canvas
>> (Extract from "The Colour of My Skin" by Reina Vaai, a student in my Advanced Criminal Law course 2014; reproduced with her permission)

This chapter will deal with two separate, although interrelated issues – that of teaching indigenous and minority perspectives and also teaching indigenous and minority students – i.e. teaching *about* us and teaching *for* us. It will use the experience of people in colonised countries to illustrate the value of teaching criminal law in context through the lenses of critical legal scholarship, including race theory. It allows law students the opportunity to critically analyse black-letter criminal law, which is often presented as neutral and non-contestable.

In short, this allows the deconstruction of criminal liability to show that it reflects culturally specific values, principles, and doctrines relating to notions of self, community, and the rights and obligations of citizens. Orthodox teaching of criminal law leaves an examination of these aspects and the often discriminatory application of criminal law processes to the disciplines of criminology and sociology. But presenting theories of harm and processes for dealing with it in other cultures as a part of teaching criminal law is a means of both broadening student knowledge and acknowledging the legitimacy of other epistemologies. Taking such an approach provides a platform for nuanced legal argument and effective lawyering.

In addition to content, the manner in which such material is taught is important. Teachers should be appreciative of drawing negative attention to minority groups and even consider the harm done by *failing* to mention cultural or ethnic identity of criminal actors for fear of upsetting students. In criminal law, social and economic inequalities as well as differential policing and enforcement practices may result in differential rates of apprehension, charging, conviction, and punishment between ethnic groups. Positive minority student engagement should take account of these political realities as well as different learning and communication styles and preferences between groups. For example, the signature pedagogy of law teaching, the Socratic method, places high value on an open form of inquiry in front of a large group, which is challenging to some minority cultures.

Being an indigenous teacher or student – the 'cultural sherpa': Let me show you the ways of my people...

Like every Māori law student, I have had the experience of sitting in a criminal law classroom feeling the myriad of emotions that comes from knowing that we have a particular place in the justice system. I have no doubt that this phenomenon resonates with other minority teachers of criminal law. There is a sense of shame, embarrassment, anger, frustration, and indignation at opening a casebook to see row after row of case citations featuring our names. Whereas outsiders may have no connection or give no more than a passing thought, if any, to these names, these are our relatives – brothers, fathers, cousins, uncles, aunties. These are people convicted of significant harms, of damage to families, communities – mostly our own.

The fact of our over-representation can be overlooked in taking a purely doctrinal approach to teaching criminal law. This may even be done by well-meaning teachers, who are wary of raising the spectre of race or culture and its relevance to criminal liability and punishment.

The law school classroom can serve to highlight social and economic disparities in the community. Law schools tend to attract high-achieving students, often from privileged backgrounds, mostly from non-minority communities. Over the past 30 years, the presence of minorities has been bolstered by the operation of affirmative action entry schemes. Whilst clearly aimed at long-term social good – a more diverse legal practice community who are better equipped to communicate with and represent minority clients – minority students can still feel marginalised and negatively labelled due to their status as Targeted Admission Scheme students. Anything that may draw attention to them in the classroom may therefore be risky.

As a criminal law teacher, I am no more detached from these feelings than minority students. I continue to feel the rage and despair of our entanglement in socially harmful behaviours. I am sickened by the perpetration of unspeakable violence against our women and children by our men. The legal realists told us that law is both personal and political. This is more than evident in our experience as Māori of criminal justice. I am mindful of the hurt Māori students feel at seeing and hearing of our transgressions in the sterile environment of a lecture theatre. There is also the shame at the deficit focus of the criminal system – that the person, their identity, culture, history is boiled down to elements of liability and aggravating or mitigating factors in punishment for an incident that may have occurred within the blink of an eye.

Aside from considering the reaction and turmoil of Māori (or other minority) students, how can a teacher connect to students of other identities to ensure they have appropriate knowledge and understanding of the context in which criminal law operates and how it impacts upon minority communities? First, all teachers should 'own' their privilege and status. I acknowledge my position as an academic and commentator, as well as being amongst the most privileged of my community – educated, middle class, and Māori. I appreciate the responsibility that comes with this position – to share my own life, experiences, and opinions with them and to expose the subjectivity of law.

Any minority person can recount the experience of being characterised as the 'cultural sherpa' in some context or situation; the outsider tasked with guiding the majority through a task or experience, or explaining things from a minority perspective. This can be the position of a minority scholar teaching criminal law. There are both advantages and disadvantages to being in this position. 'Insider privilege' allows you to raise often contentious matters of race, culture, and ethnicity in ways that outsiders cannot. You have the benefit of being able to describe and analyse race and culture politics from a place of lived experience, rather than as the interested anthropologist or social scientist. The corollary to this is of course being wary of not presenting your perspective as an essentialised one – the 'authentic' position as it were. This is where it is important to present your approach as a personal, subjective one.

This does not, however, mean that non-minority teachers should avoid contentious matters concerning race or minorities in criminal law. Avoiding the topic is a sin by omission. Non-minority teachers have the opportunity to model how to be mindful of the diverse nature of the student body, as well as sensitive or difficult matters that may arise in teaching content or materials. The establishment of a classroom culture that encourages and expects questions, active listening, discussions, and debates is crucial. Sometimes deferring to a minority guest lecturer may be appropriate. This also provides an opportunity to model the benefits to be gained in being exposed to multiple perspectives and their relevance to developing critical thinking and analysis. Where this is not possible, selection of materials to express diversity of perspectives is also useful, as is ensuring that you are informed about and aware of minority issues and histories.

Teaching broader social context – the relevance of ethnicity and socio-economic positioning

The fact of Māori criminality is so deeply entrenched in New Zealand legal culture that it is invariably the elephant in the room when discussing, teaching, or analysing criminal law. It is so obvious that is does not bear mentioning. In my view, this is a grave error – and effective teaching, learning, and, eventually, legal advocacy, representation, and reform requires direct confrontation of this issue.

The most significant contextual factor in New Zealand criminal law is the position of Māori, so this requires direct and deliberate acts of teaching to flesh out the factors that caused this situation. We are inextricably entangled in criminal law in New Zealand – a pattern that is replicated by other colonised indigenous and minority peoples around the globe. Although only 15% of the general population, Māori constitute approximately half of all offenders and are more likely to be apprehended, charged, and convicted than other demographic groups. In terms of punishment, Māori offenders are more likely to be subject to custodial sentences and other non-fiscal penalties. As criminal behaviour tends to occur within communities, Māori offending is most likely to be perpetuated upon ourselves, with Māori rates of victimisation far surpassing those of non-Māori and particular disparity evident in rates of intimate partner violence suffered by Māori women. (Quince 2007, pp334–35).

Our over-representation as offenders and victims is mirrored by our under-representation as lawyers, judges, law makers, and agents of enforcement. The study and practice of criminal law in New Zealand is heavily populated by Māori people – although it can be difficult to fully appreciate this in a lecture theatre overwhelmingly populated by non-Māori students being taught in a traditional format.

It is, therefore, extremely important to lay the appropriate foundation within which we can consider and evaluate the workings of our criminal justice system. Rather than leap straight into case method or discussion of legal doctrine, my first port of call in laying the groundwork for criminal law teaching is to describe the features of our system, including how the criminal law was 'received' upon colonisation by the British, usurping the existing autochthonous legal system of the tangata whenua. It is interesting that the constitutional validity of indigenous custom law is visibly contested in the domain of Public Law teaching (Angelo 2011, pp152–60), but remains invisible in orthodox criminal law teaching. In criminal law, the legitimacy of the coloniser's law is assumed, and not discussed in any teaching texts to my knowledge, and this can preclude discussion of pre-existing legal regimes.

The relevance of socio-economic positioning and marginalisation is also a crucial part of the contextual framework to illustrate the social, historical, and economic construction of criminality. Through a combination of a historical overview of the colonial process and an introduction to various criminological theories – strain/subcultural theory, Marxist and structuralist criminology, counter-colonial criminology, and the emerging field of indigenous criminology – students are exposed to some of the strands of thought that consider how we got to the present state of affairs in terms of Māori in criminal justice. These are, of course, complex and intersecting issues that may serve to connect students with studies in other disciplines, such as criminology, sociology, history, and politics.

As well as providing a fuller contextual picture in the classroom, providing students with authentic learning experiences outside of the classroom can enrich their learning and understanding of class and race in criminal justice. As part of our criminal law curriculum each year, students are required to undertake a court observation and submit a reflective write-up of their experience. One of the most commonly cited observations is the shock expressed at the racial apartheid evident in the courtroom – Pakeha (European) people are the judges, lawyers, and law enforcement agents, while brown people, predominantly Māori, are present in the dock and in the public gallery. Exposure to this everyday reality of criminal justice in New Zealand assists students in understanding the relevance of being able to understand Māori culture, values, and patterns of communication in order to provide effective advocacy or analysis of behaviours.

The dissonance between the demographics of the classroom and of the courtroom is a pattern in many (if not most) common law jurisdictions. It is certainly the case with respect to over-representation of indigenous peoples in Australia and Canada, as well as black and other ethnic minorities in the United Kingdom and other jurisdictions. It would, therefore, be a valid learning opportunity for any criminal law teacher to enable students to experience this divide by providing for fieldwork in their assessment.

Māori legal theory

One of my core strategies in forcing students to move away from the "deficit" mindset when considering how Māori are engaged in and affected by the criminal law is to teach a set of classes dedicated to describing and analysing a Māori conception of criminal law. This demonstrates the cultural specificity of our New Zealand system – and the fact that it embeds particular cultural values and norms that are not in fact universal. In these classes, I set out a Māori conception of legal personality, of harm and criminalisation, and of processes for responding to harm. This approach illustrates the completely different worldview through which Māori characterise relationships, and how to frame and address wrongdoing.

Exposure to an entirely different legal system and epistemology for framing and dealing with harmful behaviour is intended to have several benefits. This module requires all students to confront the assumed universality, neutrality, equality, and fairness of our criminal law. It also encourages students to think about engaging with and understanding the cultural context in which Māori entangled in criminal justice as offenders or as victims find ourselves. Finally, discussion of our own ways of thinking, being, and doing allows us to move away from a negative mindset in relation to Māori. As I inform our students, we are more than a criminogenic profile, which presents us as people with issues with violence, addictions, and victimisation. Those behaviours are not who we *are* – those are symptoms of our marginalisation and colonisation. Prior to colonisation, Māori lived with our own system of laws and social regulation, and while the everyday application of those laws have been largely usurped by Western law, the foundational principles and values of tikanga Māori (Māori custom law) continue to provide a living framework of beliefs that many Māori still subscribe to.

I liken the current position of Māori offending and victimisation to snapshots within a much longer epic feature film to illustrate the influence of past Crown action on the social construction of Māori as vulnerable members of contemporary New Zealand society. This history is presented to provide the backdrop to the very deep structural inequities between demographic groups in New Zealand – gaps that explain, but do not justify, our unenviable place at the top of the offending scale. This general contextual information is also used to drill down into an alternative analysis of cases.

Case analysis

Certain cases are amenable to being deconstructed for a Māori analysis of facts and relevant principles and processes for addressing the alleged harm. One such example is *Police v Kawiti* [2000] 1 NZLR 117. Ms Kawiti was charged with driving with excess blood alcohol and driving while disqualified. She claimed she drove because she was in terrible pain following an assault and was fearful of further harm from her partner. Kawiti was denied the defence of duress of circumstances on the basis that the source of the threat was a person. The defence of duress by threat is codified in New Zealand and requires the person making the threat to be present at the time of offending.

While Tolmie (ch 15) considers the circumstances of *Kawiti* to present a teaching opportunity in respect of concepts of equality, I also view Kawiti's story as one reflecting 'missed' information and analysis from a Māori custom law perspective. For example, the reported facts of the case state that Kawiti and her partner Mr Nathan (both Māori) were attending an unveiling at one of his family's marae in Taipa. Due to a past incident, the pair chose to sleep in the car, rather than in the marae complex. Following excess consumption of alcohol by the pair, they ended up having an argument, during which Ms Kawiti was violently assaulted by Nathan. The case refers to her being

> kicked with a karate-style kick to the shoulder which dislocated the shoulder joint. She was punched and stomped on when she was on the ground. Other members of the group urged Mr Nathan to kick Ms Kawiti again and he did so.
>
> (pp118–119)

Following the assault, Ms Kawiti drove just under a 100 kilometres to a hospital, seeking treatment for her injuries, which she described as "excruciating" (p119).

The Court does not delve deeply into Kawiti's reasons for not seeking help from the immediate vicinity – part of their assessment of the defendant's alternatives to breaking the law in terms of options available and proportionality between the harm done and the harm avoided. She testified that she "could not stay at the marae as she did not know anyone and had not been properly introduced during the protocols by Mr Nathan" (p119).

These facts are skirted over lightly by the Court, although they mask significant issues from a Māori custom law perspective. Māori law and identity is tribal, so that each tribal district is a jurisdiction with its own tikanga (law) and kawa (protocols). Citizenship or membership of a tribe is determined by whakapapa (genealogy) and whenua (geography or territory).

Laws governing both permanent and temporary migration set out guiding principles and protocols to be followed when outsiders venture into foreign territory. In the Māori conception of citizenship, persons from other places are designated as "waewae tapu" (sacred feet) – a status that means that they have no right of standing in the community. The host community is required to welcome visitors through ceremonial protocols, which establish the purpose for the visit and relate connections between the groups gathered. There are very strong expectations in terms of manaakitanga – host responsibilities – and the connection between the fulfilment of these functions and mana, or reputation and authority.

Applying these principles and processes of Māori law to an analysis of the *Kawiti* case provides students with a very different lens through which to assess Kawiti's situation and her reaction to it. As a manuhiri or visitor, she has no standing at Mr Nathan's marae. His whanau or family has failed in their obligations to her by not appropriately undertaking the proper migration and hospitality protocols. Kawiti's outsider status means that, from a Māori point of view, her reaction is both understandable and justified.

The Māori conception of legal personality is also relevant. Each person is considered inherently tapu – a sacred status referencing the whakapapa or genealogical connections between humans and the atua or gods. On another level, the female gender has particular tapu associated with child-bearing capabilities and child-raising responsibilities. These various conceptions of tapu provide the rationale underpinning the prohibition of interpersonal assault. For one human being to hit another one is to breach the tapu – the personal integrity, dignity, and sacred being of the other. (Quince 2007, p338)

Māori law also conceptualises responsibility as a collective enterprise. While harm may be committed by an individual perpetrator, liability for that harm rests with the groups to which that person belongs – their whanau, hapu, or iwi (family, sub-tribe, or tribe) – depending on the nature and level of harm caused and the context in which it occurred. In these circumstances, Mr Nathan's failure to introduce Kawiti properly would be deemed the fault of his family – as it is their responsibility to have raised and educated their son to abide by the norms and protocols of their people. Similarly, the terrible assault committed upon Kawiti by Nathan would be laid at the feet of his wider family. In Māori eyes, all activities that occur within any given location are thought to impact positively or negatively upon the mana or reputation or authority of the local people. (Quince 2007, p338)

This extra information serves multiple purposes. In a narrow sense, it allows for an alternative reading of the facts and how these are applied to the particular legal rules – for example, the court's assessment of reasonable alternatives for Kawiti. In a broader sense, it provides students with the opportunity to consider how this conflict is framed in another culture and legal system.

Another teaching example is provided by the case of *R v Maurirere* [2001] NZAR 431, also concerning the statutory defence of compulsion. Maurirere and her partner (again both Māori) had been drinking at a pub when she decided they had both had too much to drink to consider driving home. Whilst trying to take the car keys to prevent her partner from driving, he assaulted her in the car by hitting her across the face repeatedly and saying, "Drive this fucking bloody car otherwise I'll smash you and the car up" (p433). Maurirere drove as a result of the threat and was apprehended by Police. She was found to be in excess of the breath alcohol limit.

In evidence, Maurirere referred to previous assaults at the hand of her partner, including receiving black eyes, having children's bikes tramped on her, being dragged by the hair, thrown down a bank, and booted in the head. She claimed that she considered running back to the tavern but reasoned that her partner would have cut her off (p432).

At trial, the judge determined that there was insufficient evidence to support the defence being left to the jury. There was no threat of grievous bodily harm, and there were realistic and available opportunities for the accused to avoid breaching the law. She could have gone back into the tavern and asked for help. On these grounds, the trial judge decided the evidence "fell well short of establishing the basis of a defence of compulsion" (p434). The Court of Appeal upheld this decision.

A contextual analysis of this case requires consideration of theories of marginalisation, deprivation, and intersectionality. Intersectional theorist Kimberle Crenshaw (1991) uses a three-part framework to explain how the minority woman's experience of law is qualitatively different than a single axis analysis by race or gender. "Structural intersectionality" considers socio-economic or structural factors that result in minority women having different life experiences than either minority men or non-minority women. The second arm, "political intersectionality" refers to the often conflicting agendas of anti-racism and feminism, which requires minority women to subordinate one aspect of her identity to another. The third aspect, "representational intersectionality" is where women of colour are often marginalised by popular imagery or representations of themselves – in the media, popular culture, or public discourse. Each of these aspects can be applied to the case of Ms Maurirere.

This incident occurs in a socio-economically deprived area of New Zealand – in a small predominantly Māori town frequently marred by gang, family, and intimate partner violence. It is a town that has borne the brunt of radical economic reforms in the 1980s, whereby the majority of adults were rendered unemployed due to the sell-off of state assets, and its economy has never recovered. Maurirere and her partner are likely the children or grandchildren of such families – underemployed, undereducated, and living on the margins of functional society. The abuse and over-consumption of alcohol is also an embedded phenomenon in the culture of such towns. This context provides a backdrop to a community of individuals at the edge of societal norms and at risk of over-criminalisation.

In my view, Maurirere's reaction to being stopped by the Police is evidence of her appreciation of political intersectionality. The case reports, "She said nothing to the Police about being compelled to drive" (p433). Māori have a well-documented fraught relationship with the Police over nearly two centuries. In addition to specific flashpoints – the suppression of rebellion, protests, and heavy-handed treatment on many highly publicised occasions, the Police are viewed with mistrust and as agents of the Crown who represent invasion, dispossession, and discrimination. As well as negative historical experiences, the contemporary Māori experience of Police is characterised by over-surveillance, harassment, and misunderstanding (Quince 2007, p346). Viewing Maurirere's interaction with Police from a Māori perspective might then explain her failure to disclose the threat and prior assault. She and her partner are Māori. Māori do not trust the Police. Despite being a victim of crime, and presumably possessing an awareness of the wrongfulness of intimate partner violence, Maurirere is placed in a position where she has to either prioritise her victim status as a woman, *or* protect her partner as a fellow Māori – by not 'narking' on him to the Police. There is significant pressure amongst minority communities not to involve the authorities, especially law enforcement, in community matters.

Finally, representational intersectionality may be said to be relevant in analysing the Court's response to Maurirere's history of victimisation as well as the seriousness of the threat faced. Their analysis of the facts betrays a lack of understanding and appreciation of intimate partner violence and also idiomatic language to convey threats, as if the kind of language used here and this behaviour is normalised for women like Maurirere – Māori women in violent partnerships. The Court is quick to dismiss the threat as not meeting the required threshold of serious bodily harm. It is difficult to imagine that any of the three Pakeha male judges in the appellate court have ever been told that they would be 'smashed' by another human being, let alone by someone of the opposite gender who is bigger and stronger than they are. The judge at first instance dismissed evidence of a relationship characterised by violence as a series of discrete and unrelated incidents with no bearing on the matter at hand: "The accused mentioned three prior instances, but did not relate those in time, particular or circumstance to the events of the evening that we are concerned with" (p434).

My argument is that the position of women like Ms Maurirere can be viewed through the prism of intersectional theory – which attempts to account for and explain the intersecting axes of identity – including race, gender, and class. Her life, experiences, and responses to life incidents are conditioned by her identity as a Māori woman living in relative deprivation, with a documented history of victimisation. Similarly, the legal experts tasked with deciding her case do not have the required nuanced understanding of her position and the realistic choices open to her at that time.

The connection between mindfulness and effective lawyering

The strategies described earlier are part of a broader attempt to mould students into legal thinkers and practitioners who are mindful and effective. 'Mindfulness' is somewhat of a buzzword in the contemporary lexicon, essentially referring to the seemingly obvious goal that we should have an awareness of and empathy for others, whilst acknowledging our own position and limitations (see, for example: Montgomery 2007; Rogers 2012). In respect of legal education and the practice of law, I view the goal of mindfulness as reflecting the human focus of law as a discipline centred upon communication and problem-solving. In the classroom, this can be done with careful planning in terms of curriculum content and assessment, to reflect the diversity of humanity involved in criminal justice interactions.

Effectively listening to clients requires finely tuned skills and emotional intelligence in what can often be times of high stress – particularly in the criminal justice field. This includes the need to cope with vicarious trauma and may require skills of cultural competence in order to transcend difference. For example, when dealing with Māori (as defendants, witnesses, or victims), advocates should be aware of and appreciate non-verbal communication through body language and the significance of silence in Polynesian cultures. There is also likely to be enhanced communication when a relationship is properly established through the making of personal connections –i.e. introducing who you are to your client, where you come from, your family, and your place in the community. This is contrary to some views of the practitioner/client professional relationship as being predominantly arm's length and transactional.

Part of the lesson learned from legal realism is that law is both personal and political. In criminal law teaching, it is important to consider how the personal identity of students impacts upon their ability to understand and relate to the material supporting the teaching as well as the system that it emanates from. Sheldon and Krieger (2007) maintain that student wellbeing is connected to their ability to be themselves. In my experience, there is a common perception amongst law students about what a 'real' lawyer looks and sounds like, as well as what their values and worldviews might be. This partly reflects the lack of visible role models in the profession and also in popular culture. These perceptions cannot change without active manipulation and deliberate exposure to diversity and pluralism.

Alongside the necessary emphasis on doctrinal education should be some commitment to acknowledging how difficult it can be to work in the criminal justice field. Criminal practitioners are exposed to evidence, information, and accounts of extreme human behaviour. We establish rapport and relationships with wrongdoers and their victims. We see and hear things that ordinary people are never privy to. Criminal law educators have a responsibility to discuss this openly.

The challenges of addressing culture and ethnicity in criminal law teaching are significant, although this is not a reason to maintain a pretence that criminal law is race-neutral. Our obligation as teachers is to at least name and discuss the complexities of race, class and colonisation upon matters of offending, policing, and victimisation. Across the common law world, the context in which criminal law and justice is both taught and practiced is far more cosmopolitan and diverse than the society in which the common law was developed. We are morally and ethically bound to ensure that our teaching thoroughly prepares our students for the challenges of lawyering in these communities.

References

Angelo, Anthony H, *Constitutional Law in New Zealand* (Wolters Kluwer, The Netherlands, 2011).

Crenshaw, Kimberle, "Mapping the Margins: Intersectionality, Identity Politics and Violence Against Women of Color" (1991) 43 *Stanford Law Review*, 1241.

Montgomery, John E, "Incorporating Emotional Intelligence Concepts into Legal Education: Strengthening the Professionalism of Law Students" (2007) 39 *University of Toledo Law Review*, 323.

Quince, K, "Māori and the Criminal Justice System in New Zealand" in J Tolmie and W Brookbanks (eds.), *Criminal Justice in New Zealand* (Lexis Nexis, Wellington, 2007) 346.

Rogers, Scott L, "Mindful Law School: An Integrative Approach to Transforming Legal Education" (2012) 28 *Touro Law Review*, 1189.

Sheldon, KM and Krieger, LS, "Understanding the Negative Effects of Legal Education on Law Students: A Longitudinal Test of Self-Determination Theory" (2007) 33 *Personality and Social Psychology*, 883–897.

Chapter 15

Introducing feminist legal jurisprudence through the teaching of criminal law

Julia Tolmie

This chapter has three aims: (i) to outline why it is important to introduce feminist jurisprudence (and particularly as it concerns violence against women) into the teaching of criminal law, (ii) to suggest one of a myriad of ways this can be done given some of the countervailing demands of teaching the subject, and (iii) to use a small portion of the rich array of feminist research to illustrate how this material might be used to engage students with some of the bigger social justice issues involved in the operation of criminal law.

Why should feminist legal jurisprudence be integrated into the teaching of criminal law?

The current prison population of New Zealand demonstrates the significance of gender in the processes of criminal justice. In December 2014, there were 8,080 male prisoners and 561 female prisoners (Department of Corrections 2015). Criminal perpetration is overwhelmingly (although not invariably) a male phenomenon. This is no doubt reflected in other jurisdictions.

Women, and particularly socially marginalised Indigenous and ethnic minority women, are, however, deeply affected by crime. Women are the majority of victims of certain forms of violent offending – family violence and sexual violence (Morrison, Soboleva and Chong 2006; Ministry of Justice 2003). In New Zealand, for example, police statistics show that about one in five assault victims over a period of four months is a Māori woman, yet Māori women make up just 7% of the overall population (Statistics New Zealand 2015).

Less typically, women, again disproportionately socially marginalised Indigenous women, are also processed as offenders. A unique feature of women's offending is that it frequently takes place within the context of their victimisation (Miller and Meloy 2006; Swan and Snow 2006).

This account makes the point, as developed by Quince in chapter 14 that gender is only one relevant factor in patterns of perpetration and victimisation; race-based marginalisation is also a feature. Māori women have not been, however, impacted identically to Māori men (Mikaere 1998) by the process of colonisation (and the resulting intergenerational legacies of cumulative and compounding trauma, social breakdown, and economic marginalisation). Kimberlee Crenshaw's groundbreaking work describes how the *intersection* of multiple axes of oppression (such as racism and sexism) creates quantitatively and qualitatively different experiences from those who experience only one of those axes (Crenshaw 1991). Māori women, for example, are not criminalised in the same numbers as Māori men, but they are over-criminalised relative to non-Māori women at rates that exceed the over-criminalisation of Māori men when compared to non-Māori men (Quince 2010).

Despite these clear patterns, criminal law has traditionally been taught as a neutral body of principles that applies impartially and equally to all individuals. Equality concerns that have engaged judges and lawyers have been largely "formal" (Graycar and Morgan 2002, chapter 3) – how to treat like cases alike rather than exploring the justice of treating those who are very differently situated as though they are in the same position.

Engaging with the different theoretical movements within feminist legal jurisprudence (particularly intersectional feminism or critical race feminism) and the more recent theorising of masculinity and whiteness (for example, the invisibility of race as a privilege of whiteness), offers a rich body of jurisprudence that can be drawn upon to return some intellectual honesty to the teaching of criminal law. These bodies of theory expose the claim that law is objective and impartial as a power claim that has the effect of elevating particular sets of privileges, life experiences, and values into unchallengeable norms that can be applied to all people. The result is that certain women (and men) are particularly vulnerable to criminalisation and certain experiences of victimisation are not well recognised and are addressed badly.

Many of our students will be from backgrounds of relative privilege and will in their careers be called upon to advocate for, and pass judgment on, those who occupy social positions and lives that they will never experience. We are failing these students if we allow them to imagine that their own values reflect a neutral set of norms that can be non-reflexively applied. When this happens, we can see a serious disjunction emerge in the application of the criminal law. Such as, for example, the framing of those who are living lives with high levels of entrapment in terms of autonomy and choice – because autonomy and choice are characteristics of privileged and well-resourced lives (*Ahsin* [2014] NZSC 153; *Paton* [2013] NZHC 21).

Offences of violence often occur within the family, have a burden of harm beyond the immediate harm caused, and are significantly under-reported. The New Zealand Police say that 30% of adult sexual assault, 70% of child abuse, 65% of serious assaults, and 50% of homicides that are reported to them are family violence, yet only 18%–20% of family violence is reported to the police (Nimo 2012). The burden of family violence at the most dangerous end of the continuum largely falls on women and children – again, disproportionately socially marginalised Indigenous women and children (Nimo 2012).

Some would suggest that violence against women lies at the heart of much community breakdown and other flow-on criminal offending today (Marchetti

2008) and is a legacy of the state violence of colonisation via intergenerational transmission (Atkinson 2002). If one considers the central role mothers play in most families in ensuring the well-being of young children and the role that women play in holding families and communities together, then it is clear that harm done to women will have far-reaching negative effects beyond the lives of those women who are immediately affected (Lajeunesse 1993). In light of this, it is an abdication of our professional responsibility as law teachers not to address the subject of violence against women and expose students to what the experts have to say about it.

Engaging with feminist theory

How one introduces feminist theory into an entry-level course such as Criminal Law is a subject on which there will be a plethora of opinions. Does one reorder the teaching of the course around social phenomena – such as violence against women – traversing the "historical and social context, philosophical and political arguments, enforcement practice and principles" (Lacey 1992, p. 86) each subject raises? This would certainly avoid coming at important issues through the fragmented, elliptical, and politicised lens of criminal law and theory.

On the other hand, there are competing demands. Put simply, there is the risk that students will not have enough understanding of conventional interpretations of the law to know what they are meant to be critiquing. Of equal importance is the fact that a student with an 'outsider voice' and a passionate engagement with social justice issues will find themselves being dismissed as 'polemical' if they are not competent in legal reasoning and rules. Even with scrupulous lawyering, there is no guaranteed listening for such a voice. A tension exists between the need to deliver an understanding of legal doctrine and theory, along with traditional lawyering skills, and the parallel obligation to engage students in the critical analysis of those rules and skills. My own approach today is to embed critical material throughout a course organised around traditional doctrinal categories.

Here I highlight some examples from the rich array of feminist jurisprudence that can be used to stimulate students to think critically about aspects of the operation of the criminal law. These examples assist in critiquing notions of equality in relation to the development and operation of legal doctrine, the values that go into normative standards, the construction of facts (the use of language and interpretive schema), and the value of the systemic criminal justice response to social phenomena such as family violence.

Beginning an equality analysis

The criminal law is rife with examples of doctrine that appears facially neutral yet differentially impacts on the lives of those it applies to. A New Zealand example starts from understanding the nature of intimate partner violence

(IPV): It is a pattern of harmful behaviour by the perpetrator that has a cumulative and compounding effect on the victim over a period of time. As such, it differs from other forms of violence. It has been described as a form of "social entrapment" with three dimensions (Ptacek 1999, p. 10):

> (1) . . . the social isolation, fear and coercion that men's violence creates in women's lives; (2) . . . the indifference of powerful institutions to women's suffering; and (3) . . . the ways that men's coercive control can be aggravated by structural inequalities of gender, class and racism.

Evan Stark (2007, p. 15), speaking from more than 20 years of experience in working with victims of violence, comments:

> Coercive control entails a malevolent course of conduct that subordinates women to an alien will by violating their physical integrity (domestic violence), denying them respect and autonomy (intimidation), depriving them of social connectedness (isolation) and appropriating or denying them access to the resources required for personhood and citizenship (control).

The very nature of coercive control (particularly as the victim's vulnerability increases) makes it close to impossible for many women to successfully and safely remove themselves and their children from a violent partner. The abuse is directed at isolating the victim from potential support and undermining her self-determination. It is tailored for the particular victim and designed to be effective even when she is not in the presence of the abuser.

The second dimension of entrapment speaks to the fact that help within our current family violence system is sporadic, unpredictable, and, frequently, unavailable for victims in the most dangerous cases of family violence (Richardson and Wade 2010). The New Zealand Family Violence Death Review Committee has mapped the fragmented and siloed nature of the family violence system – which also currently places responsibility for addressing the abuse on the victim (Family Violence Death Review Committee 2016, pp. 24–25).

Third, racism, sexism and social marginalisation make some women particularly vulnerable. These women face higher levels of violence, cumulative experiences of abuse (including intergenerational violence), have no one in their extended social networks who does not normalise their abuse or who has the resources to protect them, have insufficient resources and dependant children to provide for, and encounter entrenched racism in the institutions tasked with protecting them. Gang-affiliated women are dealing not just with one abusive man but with an abusive and hierarchical male collective that is likely to have more power in their immediate lives than, for example, the police. Many of the women facing the most extreme levels of violence are therefore not only in dangerous relationships, but in "dangerous social positions" (Richie 2000). A raft of co-morbidities frequently accompanies family violence in these situations – for example, substance abuse and mental health issues, as women self-medicate untreated trauma histories.

Whilst these are the documented realities of family violence, there are still very high levels of ignorance in the community about how it operates. Most people still believe, for example, that it is relatively easy to seek help and/or leave an abusive relationship (*Paton* [2013] NZHC 21).

Against this background, it is interesting to examine the legal rules that give shape to the self-preservation defences. Section 24 of the Crimes Act 1961 (NZ) sets out narrow criteria for the defence of compulsion (known in other jurisdictions as duress by threats). Two of these criteria – the requirement for a specific threat ("commit the offence or else you will be seriously hurt or killed") and the requirement that the person threatening the defendant be "present" during the commission of the offence – mean that most battered defendants who commit offences under coercion from their violent partners will not be able to raise the defence of compulsion. Many of these women offend in response to the generalised threat presented by the demands of a dangerous partner and often when he is not present (Law Commission 1981, p. 63; Loveless 2010). In other words, their circumstances may be coercive, but they will struggle to meet criteria designed to locate that coercion in the immediate circumstances of the offending.

The common law defence of 'necessity' (based on duress of circumstances), by way of contrast, does not require either the presence of the person threatening the accused or a specific threat – it simply requires emergency circumstances (*Hutchinson* [2004] NZAR 303). In *Police v Kawiti* [2000] 1 NZLR 117; (1999) 17 CRNZ 88, Kawiti was assaulted by her partner on an isolated marae where she knew nobody. She drove to the emergency department of the nearest hospital whilst disqualified and with excess blood alcohol. She was in extreme pain from a dislocated shoulder and afraid that if she stayed where she was she would be further assaulted. The police officer, who was called to take details of her partner's assault on her, charged her with driving offences (an example of how entrapment operates). Although she attempted to raise the defence of *necessity* in respect of these charges, the court determined that s 24 "limits the availability of the defence in relation to all threats by persons". In other words, if the threat comes from a person, *compulsion* is the only available defence (accepted not to be available on the facts as the person threatening Kawiti was not ordering her to drive). The result is that the defence of necessity is not available for those caught up in emergency situations created by other people.

This example creates an opportunity to explore concepts of equality. Does applying the same legal rules to everyone (a formal equality approach) result in equality here? Or do we need to consider the actual constraints of people's different lives when we develop legal rules? On this second approach, equality is measured in terms of outcomes (substantive equality); for example, do these rules provide everyone, even though they have different social resources and life circumstances, with equal access to the self-preservation defences?

MacKinnon argues that formal and substantive understandings of equality are different versions of the same thing because both involve a central norm that reflects certain lives and not others (MacKinnon 1987, p. 32). She suggests an equality analysis has limitations in achieving gender equity, for example, because gender is constructed as a difference but the norms that are used for the purposes of assessing whether laws or their outcomes are equal are male. What is the 'norm' underpinning the laws on compulsion and necessity here? Does it reflect male standards or are other factors in operation? Are there ways of running a social justice argument that transcend the problems MacKinnon has identified in equality analyses?

Notions of objectivity in the application of normative standards

The criminal law regularly sets apparently objective normative standards; for example, sexual connection without another person's consent and "without believing on *reasonable* grounds" [emphasis added] that that other person consents is sexual violation contrary to s128 of the Crimes Act 1961. The very notion that there are 'objective' standards can be unpacked using the work of Forell and Matthews (2001). They argue that reasonableness in the area of sexual assault should be judged from the "reasonable women's" point of view, as that will incentivise men to develop sensitivity to the perspectives of the women with whom they interact.

In *The Queen v Tawera* CA 208/96, 2 September 1996, a 16-year-old girl was staying with the family of the 48-year-old defendant, whom she viewed as an uncle. He got into her bed, kissed her with his tongue, kissed her breasts, licked her vagina, and then said, "Honey, can I stick it in?" and had sexual intercourse with her. It was accepted by the court that she did not in fact consent but, because she was passive and did not say anything to indicate non-consent, his conviction for rape and unlawful sexual connection was over-turned on the basis that

> we find it difficult to see how on an objective appraisal it can be said absence of belief in consent on reasonable grounds has been established beyond reasonable doubt. On analysis there is nothing in the complainant's evidence, the surrounding circumstances, or the appellant's evidence which objectively indicated the complainant was not consenting.
>
> (*Tawera*, pp4–5)

Students can be asked whether this would have been the outcome if 'reasonable grounds' for his belief in consent were judged from a reasonable woman's point of view? Is there sufficient commonality in women's experiences that it is possible to imagine a reasonable women's standard? What function do/ought 'objective' normative standards play in the operation of the criminal law?

The construction of facts

One of the most problematic aspects of the operation of the criminal law is not the legal rules but how the facts that they apply to are constructed. This subject can be difficult to access because the process of constructing facts is invisible in most legal judgements. The facts are simply presented by the judge or found by the jury. It is, however, possible to render visible and critique the process by which certain facts are constructed as 'true' (and therefore attract particular legal consequences) using jurisprudence to analyse the operation of language and 'stock stories'.

The use of language

Post-modern feminist jurisprudence exposes the degree to which language mediates and therefore generates human experience. By way of illustration, case law struggles with the issue of whether harm to a foetus is bodily harm to the mother (*A-G's Reference (No 3 of 1994)* [1998] AC 245; *Harrild v Director of Proceedings* [2003] 3 NZLR 289; *R v King* (2003) 59 NSWLR 472). Clearly, the mother and child are beings with distinct genetic make-ups. On the other hand, they are profoundly interconnected. The law has oscillated between viewing the foetus as a separate independent person (rendering the mother a kind of breeding bag) and viewing the foetus as a part of the mother's body (not unlike a limb, but with future independent existence). Luce Irigaray (1985a, 1985b) imagines the possibility of language and therefore social meaning originating in women's life experiences. She suggests that certain possibilities, that are currently constructed as incompatible and contradictory (because meaning is generated in current linguistic structures by the use of binary opposites), might both be true. For example, a state of being that is "not two but not one". A foetus, for example, might be both its own person and yet *also* profoundly one with the mother (Karpin 1994).

At a less fundamental level, Coates and Wade expose how the language used by legal professionals to describe family violence on particular sets of facts is highly value laden. This language tends to serve the functions of concealing the perpetrator's responsibility for the abuse and the extent of the violence, as well as blaming the victim and concealing her resistance (Coates and Wade 2007; Wilson, Smith, Tolmie and De Haan 2015). "Dysfunctional", "volatile" (*Tamati* HC Tauranga, 27 October 2009) and "rocky" (*Wharerau* [2014] NZHC 2535) relationships are words used to describe long-term patterns of violent offending/victimisation (including ongoing criminal assaults resulting in injury and repeated rapes). In these descriptions, the violence does not belong to the perpetrator but to the relationship and is therefore partly the responsibility of the victim. Her resistance to the abuse is rendered invisible – supporting an understanding of her as 'choosing' to be abused.

Language not only frames facts and ways of thinking about reality; it is also used to elicit information from witnesses that can be used in court to construct the truth of what happened. Australian socio-linguist Diana Eades argues that the process generally used in the criminal justice system to gather information is impregnated with ethnocentric assumptions (Eades 1992). For example, Eades suggests that in the Australian Aboriginal English-speaking context, information is not freely available for the asking and direct questions built on a one-way information exchange are not a culturally appropriate means of eliciting significant and/or personal information. Furthermore, Aboriginal English speakers will often provide answers that are 'compliant' rather than 'true' without any intended dishonesty. They will have silences that they need to get comfortable or think uninterrupted by non-Aboriginal English speakers (including their own lawyers) and will give evasive answers when inappropriate means of eliciting information are adopted. There is a lack of similar socio-linguistic research in New Zealand, but such issues are likely to be no less pertinent in respect of Māori, Pasifika, and other cultures (although clearly specifics will differ).

Such issues may be further complicated in cases involving female offenders. Women's experiences of victimisation often underpin their offending, and yet victimisation can cause trauma that will affect recall and may also make disclosure extremely difficult.

The case of *R v Kina* Queensland Court of Appeal, CA No 221 of 1993, 29 November 1993, illustrates these points. Robyn Kina was an Aboriginal woman who was tried and convicted in Australia in 1988 for the murder of her de facto husband (a conviction set aside in 1993). Whilst in prison, Kina developed a relationship of trust with a social worker to whom she was able to disclose the full extent of the deceased's brutality towards her (including anal and gang rapes). She had been unable to provide this information to her young non-Aboriginal male lawyers who had asked her a series of questions but had not acquired enough information to lay the foundations for a proper defence (although they believed at the time that they had established a rapport with her). There were no language difficulties for which an interpreter was necessary.

Stock stories

A useful film to stimulate discussion about how we construct factual meaning is *Raw Deal: A Question of Consent* (although it shows footage of a rape and students will need the opportunity to decide whether they personally wish to see it – particularly those who may be triggered because of their own abuse histories).

What is interesting about the film is that multiple people watching the same footage have different accounts of what they see. Some read the complainant as having 'consensual sex', notwithstanding that she indicates that she is not prepared to have intercourse. Others read what transpired as rape – legal doctrine requires consent to exist at the time of the act to the act itself. How then is it possible to read the complainant as consenting when she consents to some sexual activities but draws the line at intercourse?

There are those who argue that rape myths distort juries' perceptions of what happened and make conviction in sexual assault trials difficult. MacKinnon goes beyond this, arguing that dominance and submission (and the eroticisation of dominance and submission) are built into hetero-sex and understandings of what it means to be a man and a woman. In her argument, gender roles, and how they play out in the expression of heterosexual sexuality, are power roles (MacKinnon 1987) blurring the line between sex and rape. What this account does not do is address how gender intersects with class and race to generate the readings of sexual and other violations.

Julia Quilter employs "an interpretive schema" to examine how facts are constructed in rape trials (Quilter 2011). A schema takes a collection of particulars and includes/excludes certain things as significant:

> The schema . . . structures how the "reader" will "interpret" the situation, meaning that the institutional features (the schema) will itself be reproduced through the interpretation.
>
> (Quilter 2011, p. 30)

Quilter describes, for example, how reform of the sexual offences has removed the need to prove victim resistance, recent complaint, and corroboration and yet such reforms have had little effect on courtroom practices. This is because rape law has an interpretive schema "with a highly sedimented history". This means that such reforms are unreadable because they are circumvented and co-opted back into the old story. The schema is:

> The location was (not) remote   +
> There was (no) physical injury   +
> She did (not) recently complain of rape +
> She was (not) of 'good fame'
> = she is (un)believable; she had sex/she was raped.
> (Quilter 2011, p. 31)

Quilter uses an actual case to illustrate both the prosecution and defence arguing opposite factual interpretations whilst utilising the same schema. The complainant was a 19-year-old who alleged that she was raped by her 30-year-old boss at a Christmas party. An issue in court was whether the location of the rape was close enough to/far away from those at the party that she could/could not have called out for help. Neither pointed out how implausible it was that a teenager would call to her colleagues to come and witness her in a violating, frightening, and shameful situation with her boss.

Raising larger systemic questions about the criminal justice response

When the criminal justice system was evolving, issues affecting women, such as family violence, were often not publicly visible. Consequently, the justice response is arguably not well designed to respond to these issues.

If family violence is a pattern of harm by the perpetrator that has a cumulative and compounding effect on victims (including hidden and future victims), then it requires a preventative rather than a reactive response. This cannot be a one-off intervention. What is required are conscious strategies for achieving victim safety through the ongoing management of perpetrators. This requires a larger repertoire of interventions than are currently available, including interventions that have the capacity to address intergenerational trauma and accommodate structural inequity.

Instead, our criminal justice system fragments patterns of harm into one-off de-contextualised incidents that it then reacts to, fragments types of abuse into distinct phenomenon (for example, child abuse and intimate partner violence) to be addressed separately, and individualises the larger social problems that are entwined with these forms of abuse.

This raises bigger issues about the design and operation of the criminal justice system. If it is to be part of the response to social problems – such as family violence – how might it need rethinking?

Conclusion

In this chapter, the case has been made for introducing feminist perspectives into the teaching of criminal law. I have drawn examples from the rich (and at times contradictory) body of feminist scholarship to illustrate how such material could be introduced into a traditional teaching format in order to stimulate a critical engagement with different aspects of the operation of the criminal law. These include the development of the legal rules, the use of normative judgements in the application of those rules, the construction of the facts that the rules are applied to, and the systemic response framework.

Taking such an approach raises many issues of methodology and process that are not addressed in this chapter because of space constraints. For example, feminist jurisprudence has strongly critiqued the use of a neutral rather than personal voice in legal writing because of the manner in which it eradicates subject positioning from the process of knowing and speaking (Williams 1991) – making a dishonest claim to objectivity and neutrality. Should this critique be introduced into the teaching of criminal law or should cultural competence be fostered by immersing students in traditional legal methodology before alternative critical possibilities are opened? When I teach women and the law, I allow students to drop standard legal conventions in how they use language and, particularly, the speaking voice. In criminal law, however, students are just starting out. They need to learn those conventions so that they can choose to use them when they need to and use them self-consciously and strategically.

Bibliography

Atkinson, J. (2002) *Recreating Songlines: The Transgenerational Effects of Trauma in Indigenous Australia* Melbourne: Spinifex Press.

Coates, L. and Wade, A. (2007) Language and Violence: Analysis of Four Discursive Operations 22 *Journal of Family Violence* 511.

Crenshaw, K. (1991) Mapping the Margins: Intersectionality, Identity Politics, and Violence Against Women of Color 43 *Stanford Law Review* 1241.

Department of Corrections, New Zealand (2015) *Prison Facts and Statistics*.

Eades, D. (1992) *Aboriginal English and the Law* Brisbane: Queensland University Law Society.

Family Violence Death Review Committee, New Zealand (2016), *Fifth Report: January 2014 to February 2015*, Health and Quality Safety Commission.

Forell, C. and Matthews, D. (2001) *A Law of Her Own: The Reasonable Woman as a Measure of Man* New York: New York University Press.

Graycar, R. and Morgan, J. (2002) *The Hidden Gender of Law* (2nd edn) Sydney: The Federation Press.

Irigaray, L. (1985a) *Speculum of the Other Women* New York: Cornell University Press.

Irigaray, L. (1985b) *This Sex Which Is Not One* New York: Cornell University Press.

Karpin, I. (1994) Reimaging Maternal Selfhood: Transgressing Body Boundaries and the Law 2 *Australian Feminist Law Journal* 36.

Lacey, N. (1992) Reconstructing the Traditional Syllabus. In Birks, P. (ed.) *Examining the Law Syllabus: The Core* Oxford: Oxford University Press, 85.

Lajeunesse, T. (1993) *Community Holistic Circle Healing: Hollow Water First Nation* International Institute for Restorative Practices.

Law Commission, New Zealand (1981) *Some Criminal Defences with Reference to Battered Defendants* 63.

Loveless, J. (2010) Domestic Violence, Coercion and Duress [2010] *Crim LR* 83.

Mackinnon, C. (1987) *Feminism Unmodified: Discourses on Life and Law* Boston: Harvard University Press.

Marchetti, E. (2008) Intersectional Race and Gender Analysis: Why Legal Processes Just Don't Get It 17:2 *Social and Legal Studies* 155.

Mikaere, A. (1998) Collective Rights and Gender Issues: A Māori Women's Perspective. In Tomas, N. (ed.) *Collective Human Rights of Pacific Peoples* Auckland: International Research Unit for Māori and Indigenous Education 79.

Miller, S. and Meloy, M. (2006) Women's Use of Force: Voices of Women Arrested for Domestic Violence 12:1 *Violence Against Women* 89.

Ministry of Justice, New Zealand (2003) *National Survey of Crime Victims*.

Ministry of Justice, New Zealand (2015) *Strengthening New Zealand's Legislative Response to Family Violence: A Public Discussion Document*.

Morrison, B., Soboleva, N. and Chong, J. (2006) *Conviction and Sentencing of Offenders in New Zealand 1997–2006* Wellington: Ministry of Justice.

Nimo, B. (2012) *Stakeholder Update: Police Family Violence Process Changes*. Powerpoint presentation to the New Zealand Family Death Review Committee (copy on file with author).

Ptacek, P. (1999) *Battered Women in the Courtroom: The Power of Judicial Responses* Boston: Northeastern University Press.

Quilter, J. (2011) Reframing the Rape Trial: Insights from Critical Theory About the Limitations of Legislative Reform? 35 *Australian Feminist Law Journal* 23.

Quince, K. (2010) The Bottom of the Heap? Why Māori Women are Over-Criminalised in New Zealand 3 *Te Tai Haruru: Journal of Māori Legal Writing* 99.

Richardson, C. and Wade, A. (2010) Islands of Safety: Restoring Dignity in Violence Prevention Work with Indigenous Families 5:1 *First Peoples Child & Family Law Review* 137.

Richie, B. (2000) A Black Feminist Reflection on the Antiviolence Movement 25 *Signs* 1133.

Stark, E. (2007) *Coercive Control: How Men Entrap Women in Personal Life* Oxford: Oxford University Press.

Statistics New Zealand Recorded crime statistics – unique victims, www.stats.govt.nz Stuff (2015) http://www.stuff.co.nz/national/crime/63995633/māori-women-most-likely-to-be-assault-victims-stats.html

Swan, S. and Snow, D. (2006) The Development of a Theory of Women's Use of Violence in Intimate Relationships 12:11 *Violence Against Women* 1026.

Williams, P. (1991) *The Alchemy of Race and Rights: Diary of a Law Professor* Cambridge, MA, and London, England: Harvard University Press.

Wilson, D., Smith, R., Tolmie, J. and De Haan, I. (2015) Becoming Better Helpers: Rethinking Language to Move Beyond Simplistic Responses to Women Experiencing Intimate Partner Violence 11:1 *Policy Quarterly* 25.

Chapter 16

Choice

Kris Gledhill

Introduction

Several contributors to this book have argued that criminal law courses can and perhaps should de-emphasise the extent to which criminal law is a matter of neutral principle and instead explain that it is a product of or reveals wider contexts, which students should be equipped to critique: see chapters 13–15. There is also doubt cast on whether there are any general principles: see in particular chapter 9. The focus of this chapter is a critique of another aspect of the traditional course, namely the use of violent and property offending as the specific offences invariably taught in detail to illustrate the principles or themes in the law. In essence, it is suggested that the teachers of criminal law should cast their net wider and consider making use of a range of other offences. It is not suggested that the traditionally-taught offences are inadequate for the purpose; rather, it is suggested that they do not hold any superior status and that lecturers should use their academic freedom to construct a course using different specific offences if they so wish, that there are benefits from doing so, and that larger law schools that teach criminal law in more than one stream should consider offering students a choice of the specific offences that will be taught.

It seems patently sensible that course design should start from the application of educational research as to how best students learn, and with that background, set out the goals for the course (i.e. what the students should be able to understand by the end of the course), identify strategies for securing the best prospect of students achieving the relevant learning outcomes, and design a process for evaluating that (Ramsden 1992, 2003). Cownie suggests that this is not common and that both legal academics and those in other fields adopt a complacent attitude:

> it appears to be very common for academics to take a very pragmatic and uninformed approach to teaching. . . . Anecdotal evidence appears to play a large part in the construction of many lectures and tutorials . . . Conscientious preparation for teaching appears to demand that one be up-to-date as regards the latest research in the area . . . but little thought is given to any but the most basic of the pedagogic aspects of teaching.
>
> (Cownie 1999, p. 44)

As is identified in chapter 1, there is a remarkable level of similarity over time and continents in the structure of criminal law courses and the infrastructure of teaching in the form of the main textbooks. In the absence of evidence that this is the result of informed course design, based on research that this is the best way to secure the goals of teaching criminal law, it looks like complacency plays a prominent part. Untrammelled academic freedom as to setting the goals for a criminal law course may be constrained by the need to offer content that will meet the requirements of professional regulatory bodies. However, as is also noted in chapter 1, the professional bodies often use language that allows a significant amount of academic freedom, because what they typically require is the learning of basic doctrines, and where there is a more prescriptive approach, the higher level of specification can no doubt be subject to discussion between the academy and the profession.

Where there is more prescription, it typically reflects the standard criminal law course. And yet the detailed prescription in Australia has not prevented the radically different approach described by Gans in chapter 8 as to the course constructed at Melbourne Law School and the text he authors based on that, despite the apparent requirements of the Australian admitting bodies. Indeed, there is something of a theme in Australian law schools of avoiding prescriptions: see also Steel, who in chapter 9 outlines the aim of a text he co-authors to undermine a false view that criminal law contains a set of unifying principles, and the evidence from chapter 1 that several law school course prescriptions suggest that offences other than those in the traditional courses are regular features.

The wider point arising from these chapters is that academic freedom may not be constrained to any great extent by the requirements of the profession and that the constraint is more self-imposed or imagined or arises from lethargy. That being so, a criminal law course can be structured by using offences that are not commonly taught but which allow both doctrine and wider policy considerations to be learned and critiqued and core skills, including transferable skills, to be developed. Recognising the validity of a significant range of offences in teaching criminal law means that the current monaural scheme – with the exceptions noted earlier demonstrating that there is nevertheless a rule – can be replaced by a range of courses, providing choice for both the lecturers and the students.

To support this suggested approach to the use of alternative structures for a criminal law course, the following building blocks are put together. First, the question of what a criminal law course will wish to achieve is explored; next, two particular areas of criminal law that seem rarely to be taught – drugs law and driving law – are examined to demonstrate how they are exemplars for the illustration of significant points of doctrine and relevant policy or wider jurisprudential considerations; and, finally, some of the arguments likely to be made by those who react against suggestions for change to what is familiar are considered, together with an outline of the benefits that should flow from expanding the range of ways of teaching criminal law.

The learning outcomes from a criminal law course

Criminal law is a core course for various reasons, including the practical reason that a significant number of lawyers work in the area. There is also the fact that criminal sanctions are a central part of the regulation of society through legal as opposed to moral or other forms of pressure, and, moreover, they involve special elements of stigma and penalty that mean that all those involved in the administration of the legal system – whether as practitioners or as lawyers involved in public policy advice – should have an in-depth knowledge from the outset. In short, it is an area that requires staffing by lawyers. In addition, as is outlined elsewhere, criminal law – often an early course for students – may also be an introduction to various other substantive aspects of the law, such as statutory interpretation, the overlap between social policy and law, and so is also a subject that should develop a number of skills that are transferable to other areas of the student's legal education.

The precise learning outcomes may well differ according to the approach of the particular law school or lecturer, including whether it is used to introduce various social policy or jurisprudential critiques. But, as noted by Tolmie in chapter 15, an introductory course on criminal law also has to include a suitable amount of doctrine in order to allow students to know what there is to critique. A list of learning outcomes along the following lines should not be controversial.

All offences have elements that the prosecution have to prove; these elements will always involve conduct and may also involve a fault element. The conduct may involve adverse outcomes (in which case there are also issues of causation); it may involve conduct that is permissible in some situations but not in others (such as whether it is consensual), or conduct that is problematic because it is offensive or risky, or sometimes may be just being caught up in a state of affairs and that it may involve a failure to do certain things. A fault element may be express or implied, and there are various factors in the implication; the various fault elements have particular meanings. A further set of doctrinal themes will include the methods by which liability is imposed, in the form of principal and secondary liability, supplemented by coverage of corporate and vicarious liability. Another area of doctrine will be the circumstances in which inchoate liability arises, including the rationale for it. Students will also need to know that liability can be defeated by certain justifications or excuses, and there is also a premise of volitional control that can be missing in certain circumstances.

The overall learning outcome of a criminal course will be to have students think like a criminal lawyer – namely, assessing whether the elements exist, whether the defendant is adequately linked to the elements, and whether a defence to liability exists. The traditionally-taught offences do not have a monopoly on this. Other offences that may form a relatively staple part of the practice of a criminal lawyer can achieve that: drugs and driving offences.

Learning outcomes, drugs law and driving law

Misuse of drugs law

Drugs offending may be more frequent than serious interpersonal violence. In New Zealand for the year to the end of 2014, there were 16,543 recorded drugs offences compared to 66 homicide offences, 4,056 sexual assaults, and 2,016 robberies (New Zealand Police 2015). In similarly-sized Ireland, annualised figures to the end of March 2014 showed 87 homicides, 1,947 sexual offences, and 15,651 drugs offences (Central Statistics Office Ireland). For England and Wales, in the year to the end of March 2015, there were 534 homicides, 88,000 sexual offences reported, and almost 170,000 drugs offences (Office for National Statistics UK). In each jurisdiction, there are many more recorded less serious assault offences and also theft offences: the suggestion is not that the traditionally-taught offences are not also important, but that drugs offending is also important numerically. Moreover, it will include offending at the level of importing or manufacturing that may be associated with organised criminality, involve multiple defendants, and potentially lead to very long sentences.

Drugs offending also presents a fascinating self-contained exemplar of basic themes in criminal law, often largely in a single statute. For example, New Zealand's Misuse of Drugs Act 1975 involves result crimes (e.g. dealing offences) and conduct crimes (including the offences of possession, a concept with significant nuances). New Zealand also has offences with status elements, such as that of associating with serious drug offenders (section 6B of the Summary Offences Act 1981). The full range of mens rea states is open to discussion through the 1975 statute, including whether they should be implied; the New Zealand statute also has a specific offence of theft of controlled drugs and one of handling such drugs being reckless as to whether they are obtained from crime, or laundering proceeds with a reckless frame of mind. Principal and party liability can be illustrated through drugs offending, and there are also specific offences to note – such as allowing premises to be used for drug taking – which are instances of criminalising conduct because it assists the targeted conduct of drug use. Corporate and vicarious liability principles can also be illustrated: section 17 of the 1975 Act makes specific provision for such liability. Similarly, inchoate offending can be illustrated, including through specific precursor offences, such as possession of utensils that can be used to consume drugs or importing substances that can be used to manufacture illegal drugs. There are also downstream offences, such as money laundering. In short, the major aspects of doctrine can be illustrated through drugs laws.

Further, it is an area of criminal offending that leads naturally into important areas of both doctrine and policy context and arguably provides a superior palette for some such matters. For example, doctrinal matters relating to jurisdiction and the overlap between international obligations and domestic law inevitably arise in drugs matters. Cases relating to the ongoing nature of a conspiracy, for instance, have arisen to allow jurisdiction to be exercised when drugs have merely passed through a country as part of an international shipment (*DPP v Doot* [1973] AC 807). Moreover, the structure of drug offending legislation cannot be understood without also noting relevant international treaty arrangements, which go back as far as the International Opium Convention 1912 and now the Single Convention on Narcotic Drugs 1961 and its 1972 Protocol, the Convention on Psychotropic Substances 1971 and the United Nations Convention against Illicit Traffic in Narcotic Drugs and Psychotropic Substances 1988. Similarly, there are reverse burdens of proof arising from possession of a certain amount, which leads to people being presumed to be dealers unless they prove to the contrary: this is said to be justified by the need to mount a 'war on drugs', but reveals a willingness by legislatures to ignore bedrock principles in relation to such matters as burdens of proof.

The whole strategy of criminalisation and heavy penalisation leads naturally to wider discussions. At the more traditional level, the proper ambit of the criminal law is raised, given that the whole aim of drugs law is to prevent people causing harm to themselves (and possibly to others) from consumption of substances deemed harmful: the validity of treating drugs and alcohol differently, and a range of other ethical and jurisprudential questions, arise naturally. Importantly, a significant difference between the traditionally-taught offences that are clearly mala per se and drugs offending is that it is arguably mala prohibita. Although it leads to some of the longest sentences and, in many countries, the imposition of the death penalty, there is obvious scope to discuss whether society should take a different approach – most obviously, legalisation and licensing (as in relation to alcohol or tobacco), with medicalisation of addiction, which might reduce the scope for organised criminal offending and the risks of violent offending that accompany it. This has been the approach of Portugal, with apparent success (Hughes 2010).

Indeed, the entire history of drugs law is a fascinating study of law in context, marked at the outset by overt racism against people of Chinese origin. In New Zealand, the first legislation related to opium: the Opium Prohibition Act 1901 required licences for the import of opium but expressly provided in section 3(3) that people "of the Chinese race" could not obtain a licence; and the more comprehensive Dangerous Drugs Act 1927 required warrants to allow police to search for proscribed drugs except in relation to searches in relation to opium in Chinese homes. This leads naturally to the examination of the modern context and arguments as to use of drugs laws to allow differential policing and prosecuting decisions: see Scraton and Stannard (chapter 11) and Steel (chapter 9) on the value of teaching students to understand the interplay between the law and the enforcement of the law and the potential for the latter to undermine any neutrality.

Driving offences

Driving offences, no doubt the most common by number, also illustrate well many doctrinal points that students need to learn and do so in a context that is familiar for most, which might assist comprehension. For example, illustrating the distinction between social welfare offences and those that are at a high level of criminality and mala per se – from driving a car without a current warrant of fitness to causing death by reckless driving – is possible. Further, most offences are based on the risk of adverse consequences (speeding offences, driving whilst impaired through alcohol or drugs); the impact of actual adverse outcomes is revealed by the existence of separate offences. Similarly, there are status offences – such as driving without a proper licence for the vehicle type or whilst disqualified.

Driving offences raise interesting questions as to the nature of criminality, including the distinction between mala per se and mala prohibita offending. For example, as legal limits as to permissible blood-alcohol levels have decreased over the past few decades, changes in societal attitudes towards drink-driving may mean it is now considered mala per se to take the risk of mixing intoxication and driving, but regular drink-drivers may take a different view. Similarly, public debate about speeding offences regularly involves comments to the effect of enforcement being more about revenue raising than about responding to the fact that speeding makes any crash so much more serious and so should be viewed as mala per se.

Party liability questions also arise and in interesting situations such as when bar staff or private hosts provide alcohol to someone they know will drive; corporate and vicarious liability matters also arise in relation to driving offences in the course of employment. This may extend to serious offences in which deaths occur in situations caused by poor maintenance, which may raise questions of causation, corporate, and omission liability and possibly joint liability if the conduct of the driver is also implicated. There is no shortage of inchoate offending, including in corporate settings, such as where employers and drivers collude to avoid limits on driving hours or employers encourage such behaviour.

The overlaps between substantive law and social policy matters relating to the risks of police targeting certain groups also arise, and issues arise as to whether random powers to stop drivers should be allowed for reasons of public safety – given the prevalence of road deaths and injuries – or limited to situations of reasonable suspicion that an offence had been committed. There are also wider policy questions, such as whether improvements in road design or safety features in vehicles, which could be made mandatory, might be a better approach to reducing injury on the roads, rather than a motif of focusing on instances of poor driving.

The important overlap between criminal procedure and substantive law can also be illustrated: charges of refusing or failing to complete breath or blood-alcohol tests can be defended on the basis that the prerequisites to the police having a right to make the demand were not met. The context of this is the requirement that defendants can be compelled to produce the very evidence that incriminates them.

The limits of criminalisation can also be illustrated: are the laws relating to requiring seat belts or preventing mobile phone use examples of too great an interference with autonomous choices, or does the fact that someone else may have to witness or clean up the consequences of such demonstrably unsafe behaviour provide a sufficient justification for its criminalisation?

The benefits of offering choice

The brief description of the points arising from drug offending and driving matters is designed to outline the easy fit between these two common areas of offending and the general themes that a traditional course will aim to illustrate, including doctrinal concepts and public policy overlays. No doubt they are not the only self-contained areas of criminal law that could also be taught as the substantive offences that illustrate the more general matters. As to how that might be structured, other chapters in this collection illustrate the questions relevant to course construction and techniques relevant to ensuring comprehension through active learning.

Even so, it may be suggested that it is best to leave well enough alone; after all, if the traditionally-taught specific offences have withstood the test of time, why should there be change? Although the 'test of time' may reflect inertia, which is not by itself impressive as a justification, there are no doubt relevant advantages, such as the infrastructure that exists in the form of the many established texts that follow the standard structure of using interpersonal violence and property offending. However, new texts can be written, as illustrated by Gans in chapter 8.

There will also be arguments in favour of the traditional concentrations, such as that violence is what is interesting about criminal law. It would be useful to carry out research on whether that is an accurate assertion, or does it perhaps reflect a 'boys own' view of the topic? Moreover, it overlooks the ability of lecturers to enthuse students: I have heard rumours of a colleague who makes tax law interesting.

A more substantial argument may be that the seriousness of homicide and rape charges means that there are more appeals, such that a significant number of the core cases on general principles arise in that setting. Again, it would be interesting to carry out an audit of whether that is so. Moreover, it may be that homicide and rape are in many respects atypical in terms of general principles. For example, the need for reasonable grounds for a belief in consent in a rape setting, a common statutory modification of the common law, is not a regular feature of other serious offences. And the complexities of the mens rea for murder are atypical: the New Zealand statutory version, for example, includes intention as to death (which seems to be limited to direct rather than oblique intention), but also has recklessness as to death and various elements of the common law's constructive malice through a version of the felony murder rule. Steel makes the point in chapter 9 that homicide has a somewhat unusual structure; similarly in relation to property offences, Child makes the point in chapter 3 that the mens rea provisions for theft are unique.

The point arising is that if the offences typically taught are supposed to be exemplars of general principles, some of them do not fulfil that role well. An alternative viewpoint is that criminal law consists more of a collection of relatively independent areas, as is accepted in relation to the law of torts. As such, the key for student learning is the approach to adopt within the particular area of law rather than to search for general principles. The chapters by Steel and Scraton and Stannard (chapters 9 and 11) contain further discussion on whether this search is fruitful. The self-contained nature of drugs and driving, usually within a single statute, supports the viewpoint that it may be more realistic to view criminal law as a series of codes which may overlap in part and on occasion rather than forming a cohesive whole.

Moreover, the focus on crimes that are clearly mala per se may create a false impression of the criminal law and the existence of principles such as the presumption of mens rea which are undermined by the prevalence of strict and absolute liability offences: Blake and Ashworth (1996) found that 45% of English indictable offences were actually strict liability offences. Since more students will practice in the commercial rather than the criminal field, they may find that a fuller understanding of the themes that apply in a regulatory criminal setting is more important.

Supplementing this utility to the profession – and for all the unnecessary sensitivity about the trade school function (which does not seem to affect medical schools), there is the very practical point that no law school would offer a criminal law course that was designed not to allow its students to progress into practice – there is the fact that academic lawyers may more naturally tend to write in areas that they teach, with the result that there will be a comparative lack of writing on these other significant aspects of the criminal world that are important in practice. If so, is not the academy partially failing in its task of critiquing court decisions and policy with a view to securing better outcomes?

Another way to approach the issue would be to ask how a course would be constructed if there were a blank slate. One would take the relevant pedagogical aims – ensuring the illustration of important areas of criminal law doctrine, outlining the role of criminal law in implementing social policy, and so on – and construct a course around that. Without the baggage of the history of criminal law being taught in a certain way, the academic freedom to illustrate criminal law through whatever the individual academic thought best would come to the fore. As is noted in chapter 1, this is often attainable within the regulatory framework imposed by the profession and could be negotiated with them if there are constraints that reflect the traditional course. Indeed, the profession could be surveyed as to what should be taught.

An important feature that could emerge in course planning within a larger law school that has more than one stream of students studying crime is the prospect of offering to students the choice of the concentration. For example, students who envisage that they might practice in a typical high street criminal law firm might benefit from a course on 'street crime' (perhaps including drugs, public order, assaults, theft, and criminal damage), whereas students aiming for commercial practice might prefer a stream covering commercial and financial crime (perhaps focussing on theft, fraud, tax crime, and financial markets crime and with a more detailed analysis of matters such as corporate and vicarious liability). As has been noted in relation to drugs and driving matters, they may provide an easy entry into areas of legal principle that are not naturally raised by mala per se offending; financial regulatory criminal matters also have such wider questions arising, such as the use of criminal as opposed to disciplinary liability and the creation of hybrid regimes of civil penalties for non-compliance with regulatory requirements.

No doubt various other 'themes' could be developed and offered, each of which could well have particular advantages in terms of illustrating certain doctrines. This does not exclude variety within a law school that teaches criminal law in one stream: a lecturer might find it refreshing to offer the course using different foci, whether on a rotational or occasional basis.

There would no doubt be challenges to this approach that would have to be met. For instance, equitable marking between streams taught differently and the potential for disadvantage based on the availability of textbooks that focus on areas other than the traditionally-taught subjects. Moreover, it may be that certain streams of contextual teaching, such as an introduction to feminist jurisprudence, might be more suited to the traditional model: that, of course, can be a stream that is taught if that reflects the priority of the academic in question. The first step, naturally, is for lecturers in criminal law to reflect on whether their teaching is unnecessarily constrained by history and whether it meets the pedagogically sound approach to design they would adopt when creating a fresh course that was optional rather than compulsory.

References

Blake, Meredith and Ashworth, Andrew, "The Presumption of Innocence in English Criminal Law", [1996] *Criminal Law Review* 306–317.

Central Statistics Office Ireland: http://www.cso.ie/en/releasesandpublications/er/rc/recordedcrimequarter12014/

Cownie, Fiona, "Searching for Theory in Teaching Law" in Fiona Cownie (ed), *The Law School–Global Issues, Local Questions*, Ashgate, Adershot 1999, pp. 41–61.

Hughes, Caitlin Elizabeth and Stevens, Alex, "What Can We Learn from the Portuguese Decriminalisation of Illicit Drugs", [2010] 50 *British Journal of Criminology* 999–1022.

New Zealand Police, *New Zealand Crime Statistics 2014*, Police National Headquarters, ISSN 1178–1521, April 2015.

Office for National Statistics: http://www.ons.gov.uk/ons/taxonomy/index.html?nscl=Crime

Ramsden, Paul, *Learning to Teach in Higher Education*, Routledge, London 1992 (second edition 2003).

Chapter 17

The absence of regulatory crime from the criminal law curriculum

Shane Kilcommins, Susan Leahy, and Eimear Spain

Introduction

In examining the contours of the penal complex, lawyers, penologists, and criminologists are often drawn to traditional 'real crime' (homicides, violent assaults, organised crime, sexual offences, requirements of *mens rea* and *actus reus*, and general defences) whilst ignoring regulatory offences which are often enforced by specialist agencies (Lacey 2004, p. 144). They have tended to be preoccupied with the punitive regulation of the poor – a project closely tied to a police-prosecutions-prisons way of knowing – that focuses on "crime in the streets" rather than "crime in the suites" (Ashworth 2000; Braithwaite 2003). As Scott notes,

> [L]egal professionals schooled largely in appellate decisions relating to indictable offences, but also a broader society and media, [are] interested and often obsessed with homicide, sexual offences, robbery and theft. Much of the teaching of criminal law in universities also shares this focus.
> (Scott 2010, p. 64)

As a result, "[r]egulatory criminal law is all but ignored by most criminal law texts and journals" (Chalmers and Leverick 2014, p. 75).

The narrow exclusivity of this approach is a mistake: regulatory criminal law is becoming increasingly influential, not least because criminalisation is now more than ever viewed as a panacea for almost any social problem, whether in matters of competition law, environmental protection, health and safety law, or consumer and corporate affairs. There is also a new governmental approach involving the changing nature and perception of security risks and the emergence of more 'networked governance' strategies that employ civil, administrative, and regulatory mechanisms alongside criminal law instruments. This extended, somewhat fluid, institutional arrangement is very different from the traditional bifurcated representation of wrongs as either civil or criminal harms, with almost mutually exclusive formal processes for knowing and handling conflicts (Van Krieken 2006, p. 1, citing *R v Kidman* (1915) 20 CLR 425).

As a result, distinctions traditionally drawn cease to make sense – namely that, in contrast to 'ordinary' crimes, regulatory crimes are *mala prohibita* and do not involve quasi-moral "values such as 'justice, fairness, right, and wrong' but should instead be thought of in 'instrumental means-ends terms'" (Lacey 2004, p. 145); they are a 'quasi-administrative matter' and do not attract significant moral opprobrium or stigmatise those convicted (McAuley and McCutcheon 2000, p. 341), or are more likely to be victimless (or at least not have a readily identifiable victim); and for the most part, such offences do not embody a punitive or sanctioning model of justice, preferring compliance strategies instead. This conceptualisation remains in the ascendancy, as evident in many criminal law textbooks and syllabi, but we suggest that it is time to abandon the traditional divisions which have so structured our thinking and teaching. The teaching of criminal law should be extended beyond a focus on a relatively narrow taxonomy of offences and contestable principles – such as subjective culpability – to incorporate regulatory criminal wrongdoing. Rather than being afforded exceptional or epiphenomenal status, its extensive use, infrastructural arrangements, and modes of operation requires us to re-consider the purposes, principles, and boundaries of criminal law and how it is taught.

Public protection

It is hardly contentious that our criminal justice system is founded on the identification of public protection and security as 'essential goods' to enable us to flourish and go about our lives free from the threat of injury or harm. What is striking is the ongoing perception that regulatory crime does not threaten our security in the same way that street crime does. This is a fallacy. Though it may appear more remote, more victimless, and may often be less dramatic, misconduct in the banking and corporate sectors, in the workplace, in the environment, and in the distortion of competition in the market poses as much, if not more, of a threat to our everyday lives as ordinary crime (with the potential to impact more people). Our security can be affected by such matters as workplace injuries, loss of jobs, loss of reputation, and the consequent devaluation of share prices and pension funds, threats to the environment, increased taxation, and increased costs for consumers. Habermas noted that our legal system needs to move away from "personal references and towards system relations" including "protection from environmental destruction, protection from radiation poisoning or lethal genetic damage; and, in general, protection from the uncontrolled side effects of large technological operations, pharmaceutical products, scientific experimentation, and so forth" (Habermas 2008, pp. 432–435). Most criminal law syllabi in Ireland (and elsewhere – see chapter 1) continue to focus on 'personal references' – assaults, homicides, sexual offences, criminal damage – and remain rooted in 'crime in the street' harms to individuals. By ignoring the 'systems risks', they facilitate a very narrow understanding of what constitutes a threat to our security, fastened to a very traditional outlook that views regulatory wrongdoing as having comparatively benign effects (Wright and Friedreichs 1991, p. 105).

Compliance and sanctioning strategies

One of the principal difficulties with only teaching criminal law through a 'police-prosecutions-prisons' prism is that it assumes that sanctions are a point of first resort for all types of offending behaviour. Though such an assumption works well in relation to most serious ordinary crime, it does not properly capture the realities in respect of low-level offences, nor the possibilities available in respect of regulatory wrongdoing where there is an emphasis on promoting an entrepreneurial spirit. Compliance rather than sanctioning techniques will often be called for in this setting. They are orientated towards persuasion and dialogue and are designed to promote good working relationships (Macrory 2006; Hamilton 2010, p. 17; Lynch-Fannon 2010, p. 127). A sanctioning approach to all regulatory wrongdoing would, it is argued, have very negative consequences:

> it undermines the coercive power of the criminal law, dilutes its expressive power, over-deters otherwise desirable business activities, conflates blameworthiness with imprisonment, creates incentives for prosecutors to abuse their powers, fuels an appetite for enhancing prison terms, increases social costs and punishes people for actions that in some instances are not even civil wrongs, let alone undertaken with the taint of moral wrongfulness.
> (Gopalan 2010, p. 2)

While the relatively equal effect of prison is often seen as advantageous, it can also be argued that if the cost of imprisonment is the same for offenders with different earning capacities, imprisoning those with very high earning capacities is a waste of social capital, especially if the objectives of incarceration can be achieved through other means (Gopalan 2010, p. 2). An appreciation of the competing arguments in this sphere "requires an analytical eye and an appreciation for nuance and competing views" (Shover and Cullen 2008, p. 171), and the inclusion of the topic in the criminal curriculum offers instructors an opportunity to develop important skills in undergraduate law students.

There is significant merit in the adoption of compliance strategies and, importantly, their exploration in criminal law syllabi. The line between poor business decision making and criminal activity is far from clear cut. Moreover, white-collar crime is difficult to detect because it often occurs in private, behind closed corporate doors. It is also the case that proof is difficult in these cases and often resource intensive. It is for this reason that the area of regulatory crime still, by and large, remains predominantly orientated towards a compliance model of enforcement (McGrath 2015). This is facilitated by a wide range of strategies that favour the employment of negotiation, consultation, and persuasion, rather than an exclusively sanctioning approach that would potentially polarize the various parties involved. These strategies include audits, warning letters, notices, injunctions, guidance, binding directions, and the suspension and revocation of licences (O'Neill 2008; Appleby 2010). As Scott (2010) has recently noted,

> The enforcement strategies of enforcement agencies have been arrayed in a pyramidal approach to enforcement in which the object is to maintain as much enforcement activity as possible at the base of the pyramid. . . . This approach is said to be effective not only with businesses which are orientated to legal compliance, but also with the "amoral calculators" for whom compliance becomes the least costly path when they know there is a credible threat of escalation to more stringent sanctions.
>
> (p. 73)

The nuances and circuits that run through this pyramidal structure – with compliance at the bottom and sanctioning at the apex – is not currently captured in criminal law syllabi in universities in Ireland. In this regard, the curriculum is quite one dimensional and divorced from the 'action' and practice of criminal law. It also fails to capture the breadth of criminal law purposes. A compliance model of justice, for example, speaks primarily to the 'good man' who seeks to act in good faith and employs the law as a normative guide to conduct and action and not to the 'bad man' who seeks to evade the strictures of the law. In order to encapsulate both forms of conduct, the compliance model must also be supported by a sanctioning model which can act as a platform for the expression of collective outrage. The criminal law is designed to uphold moral sensibilities, and it permits a powerful message to be conveyed in relation to the anger felt by ordinary citizens about the commission of certain crimes. It also acts as an important safety valve by limiting the 'demoralising effects' on society of the consequences of serious misconduct (McGrath 2012, p. 72; Robinson 2014).

Traditionally, it had been said that the focus of the sanctions for many of these regulatory offences was more 'apersonal' in nature than their ordinary counterparts. The argument was that "these were not real crimes to which stigma should attach, but were rather in the nature of administrative regulations with non-stigmatising penalties such as fines" (Lacey 2004, p. 161). The traditional lack of a mens rea requirement operated as the "doctrinal marker of these defendants less than fully criminal status from a social point of view" (Baldwin 2004; Lacey 2004). But regulatory agencies have increasingly grown considerable teeth as regards prosecution. For example, on conviction on indictment for competition law offences in Ireland, undertakings are liable to a fine of up to the greater of €5 million or 10% of the turnover of the undertaking in the financial year ending in the 12 months prior to conviction. Individuals are subject to the same fine limits and/or a term of imprisonment not exceeding ten years. The apex of the pyramid now occupies a space which views regulatory wrongdoing as 'real crime' and has adopted multiple strategies with potentially serious individual consequences, and the exclusion of regulatory crime from criminal law syllabi in these circumstances is a serious shortcoming.

Governance

Criminal law teaching remains predominantly focused on offences that are pursued exclusively by centralised policing (the Gardaí) and prosecuting authorities (Director of Public Prosecutions). This tends to ignore the emergence of new mechanisms and modes of governance for dealing with criminal wrongdoing. Since the 1990s, we have increasingly witnessed the extensive use of regulatory criminal and civil strategies in areas such as competition law, environmental protection, health and safety law, and consumer and corporate affairs (Scott 2010, p. 69). These strategies are supported by a wide range of criminal sanctions available summarily and on indictment. Durkheim neatly captures this expansion in criminalisation, juxtaposing it with the decline in severity in penal punishments:

> Seeing with what regularity repression seems weaker the further one goes in evolution, one might believe that the movement is destined to continue without end; in other words, that punishment is tending towards zero . . . For there is no reason to believe that human criminality must in its turn regress as have the penalties which punish it. Rather everything points to its gradual development; that the list of acts which are defined as crimes of this type will grow, and that their criminal character will be accentuated. Frauds and injustices, which yesterday left the public conscience almost indifferent, arouse it today and this insensitivity will become more acute with time.
> (Durkheim 1992, pp. 46–47)

The emergence of this regulatory criminal framework is significantly different from the unified monopolies of centralised control underpinning policing and prosecution in the modern State. Arguably these new techniques and strategies can be seen as part of a pattern of more, rather than less, governance, but taking 'decentred', 'at-a-distance' forms. Prior to the nineteenth century, the institution of local policing was heavily orientated towards the "creation of an orderly environment, especially for trade and commerce" (Braithwaite 2005, pp. 13–14). It did not focus exclusively on offences against persons and property, but also included the regulation of "customs, trade, highways, foodstuffs, health, labour standards, fire, forests and hunting, street life, migration and immigration communities" (Braithwaite 2000, p. 225). Throughout the nineteenth century, however, the State very gradually began to monopolise and separate the prosecutorial and policing functions, particularly for serious crimes. In terms of policing, this meant that uniformed paramilitary police were preoccupied with the punitive regulation of the poor to the almost total exclusion of any interest in the constitution of markets and the just regulation of commerce became one of the most universal of globalised regulatory models.

From the mid-nineteenth century, factories inspectorates, mines inspectorates, liquor licensing boards, weights and measures inspectorates, health and sanitation, food inspectorates, and countless others were created to begin to fill the vacuum left by constables now concentrating only on crime. Business regulation became variegated into many specialist regulatory branches (Braithwaite 2005, pp. 15–16). In Ireland, these specialist agencies included the Bacon Marketing Board, the Irish Tourist Board, the Racing Board, the Health Authorities, CIE (Ireland's national public transport provider), the Irish Greyhound Board, and the Opticians Board. Similarly, during the course of the nineteenth century, conflicts were no longer viewed as the property of the parties most directly affected. Previously strong stakeholder interests in the prosecution process, such as victims and the local community, were gradually colonised in the course of the nineteenth century by a State apparatus which acted for rather than with the public.

Now, however, the Office of the Director of Public Prosecutions is, to some extent, increasingly losing its monopoly role. The number of administrative agencies that have entered the criminal justice arena, colonising the power to investigate regulatory crimes in specific areas and to prosecute summarily, has increased dramatically in Ireland in recent years. They include the Revenue Commissioners, the Competition Authority, the Director of Consumer Affairs, the Environmental Protection Agency, the Health and Safety Authority, and the Office of the Director of Corporate Enforcement. Significantly, these agencies have both investigative and prosecution functions, with each pursuing their own agendas, policies, and practices. Moreover, very wide powers of entry, inspection, examination, search, seizure, and analysis are given to some of these agencies (Considine and Kilcommins 2006). Another striking feature of this regulatory infrastructure is the proliferation of hybrid enforcement mechanisms that can be employed by the agencies or, on occasion, by private parties. These mechanisms have also contributed to a more general 'blurring of legal forms" (Ashworth 2000, p. 237) and conflating the functional distinctions that exist between criminal and civil law, as well as between regulatory wrongdoing and ordinary wrongdoing (McGrath 2015). Criminal law syllabi which continue to focus on centralised policing and prosecuting authorities and exclude from consideration the wide variety of enforcement agencies and mechanisms employed today cannot be said to accurately reflect the modern criminal law. It is contended that a fuller integration of new mechanisms and modes of governance for dealing with criminal wrongdoing in criminal law curricula is both desirable and necessary (Baer 2014, p. 790).

Information sharing and mandatory reporting

Prior to the centralisation of power in centralised police and prosecution forces, the old system of law enforcement was heavily reliant on a network of rewards, victims, thief-taking, and accomplice-driven prosecutions. As the

State increasingly began to monopolise investigative and prosecutorial functions during the nineteenth century, recourse to local networks was minimised; where these practices continued – for example with informants – they were downplayed. The centralised state apparatus – as expressed through the police and public prosecutors – thus completely monopolised the crime conflict. Commitment to this way of doing justice still informs criminal law teaching in Ireland. Though it remains largely true of the investigation and prosecution of 'ordinary' offences, it fails to adequately capture new circuits of information gathering in the regulatory sphere. New regulatory approaches are beginning to throw up investigative and prosecutorial networks that in part rely on information gathering beyond the traditional reach of the police and prosecution agencies.

What is emerging in recent years is the increasing adoption of a more variegated approach to the detection, investigation, and punishment of offences, straddling both civil and criminal jurisdictions. More specifically, legislation increasingly permits authorities, including the Competition Authority, An Garda Síochána, the Revenue Commissioners, the Insolvency Service of Ireland, the Director of Corporate Enforcement, and the Irish Takeover Panel, to share information with each other. In some instances, individuals are required to become 'information reporters' (Horan 2011, pp. 1529–1540). Auditors, tax advisers, lawyers, accountants and liquidators are all bound by statutory requirements (section 447 of the Companies Act 2014 and section 59 of the Criminal Justice (Theft and Fraud Offences) Act 2000) to report information to relevant authorities. Very broad and generic obligations to disclose information have also recently been enacted in Ireland, and it will become increasingly important for lawyers to understand their obligations in this regard and to inform clients, yet criminal law syllabi continue to ignore this development.

In addition to facilitating exchange of information and compelling certain parties to become information reporters, the authorities are increasingly also seeking to protect and encourage witnesses to come forward and provide evidence. 'Whistle-blowers' have been crucially important in Ireland on lifting the lid on various abuses such as the care of the elderly and corruption in banks. Encouraging such witnesses to provide information ordinarily takes two forms: protection and/or immunity. The Protected Disclosures Act 2014, for example, provides extensive protection for public-sector workers in Ireland in respect of wrongdoings such as health and safety threats, misuse of public monies, mismanagement by a public official, damage to the environment, or concealment or destruction of information relating to any of the foregoing. Other relevant statutes are section 6 of the Unfair Dismissals Act 1977; section 27 of the Safety, Health and Welfare at Work Act 2005; section 87 of the Consumer Protection Act 2007; section 26 of the Employment Permits Act 2006; and section 20 of the Criminal Justice Act 2011. The "reconstruction of criminal justice in decentralised ways so that it responds to local needs, reflects local morality, and takes advantage of local knowledge" (Bayley 2001, pp. 211–212) is an important development in the field, and law students and lawyers alike will be required to appreciate the significance of this shift both for professionals and the public.

Causation

One of the difficulties of teaching criminal law with a focus on the relatively narrow traditional range of offences is that it implicitly paints a picture of the types of persons committing crimes. It will inevitably contain a "disproportionate number of those who are poor, uneducated and unskilled" (McCullagh 1995, pp. 411–412). Criminal law teaching can in part help inculcate a set of attitudes towards the legal system in society by exhorting, in particular, its legitimacy on the basis of its neutral nature, whilst ignoring the underlying structural inequalities of power which are imbricated in the cross-currents of society. The ideology of objectivity, egalitarianism, and the strict application of rules can mask and mystify law's partiality, particularly its capacity to preserve and maintain the status quo for those in power (Horwitz 1992, p. 266). As Norrie (2001) suggests, "The cunning of the law lies in its ability to mask the one-sidedness of its instrumental content through its formal character as a logic of universal individualism" (p. 23). Hiding behind the 'false consciousness' of black-letterism are the variety of hierarchical interests that it serves. Apart from legal education (Kennedy 1990, p. 45), this also has implications for legal practice, particularly the notion that what lawyers actually do is apolitical and independent, merely following the inner technical logic of the law. This might be reassuring, but it is a denial of the political and social realities of legal practice:

> [B]lack-letterism works as a convenient mode of denial. It enables legal academics and lawyers to engage in what is a highly political and contested arena of social life – namely, law – and to pretend that they are doing so in a largely non-political way. The main advantage of this is that they can go about their daily routines without assuming any political or personal responsibility for what happens in the legal process. However, the insistence that lawyering is a neutral exercise that does not implicate lawyers in any political process or demand from scholars a commitment to any particular ideology is as weak as it is woeful. Such an image is a profoundly conservative and crude understanding of what it is to engage in the business of courts, legislatures and the like.
> (Hutchinson 1999, p. 302)

In addition to difficulties with the portrayal of criminal law as neutral and value free, criminal law teachers who exclude regulatory crime from the curriculum implicitly construct a very narrow view of criminal typology, giving the impression that it is only certain socio-economic classes that commit crime. The crimes of the powerful remain at the margin of attention. This is in spite of considerable change in criminological discourse in relation to white-collar crime and state crime.

Paradigmatic criminal law

At a more technocratic level, many aspects of regulatory crime operate in opposition to the general trend of paradigmatic criminal law which permits general defences, demands both a conduct element and a fault element, and respects procedural standards such as a legal burden of proof beyond reasonable doubt. Pure doctrines of subjective culpability and the presumption of innocence are increasingly abandoned within this streamlined regulatory framework to make up for difficulties of proof in complex cases. The increasingly instrumental nature of criminal legal regulation is evident, for example, in the introduction of 'reverse onus' provisions that require the accused to displace a presumption of guilt. While this development is not uncommon in some other areas of law, for example, in relation to drugs offences, it is more pronounced in the regulatory criminal arena.

The system of justice that applies in the regulatory realm is thus more inculpatory in orientation than its ordinary criminal counterpart. It is also evident in the instrumental fault element requirements of criminal regulation. The attachment of a subjective mental element to wrongdoing in conventional criminal law is often severed in the regulatory criminal arena where objective standards of culpability apply. Moreover, any defences that might exist in the regulatory area are also more specialised than might be the case in the general defences that apply in criminal law. For example, in competition law, it is a specific defence to show that the agreement, decision, or concerted practice complained of benefited from a declaration from the Competition Authority that the practice contributes to improved production or distribution of goods and services, or promotes technical or economic progress.

Employing instrumentalist reasoning can also give rise to difficulties, particularly in relation to constitutional justice and due process safeguards. These difficulties have manifested themselves in relation to, for example, the imposition of administrative sanctions (*McDonald v Bord na Gcon* [1965] IR 217); definitions of a crime and double jeopardy (*Registrar of Companies v District Judge David Anderson and System Partners Limited* [2005] 1 IR 21); the privilege against self-incrimination (*DPP v Collins* (Unreported, Circuit Court, 27 September 2007) cited in Duggan 2008, p. 70); the burden of proof (*PJ Carey Contractors Limited v DPP* [2012] IR 234); proportionality of sentencing (*DPP v Hughes* [2012] IECCA 85; *Paul Begley v DPP* [2013] IECCA 32); and *mens rea* requirements (*CC v Ireland and Others* [2006] IESC 33; The Employment Equality Bill 1996 [1997] 2 IR 321); *Brady v Environmental Protection Agency* [2007] IEHC 58).

As these regulatory criminal practices become more embedded, they are increasingly tested in the courts, given their instrumental desire to maximise efficiency, enhance control, and minimise risk. The flow of power into these civil and regulatory spheres is challenging for a due process system that emphasises the primacy of individual rights. The institutionalised nature of accused rights has ensured that they cannot be easily "trumped for collective policy reasons such as risk management, security and public protection" (Dworkin 1977, pp. 93–94). They remain very much part of the topography in the Irish criminal process, carrying a "threshold weight" "which the government is required to respect case by case, decision by decision" (Dworkin 1988, p. 223).

When due process and regulatory values and outlooks meet, as they increasingly do, it makes for an interesting battleground – a site for struggle and competing claims about security, instrumental effectiveness, governance, and liberal principles. These tensions are often, however, not captured in criminal law teaching, which continues to perpetuate the myth of regulatory exceptionalism (usually in relation to strict liability offences only). The practice and operation of regulatory criminal law needs to be more fully embraced to highlight its growth and the tensions it creates for a traditional criminal law model rooted in an 1861 Offences against the Person Act conception of wrongdoing.

Conclusion

It is clear that the traditional preoccupation in criminal law syllabi with well-accepted forms of criminal activity (e.g. assault, theft, murder, sexual offences), to the exclusion of regulatory crime, promotes a myopic vision of criminality amongst students. When students do not learn about regulatory crime alongside 'real crimes', their understanding of regulatory crime as less harmful and less threatening is re-enforced. Given the available evidence of the threat posed to society by 'systems risks' and the proliferation of regulatory offences in recent decades, a criminal law syllabus which focuses exclusively on traditional criminal offences fails to paint a complete picture for students. Moreover, their learning is fragmented, as their understanding of this form of criminal activity is relegated to learning within commercial or company law context where the appreciation of this activity as a crime is lost. Particularly problematic in this regard is the failure to teach students how our traditional understanding of the structure of criminal offences (requiring conduct and fault elements), criminal defences, and procedural safeguards differs when applied to regulatory crime. A departure from the traditional approach to exploring the contours of the criminal law is required and should encompass the broad sweep of offences and enforcement agencies, as well as recognise the variegated approach to the detection, investigation, and enforcement of offences in the twenty-first century.

References

Appleby, P. (2010) 'Compliance and Enforcement – the ODCE perspective' in Kilcommins and Kilkelly, eds, *Regulatory Crime in Ireland*, Dublin, First Law.
Ashworth, A. (2000) 'Is the Criminal Law a Lost Cause?', *Law Quarterly Review*, 116, 225–256.
Baer, M. (2014) 'Teaching White Collar Crime', *Ohio State Journal of Criminal Law*, 11, 789–793.
Baldwin, R. (2004) 'The New Punitive Regulation', *Modern Law Review*, 67(3), 351–383.
Bayley, D. (2001) 'Security and Justice for All' in H. Strang and J. Braithwaite, eds., *Restorative Justice and Civil Society*, Cambridge: Cambridge University Press.

Braithwaite, J. (2000) 'The New Regulatory State and the Transformation of Criminology', *British Journal of Criminology*, 40, 222–238.

Braithwaite, J. (2003) 'What's Wrong with the Sociology of Punishment', *Theoretical Criminology*, 7(1), 5–28.

Braithwaite, J. (2005) *Neoliberalism or Regulatory Capitalism*, Occasional Paper 5, Canberra: National University of Australia.

Chalmers, J. and Leverick, F. (2014) 'Quantifiying Criminalisation' in R.A. Duff et al., eds., *Criminalisation: The Political Morality of Criminal Law*, Oxford: Oxford University Press.

Considine, J. and Kilcommins, S. (2006) 'The Importance of Safeguards on Revenue Powers: Another Perspective', *Irish Tax Review*, 19(6), 49–54.

Duggan, G. (2008) 'Disclosure to Revenue and the Privilege Against Self-Incrimination', *Irish Tax Review*, 70.

Durkheim, E. (1992) 'Two Laws of Penal Evolution' in M. Gane, ed., *The Radical Sociology of Durkheim and Mauss*, London: Routledge.

Dworkin, R. (1977) *Taking Rights Seriously*, Harvard: Harvard University Press.

Dworkin, R. (1988) *Law's Empire*, Harvard: Harvard University Press.

Gopalan, S. (2010), 'Skilling's Martyrdom: The Case for Criminalization without Incarceration', available at http://eprints.maynoothuniversity.ie/2417/1/SG_Skillings_Martyrdom.pdf

Habermas, J. (2008) *Between Facts and Norms*, Cambridge: Polity Press.

Hamilton, J. (2010) 'Do We Need a System of Administrative Sanctions in Ireland' in S. Kilcommins and U. Kilkelly, eds., *Regulatory Crime in Ireland*, Dublin: First Law.

Horan, S. (2011) *Corporate Crime*, Dublin: Bloomsbury Professional.

Horwitz, M. (1992) *The Transformation of American Law, 1780–1860*, Oxford: Oxford University Press.

Hutchinson, A.C. (1999) 'Beyond Black-Letterism: Ethics and Legal Education', *International Journal of Legal Education*, 33(3), 301.

Kennedy, D. (1990) 'Legal Education as Training for Hierarchy' in David Kairys, ed., *The Politics of Law*, New York: Pantheon Books.

Lacey, N. (2004) 'Criminalization and Regulation: The Role of Criminal Law' in C. Parker, et al., eds., *Regulating Law*, Oxford: Oxford University Press.

Lynch-Fannon, I. (2010) 'Controlling Risk Taking: Whose Job Is It Anyway?' in S. Kilcommins and U. Kilkelly, eds., *Regulatory Crime in Ireland*, Dublin: First Law.

Macrory, R. (2006) *Regulatory Justice: Making Sanctions Effective*, Final Report, Macrory Review, London: Cabinet Office.

McAuley, F and McCutcheon, P. *Criminal Liability*, Dublin: Round Hall, 2000

McCullagh, C. (1995) 'Getting the Criminals We Want: The Social Production of the Criminal Population' in P. Clancy, ed., *Irish Society: Sociological Perspectives*, Dublin: IPA.

McGrath, J. (2012) 'Sentencing White-Collar Criminals: Making the Punishment Fit the White-Collar Crime', *Irish Criminal Law Journal*, 3, 72–79.

McGrath, J. (2015) *Corporate and White Collar Crime in Ireland: A New Architecture of Regulatory Enforcement*, Manchester: Manchester University Press.

Norrie, A. (2001) *Crime, Reason and History: A Critical Introduction to Criminal Law*, Cambridge: Cambridge University Press.

O'Neill, A. (2008) 'The Consumer Protection Act 2007-Enforcing the New Rules', *Irish Law Times*, 26, 46–52.

Robinson, D. (2014) 'Collared', *Gazette of the Law Society Ireland*, 180(1), 40–43.

Scott, C. (2010) 'Regulatory Crime: History, Functions, Problems, Solutions' in S. Kilcommins and U. Kilkelly, eds., *Regulatory Crime in Ireland*, Dublin: First Law.

Shover, N. and Cullen, F.T. (2008) 'Studying and Teaching White-Collar Crime: Populist and Patrician Perspectives', *Journal of Criminal Justice Education*, 19(2), 155–174.

Van Krieken, R. (2006) 'Crime, Government and Civilization: Rethinking Elias in Criminology', available at http://hdl.handle.net/2123/916

Wright, R.A. and Friedreichs, D.O. (1991) 'White-Collar Crime in the Criminal Justice Curriculum', *Journal of Criminal Justice Education*, 2(1), 95–122.

Chapter 18

Conclusion

Looking to the future

Kris Gledhill and Ben Livings

In this concluding chapter, we will try to draw out some of the emergent themes from the preceding chapters and to explore the implications of a fuller understanding of the state of and prospects for criminal law teaching they have enabled. In so doing, it is unlikely that we will do justice to every aspect of each of the contributors' arguments, but we hope to draw attention to their key contributions and how these might suggest potential avenues of enquiry and opportunities for further research.

In Chapter 1, we noted the marked similarity in criminal law teaching across common law jurisdictions. In acknowledging some of the reasons for this, we nevertheless pointed to the considerable scope that exists for innovation should that be thought necessary. The implicit question that underlies this volume, and which has motivated each of the contributions, is: what is the best way to teach criminal law? Or, more comprehensively, there is a desire to suggest a range of options as to the teaching of criminal law beyond that of a black-letter course of lectures structured around several weeks of general principles followed by several weeks of the details of offences of violence and property.

A number of chapters concentrate on pedagogical approaches and techniques and how these impact upon students' understanding of the materials with which they are presented. These are pertinent to courses irrespective of decisions made as to content. For example, Brown and Murray suggest that the traditional lecture might be improved through the use of technology that facilitates a degree of interaction, while the chapters by Boylan-Kemp and Huxley-Binns and Fitzpatrick suggest more fundamental change to the way in which criminal law is taught through the use of 'flipped classrooms' and 'problem-based learning'. Donson and O'Sullivan and Child address some of the conceptual challenges posed by teaching according to the classificatory and organisational principles of criminal offences, suggesting means by which to overcome some of the complexities of and inadequacies inherent in the mens rea/actus reus structure.

A further structural point raised by some authors relates to the attachment of the traditional approach to the common law, which undermines the reality of the fact that modern criminal law is largely and in some jurisdictions entirely based on statute: they suggest that this statutory basis could be better reflected in its teaching. Crofts and Tarrant address this through an account of teaching in the Australian Code States, while Gans details a course shaped by statutory interpretation.

A further theme relating to the basis of the criminal law is the importance of a contextualised approach to the subject, both within the law school curriculum and the wider socio-political context, which makes it important to outline the institutional context of criminal law and its linkages to the other parts of the curriculum, and also the way in which substantive criminal law reflects political values rather than a neutral set of principles. This manifests in a number of ways; confronting the challenge literally, Jackson and Kerrigan describe a course that integrates concurrent study of the substantive criminal law, litigation, and evidence, while Scraton and Stannard document a course that fuses critical criminology and criminal law. The chapters by Livings, Loughnan, Quince, and Tolmie also point to the importance of context. Howsoever 'context' is construed, an appropriate contextualisation of the conditions in which criminal law emerges and operates, allows for an understanding that breaks through the tightly defined, discipline-bound conception that typifies the black-letter approach. This is demonstrated by Quince and Tolmie, who both point to an understanding of the experience of criminal justice on the part of the socially marginalised as a particularly important critical window into the supposed 'value-neutrality' of the law.

A final theme that emerges from the chapters is that the traditional and narrow range of subject matter taught in most criminal law courses may present an unnecessarily limited conception of the ambit of the law. Gledhill and Kilcommins, Leahy and Spain look at the subject matter with which the course is typically concerned and identify gaps in relation to drugs, driving, and regulatory offences, and Gans joins this by pointing to the value of a course that embraces inherent variation by enabling the selection of a range of statutory provisions as the material through which to study the criminal law.

Our central purpose in putting together this collection was to demonstrate that there are options for those who wish to teach criminal law in a way that does not merely replicate with updated cases a course that was taught in generations past. The respective authors have chosen to address various facets of criminal law teaching. Each demonstrates a level of dissatisfaction with the traditional approach, and their contributions manifest a reflective will to innovate in terms of course content and lecturing methodology. They advocate moving away, to a greater or lesser degree, from the black-letter course structure, content, and pedagogy, and they identify rationales for their respective approaches. Insofar as the individual contributions comprise advice to those constructing or redesigning a criminal law course, it may not be possible to accommodate every suggestion, but the ideas presented here will help to inform and justify the approach that is adopted.

An underlying premise behind presenting a book on the options available in course design is that course structures should not necessarily be static – that what was done 30 years ago may not be the best way to approach things now. A clear justification for this suggestion for change is the view that how we teach criminal law, or indeed any other subject within a law school curriculum, should be informed by reflective choices and research rather than by simply replicating what was done previously. Of course, we do not deny the possibility that an academic lawyer may, having reflected on the options available in devising a criminal law course, decide that the traditional structure and content remains the best way to do things. This might be for a number of reasons, including a view that the existing teaching infrastructure and available textbooks provide benefits to the students.

Even if that is the outcome of reflection, the positive choice that it demands and represents demonstrates a point that should be core to academic endeavour. The importance of reflective and research-based choices as to the aims and efficacy of criminal law courses are legitimate and important subjects for research, and they warrant ongoing work. Aside from the benefits to be gained from active consideration of the appropriate content, shape, and approach of courses in criminal law, there is a role for empirical work as part of this process. This could include, but is no doubt not limited to, building on the ideas of various contributors to this collection. For example, Donson and O'Sullivan and Brown and Murray engaged in empirical research as to the efficacy of changes they introduced to course structures and to teaching methodology, and these could be followed up on a larger scale and in more detail. Similarly, arising from the views expressed by those who contend that course content should be different, consultation with various groups – 'stakeholders' being the over-used term – could assist in determining what should be the graduate attributes sought for those who have studied criminal law and what are the acceptable ways of achieving that. As Livings notes in chapter 12, the shape of the criminal law course and of the whole of the legal curriculum is affected by these stakeholders, often in an implicit way. Indeed, it is unlikely that the respective interests are well understood, such that research into their nature, and how and whether they should be accommodated and balanced, would be valuable. Such research could involve consultation with a wide range of criminal justice agencies, legal services providers more broadly construed, other potential employers, academics, and students. But because criminal law has its place within a wider curriculum, research should perhaps engage with that wider curriculum as well (noting, for example, Gans's position set out in chapter 8 that his redesigned course satisfies the demand for an understanding of statutory interpretation as a core graduate attribute for those who have completed a law degree).

This leads to a wider point. It is our view that the study of criminal law is, and should remain, a vital component of legal education, but we have the obvious bias of being employed to teach criminal law, and its centrality may not be assured. For instance, the recent *Legal Education and Training Review* carried out in England and Wales suggested that the scope of the core, 'foundation' subjects mandated for study in that jurisdiction should remain under review; it also cited a survey of 'legal services providers' (solicitors, barristers, and paralegals), which placed 'criminal law' as twelfth most important of 16 posited 'knowledge items' in academic legal education (Webb and others 2013, p. 34). Of course, this may reflect the nature of what is taught in a traditional criminal law course and the relatively narrow ambit of the substantive subjects on which there is a concentration. But it may also suggest the importance of setting out the aims of a criminal law course and the pedagogy through which to achieve it; clearly elucidated aims and research-informed pedagogies are both valuable to teaching and learning in criminal law and can also persuade stakeholders of the continued importance of its place in legal education.

Reference

Webb, J., Ching, J., Maharg, P. and Sherr, A., *Setting Standards: The Future of Legal Services Education and Training Regulation in England and Wales* (Legal Education and Training Review 2013).

Index

actus reus and mens rea: as core or threshold concepts 11, 21–32; teaching of 11–12, 21–32, 35–8, 110–11; understanding of by students 11–12, 27–32
assault offences: feminist jurisprudence and 173–8; *see also* specific substantive offences: teaching of – assault offences
assessment: design of 98

classroom response technology: use of 12–13, 46–57
complicity: teaching of 39–40, 72–82, 113
core and threshold concepts 11, 21–32
course structure *see* curriculum and course design and structure
criminal codes: teaching of 14, 83–92, 95
criminal justice: teaching of 109–10, 134–5, 162–72, 181–2
criminology and substantive law: integrated teaching of 16, 127–37; *see also* evidence, procedure and substantive law; "law in context"
curriculum and course design and structure: choice through different streams 191–3; design of assessments, role of 98; learning outcomes sought 187; limited use of research on 5–6, 185–6; practical skills, role of 142; pressures and constraints on 143; regulation by the legal profession as to 6–11, 102, 140, 186; stakeholders in 101–2, 140–2; survey of course structures 1–4; textbooks, role of 140–1; traditional structure, content of 1–5, 21, 60–1, 104, 185; traditional structure, critique of 5, 11, 13, 15, 16, 18, 19, 21, 61–3, 96, 104–13, 128–30, 139–40, 143–9, 191–3, 194–203

discretion: role of in criminal justice 99, 109–10

elements of offences: teaching of 12, 34–44, 94
evidence, procedure and substantive law: integrated teaching of 15–16, 116–26; *see also* criminology and substantive law

facts: construction of 179–82
feminist perspective: teaching of 18, 173–82
"flipped classroom" *see* SCALE-UP method of teaching

general principles of criminal law: critique of 15, 104–13; teaching of 1–4, 12, 38, 61, 94, 99–100, 104–5, 187; *see also* actus reus and mens rea

"law in context": teaching of 3, 16–18, 109–13, 139–49, 151–60, 162–72, 173–82; *see also* criminal justice; *see also* criminology and substantive law

Māori conception of criminal law 166–71
mens rea *see* actus reus and mens rea
mental capacity: teaching of 157–60
mindfulness: role of 171–2
minority and indigenous perspectives: teaching of 17–18, 162–72

non-fatal offences against the person *see* specific substantive offences: use of in teaching – assault offences, sexual offences

problem-based learning: use of 13, 60–70, 72–82
professional regulatory bodies: influence of *see* curriculum and course design and structure: regulation by the legal profession as to
prosecuting authorities and strategies: range of 198–201

SCALE-UP method of teaching: use of 13–14, 72–82
Socratic method of teaching 47–8
specific substantive offences: use of in teaching – anti-terrorism offences 4; assault offences 1–4, 18, 95, 111; Commonwealth offences (Australia) 4; computer hacking 2; corporate offences 2; course of justice, offences against 3; driving offences 2, 4, 19, 95, 189–91; drugs offences 2–4, 19, 95, 110–11, 188–9; endangerment 95; homicide 1–4, 95, 96, 110, 112; inchoate offences 39–40; money laundering offences 95; morality, offences against 3; people smuggling offences 95; pollution offences 95; property offences 1–4, 72–82, 95, 96, 112–13; prostitution 2; public order offences 2–4, 27, 95, 111; range of offences 18–19, 95, 185–93; regulatory offences 2, 4, 19, 95, 194–203; sexual offences 1–4, 95, 111; slavery offences 95; social security offences 95; summary offences 110–11; tax offences 96; trade descriptions offences 2; *see also* course structure: traditional structure, content of; elements of offences; general principles of criminal law: teaching of
statutory interpretation: teaching of 14–15, 93–102

teachers: responsibility of 12, 13, 17, 18, 34, 93–4, 142, 162–72
textbooks: structure of 4, 11, 21, 61, 100–1, 105–9, 140–1
threshold concepts *see* core and threshold concepts